T0065477

SOMEBODY
MUST COME
PREACHING

*A Collaborative
Collection of
Exposition in
African-American
Churches of
Christ*

J. Michael Crusoe, D.Min

WESTBOW
P R E S S®
A DIVISION OF THOMAS NELSON
& ZONDERVAN

WestBow Press books may be ordered through booksellers or by contacting:

WestBow Press
A Division of Thomas Nelson & Zondervan
1663 Liberty Drive
Bloomington, IN 47403
www.westbowpress.com
844-714-3454

Because of the dynamic nature of the Internet, any web addresses or links contained in this book may have changed since publication and may no longer be valid. The views expressed in this work are solely those of the author and do not necessarily reflect the views of the publisher, and the publisher hereby disclaims any responsibility for them.

Any people depicted in stock imagery provided by Getty Images are models, and such images are being used for illustrative purposes only.
Certain stock imagery © Getty Images.

Scripture taken from the King James Version of the Bible.

Scripture taken from the New King James Version® Copyright © 1982 by Thomas Nelson. Used by permission. All rights reserved.

Scripture quotations are from the ESV® Bible (The Holy Bible, English Standard Version®), copyright © 2001 by Crossway, a publishing ministry of Good News Publishers. Used by permission. All rights reserved.

[Scripture quotations are] from the Revised Standard Version of the Bible, copyright © 1946, 1952, and 1971 the Division of Christian Education of the National Council of the Churches of Christ in the United States of America. Used by permission. All rights reserved.

Scripture quotations taken from the (NASB®) New American Standard Bible®, Copyright © 1960, 1971, 1977, 1995, 2020 by The Lockman Foundation. Used by permission. All rights reserved. www.lockman.org

ISBN: 978-1-6642-2822-1 (sc)
ISBN: 978-1-6642-2821-4 (e)

Print information available on the last page.

WestBow Press rev. date: 06/14/2021

CONTENTS

Preface
Dr. James Michael Crusoe, Arlington Road Church of Christ, Hopewell, VA xi

Introduction to Preaching
2 Timothy 4:1-5 – *The Preacher, Evangelist, Teacher*
Dr. Jefferson R. Caruthers, Carver Road Church of Christ, Winston-Salem, NC xv

Honoring Preaching Giants from the East Coast:
Standing on the Shoulders of Soldiers of the Cross
Introduction by Dr. James Michael Crusoe 1

1 Corinthians 1:23-25 – *Preaching that Pleases God*
Dr. Eugene Lawton, Newark Church of Christ, Newark, NJ 4

2 Samuel 3:32-38 – *Death of a Brilliant Fool*
Joseph H. Brown, Sandy Lane Church of Christ, Richmond, VA....................... 11

2 Corinthians 5:15-17 – *Jesus, The Revolutionary*
Humphrey Foutz, Central Church of Christ, Baltimore, MD 16

Authorial Intent of New Testament "Sending"
Romans 10:15
Dr. James Michael Crusoe, Arlington Road Church of Christ, Hopewell, VA 23

Effective Church Planting: A Paradigm that Works
Interview with Douglas Anthony Goodman, Capitol Church of Christ,
Annapolis, MD 26

Beginning with Eight
Interview with Tradanius Beard, Northwest Church of Christ, Southaven, MS 31

Passing the Baton: Ministerial Transitions –
Interviews with three preachers:

1. Dr. Lovell C. Hayes, East Jackson Church of Christ, Jackson, TN 34
2. Dr. James Michael Crusoe, Arlington Road Church of Christ,
   Hopewell, VA 39
3. Ian Nickerson, Minda Street Church of Christ, Abilene, TX 44

The Man of God and Church Hurt
Dr. James Michael Crusoe, Arlington Road Church of Christ, Hopewell, VA 49

Why Expository Preaching?
David Wilson, Kings Church of Christ, Brooklyn, NY 54

The Challenge of Expository Preaching
in African-American Churches of Christ
John Davis Marshall, Aiken, SC 59

EXPOSITIONAL SERMONS

Pentateuch:
Exodus 12:40-51 – *Oh, What a Night: The Passover Lamb*
Dr. Harold Redd, Midtown Church of Christ, Memphis, TN 65

Historical Old Testament:
Ruth 3:1-6 – *A Mother-in-Law Who Mentors*
Dr. James Michael Crusoe, Arlington Road Church of Christ, Hopewell, VA 76

2 Samuel 18:18-29 – *A Biblical Response to Social Injustice –*
Are the Young Men Safe?
Dr. James Michael Crusoe, Arlington Road Church of Christ, Hopewell, VA 82

Wisdom Literature:
Job 23:1-12 – *When He Has Tried Me, I Shall Come Forth as Gold*
Dr. Loyd Clay Harris, McAlmont Church of Christ, Little Rock, AR 89

Psalm 27:1-6 – *The Power of Praise in Stressful Situations*
Dr. David L. Lane, Southern Hills Church of Christ, Dallas, TX 101

Major Prophets:
Jeremiah 38:7-13 – *A Black Man Comes to the Rescue*
Dr. Edward J. Robinson, North Tennaha Church of Christ, Tyler, TX............110

Minor Prophets:
Jonah 1:1-4, 17 – *A Disobedient Child, with a Compassionate God*
Bryan C. Jones, Newburg Church of Christ, Louisville, KY.............................118

New Testament Synoptics:
Mark 10:46-52 – *The Compassionate Christ Will Hear You If You Holla*
William Jones, North Greece St. Church of Christ, Rochester, NY.................. 127

Luke 7:36-50 – *Simon Says*
Michael L. Dublin Sr., South Central Church of Christ, Raleigh, NC.............. 138

Johannine Literature:
John 8:38-44 – *The Day Jesus Called for a Paternity Test*
Jonathan W. Morrison, Cedar Crest Church of Christ, Dallas, TX.................. 148

John 10:7, 11 – *I AM, The Good Shepherd*
Dr. Robert Davis, Drayton Mills of Christ, Spartanberg, SC 154

John 11:35-37 – *Crocodile Tears*
Dr. Lovell C. Hayes, East Jackson Church of Christ, Jackson, TN 161

Book of Acts:
Acts 8:26-40 – *The Conversion of a Black Man*
Dr. Cleavon P. Matthews Sr., Bold Believers Church of Christ, Dayton, OH.... 168

Pauline Epistles:
Welcome to Ephesians
Dr. Luis R. Lugo Sr., Northside Church of Christ, Tampa, FL 178

Ephesians 6:10-11 – *Be Strong in the Lord*
Dr. Nicholas A. Glenn, Sharpe Road Church of Christ, Greensboro, NC......... 188

Ephesus – *First Love Forsaken* – Revelation 2:1-7
Jeffrey J. Walker, Tonto Street Church of Christ, Phoenix, AZ 194

General Epistles:

Hebrews 11:32-40 – *What More Shall I Say? Faith Is the Key*
George Micheal Williams, Eastside Church of Christ, Austin, TX................... 202

1 Peter 2:11-17 – *This Is How We Do It*
Dr. Kelvin Teamer, Bouldercrest Church of Christ, Atlanta, GA 215

East Cost Preaching Giants

Dr. Eugene Lawton
Joseph H. Brown
Humphrey Foutz

Contributors

Tradanius Beard
Dr. Jefferson R. Caruthers Jr.
Dr. James Michael Crusoe
Dr. Robert Davis
Michael L. Dublin Sr.
Dr. Nicholas A. Glenn
Douglas Anthony Goodman
Dr. Loyd Clay Harris
Dr. Lovell C. Hayes
Bryan C. Jones
William Jones
Dr. David L. Lane
Dr. Luis R. Lugo Sr.
John Davis Marshall
Dr. Cleavon P. Matthews Sr.
Jonathan W. Morrison
Ian Nickerson
Dr. Harold Redd
Dr. Edward J. Robinson
Dr. Kelvin Teamer
Jeffrey J. Walker
George Micheal Williams
David Wilson

PREFACE

I have a plethora of sermon books in my library. Even as I write this, I'm looking at a number of them: *Outstanding Black Sermons: Volume 2 . . . Sermons from the Black Pulpit . . . Texts of Terror . . . Preaching in Two Voices: Sermons on the Women in Jesus' Life . . . Afrocentric Sermons: The Beauty of Blackness in the Bible . . . The African Presence in the Bible . . . From Mess to Miracle and Other Sermons . . . Best Black Sermons,* to name a few. Most recently, one of my classmates at Union University School of Theology contributed to a sermon book titled *Say It! Celebrating Expository Preaching in the African American Tradition.* And then it hit me – many preachers in our fellowship wrote sermon books, and there may be a compilation of lectures from previous church lectureships; yet, I was not aware of a collaborative effort of expositions among preachers in African-American Churches of Christ focused on Expository Preaching. Thus, the task began to reach out to an eclectic group of well-prepared preachers in churches of Christ. *SOMEBODY MUST COME PREACHING* went from vision to reality. I want to alert those who read this book of expositions to remember the difference between writing a sermon and preaching a sermon. While the Holy Spirit influences both, we must allow for the diversity of giftedness in our brotherhood. Some preachers are great orators, some are great writers, some are gifted at both. Thank God for anointing Men of God to use their gifts for the glory of God!

This is a not a sermon book on how to preach, but rather a book of sermons from a cadre of preachers representing a cross section of generations that include Baby Boomers, Generation X, and Millennials. That was intentional as we endeavor to keep the unity of the Spirit in the bond of peace. I am very happy that this collection of sermons bridges the generation gap. There is a special section honoring Pioneer Preachers, along with one of their sermons. Countless Church of Christ ministers stand on the shoulders of spiritual giants such as Dr. Eugene Lawton (Newark, New Jersey) and Joseph H. Brown (Richmond, Virginia), along with a preacher who is now with the Lord: Humphrey Foutz (Baltimore, Maryland). Each of these men influenced my ministry in Virginia.

Members of churches of Christ have a reputation of being "people of the book." In years past, that theme originated from a "proof texting" and "topical" approach. While the present trend toward expository preaching has increased, preachers in churches of Christ hold a high regard for textual, narrative and exegetical preaching that does not disconnect from the Restoration Movement plea of "speaking where the Bible speaks . . . being silent where the Bible is silent." In *Somebody Must Come Preaching*, you will see that each preacher has his own unique style of sharing the Word. You will be fascinated, encouraged, and motivated as you read the genres of Narrative preaching, Topical preaching, Evangelistic preaching, and Textual preaching. I believe the interview section regarding "being sent" and "passing the baton" are necessary in our brotherhood. The "Introduction to Preaching," along with the articles on "Expository Preaching" and "Ministerial Transition" in an African-American context give a "tool-shed" perspective of the heavenly treasure entrusted to earthen vessels.

Augustine, a North African theologian and philosopher, once stated, "When the Scriptures speak God speaks." A high view of Scripture and of preaching sustains the proclamation of the Kergyma. Expository preaching is preaching that either exposes or explains a passage of Scripture with the purpose of informing the audience of the historical, textual, grammatical, or doctrinal intent of the author, with the goal of challenging the audience to change beliefs, behavior, or biases. Stephen and David Olford gave this definition, "Expository preaching is the Spirit-empowered explanation and proclamation of the text of God's Word with due regard to the historical, contextual, grammatical, and doctrinal significance of the given passage, with the specific object of invoking a Christ-transforming response."[1]

Expository preaching is:

---

[1] Stephen F. Olford and David L. Olford, *Anointed Expository Preaching* (Nashville: B&H, 1998), 69.

1. Spiritual . . . it is the Spirit-empowered explanation and proclamation. People cannot be born again without the work of the Holy Spirit.
2. Textual . . . it must be textually determined. It is not testimony, it is the specific proclamation of the Word of God, with due regard to the historical, contextual, and grammatical context (keeping in mind its nature). YOU CAN HAVE A MESSAGE THAT GIVES TRUTHS, BUT IS NOT TEXTUAL.
3. Doctrinally focused . . . preaching should be doctrinally focused. We do not have miscellaneous thoughts; homiletics should help proclaim truths based on doctrine.
4. Purposely delivered . . . what is the purpose in this message? What are you seeking to see God do?

Key words related to expository preaching are the words "expose" and "explain." By expose, I mean to open up the text, to make the text transparent, to reveal the meaning of the text by traveling through the text. By explain, I mean to offer information and instruction concerning why the text was written, identifying and defining key words and phrases. Scripture says, "the preaching of the Cross is foolishness to those who are perishing, but to us who are being saved it is the power of God." Preaching is powerful! David Larson – When preaching has been strong in the Christian church, the church has been strong, when preaching has been weak, the church has been weak. We need strong preaching and strong churches. Emphasis on content should supersede charisma. You will find that writing a sermon is quite different from delivering a sermon. While not neglecting the importance of verbal communication (preaching is proclamation), preachers were asked to put in written form so that in the words of the Apostle Paul, "when you read you can understand my insight into the mystery of Christ" (Ephesians 3:4 NASB). What we preach comes from discourses that were written in order to be read and heard.

To my preaching brothers, THANK YOU for your contributions. The world will be a better place because of the *RHEMA WORD* that you boldly share!

Respectfully,
Dr. James Michael Crusoe

INTRODUCTION TO PREACHING

2 Timothy 4:1-5 – *The Preacher, Evangelist, Teacher*

Dr. Jefferson R. Caruthers Jr.

Scripture Text:

> *"I charge thee therefore before God, and the Lord Jesus Christ, who shall judge the quick and the dead at his appearing and—his kingdom. Preach the word, be instant in season, out of season; reprove, rebuke, exhort with all long suffering and doctrine. For the time will come when they will not endure sound doctrine; but after their own lusts shall they heap to themselves teachers, having itching ears. . . . But watch thou in all things, endure afflictions, do the work of an evangelist, make full proof of thy ministry"* (2 Timothy 4:1-5 KJV).

Jesus gave dignity to a number of behaviors while walking this earth. He provided insight into what was important to God, the Father. Perhaps the greatest insight He provided was the necessity to love, even our enemies. He demonstrated love to the extent that He made the sacrifice of dying on the cross. And He died, not only for those who sought to be His friends, but also for His enemies (Romans 5:8 KJV). It cannot be said, then, that sacrifice for others is ignoble or worthless.

Jesus also dignified service. He contrasted service with lordship. The Gentiles exercised lordship (Mark 10:42 KJV). Jesus encouraged, "And whosoever of you will be chiefest, shall be servant of all. For even the Son of man came not to be ministered unto, but to minister, and to give his life a ransom for many" (Mark 10:44-45 KJV). Providing service and ministering must both be viewed as behaviors that please God.

In addition to loving, and sacrificing, and serving, and ministering, Jesus came preaching. Matthew records, "And Jesus went about all Galilee, teaching in their synagogues, and preaching the gospel of the kingdom, and healing all manner of sickness and all manner of disease among the people" (Matthew 4:23 KJV). Preaching is as much integral to the gospel story as are love, sacrifice, serving, and ministering.

Preaching in the New Testament began with John the Baptist. The text reads, "In those days came John the Baptist, preaching in the wilderness of Judaea" (Matthew 3:1 KJV). And there were others who engaged in this ministry during the earthly walk of Jesus. Jesus instructed His disciples, "And as ye go, preach, saying, The kingdom of heaven is at hand" (Matthew 10:7 KJV).

What we address in this reflection, this message, is that in the New Testament there is not only a focus on the preaching, but we are also giving insight into the character and ministry of the preacher.

Let me quickly address that when noting New Testament information on the preacher, it is acknowledged that the treasure is the gospel, and that we are vessels. Let it be acknowledged that it matters not who plants or waters, but it is God who gives the increase. Let it be acknowledged that some preach out of envy and insincere motives, but what is important is that the gospel is preached. Let it be acknowledged that there are some who preach and glorify themselves by measuring themselves by themselves. It must always be acknowledged that the power is in the gospel.

The power is in the gospel; the gospel is to be heard, but how will one hear without a preacher (Romans 10:14 KJV)? The power is in the gospel, but the feet of those who come preaching the gospel are beautiful (Romans 10:15 KJV). The power is in the gospel, but in Paul's day and until this day there is the command to preach the gospel, being instant in season and out of season (2 Timothy 4:2 KJV).

The child of God must remember that John the Baptist was a preacher. Jesus Christ was a preacher. The men Jesus chose while on earth were commissioned to preach, to be preachers (Mark 16:15-16 KJV). And of all the ways Paul envisioned himself, he saw himself first as a preacher.

We come to understand Paul's prioritizing of preaching in his letters to Timothy. But even before then, as Paul reflected on the opportunity to reach Rome, he wrote that as much as in him was, he was ready to preach the gospel in Rome (Romans 1:15 KJV). When Paul preached, his desire was that one would hear and obey, but as necessary as baptism was for salvation, Paul said that God sent him not to baptize, but to preach (1 Corinthians 1:17 KJV). It is no wonder, then, that when Paul wrote to his younger companion who was trained by Paul to preach, he wrote, "Whereunto I am ordained a preacher, and an apostle, (I speak the truth in Christ and lie not;) a teacher of the Gentiles in faith and verity" (1 Timothy 2:7 KJV). Then, in his second communication, he wrote, "Whereunto I am appointed a preacher, and an apostle, and a teacher of the Gentiles" (2 Timothy 1:11 KJV).

We might miss something if we ignore that Paul often wrote about the faith in terms of priority. When speaking to what God gifts the church with, he wrote, "And he gave some, apostles; and some, prophets; and some, evangelists; and some, pastors and teachers" (Ephesians 4:11 KJV).

Paul saw himself primarily as a preacher who was also an apostle and teacher. He wrote in our lesson text to Timothy, who was an evangelist. But no less significant than being an evangelist was the charge to preach. As much as Paul was a preacher, apostle, and teacher, Timothy was a preacher, evangelist, and teacher.

Timothy was instructed in the role of being a preacher, evangelist, and teacher. Paul challenged Timothy to be engaged in all three of these aspects of ministry. On preaching, Paul wrote, "Preach the word; be instant in season, out of season; reprove, rebuke, exhort with all long suffering and doctrine" (2 Timothy 4:2 KJV).

On being an evangelist, Paul admonished Timothy: "But watch thou in all things, endure afflictions, do the work of an evangelist, make full proof of thy ministry" (2 Timothy 4:5 KJV). Know that whatever being an evangelist was, it involved being engaged in work.

Then on teaching, Paul wrote, "And the servant of the Lord must not strive, but be gentle unto all men, apt to teach, patient, In meekness instructing those that oppose themselves, if God peradventure will give them repentance to the acknowledging of the truth" (2 Timothy 4:24-25 KJV). Further, the ESV makes clear what is not immediately so in the KJV. Paul writes, "Command and teach these things" (1 Timothy 4:11). And, "Until I come, devote yourself to the public reading of Scripture, to exhortation, to teaching" (1 Timothy 4:13 ESV).

In the first century, John the Baptist came preaching. Jesus came preaching. The apostles came preaching. Paul the Apostle came preaching. And Timothy came preaching. Let us examine a few things about Timothy as preacher.

The Preacher's Parents

First, we appreciate this preacher's parents. If we are going to have a good influx of preachers in the church, we must always appreciate the parents who point children in the right direction while they are young. Timothy's grandmother, Lois, and his mother, Eunice, had exemplary faith (2 Timothy 1:5). This truth must certainly be the reason that Paul could say about Timothy that from a child Timothy knew the holy Scriptures (2 Timothy 3:15). This becomes all the more instructive when we consider that we live in an age when parents are not as committed to home prayers, home Bible studies, Bible school, and youth church participation. Timothy became a great preacher because of the faithful guidance and instruction of his parents.

The Preacher's Preparation

Second, we appreciate this preacher's preparation. He was prepared by the Apostle Paul. Paul reminded Timothy of the training curriculum: "But thou has fully known my doctrine, manner of life, purpose, faith, longsuffering, charity, patience, persecutions, afflictions, which came unto me at Antioch, at Iconium, at Lystra; what persecutions I endured: but out of them all the Lord delivered me" (2 Timothy 3:10-11 KJV). Timothy did not just pick up the mantle of preaching; he traveled with Paul hearing his teaching, observing his life, witnessing his commitment, and being blessed by his faith.

The Preacher's Preaching

Third, we appreciate the preacher's preaching. He was to preach the Word, a word that affirmed that Jesus Christ of the seed of David was raised from the dead (2 Timothy 2:8 KJV). Preaching shaped the first century church. Preaching informed prayer (1 Timothy 2:1-2 KJV). Preaching shaped the interaction of men and women in worship (1 Timothy 2:9-15 KJV). Preaching shaped the organization of the church (1 Timothy 3:1-14 KJV). Preaching shaped the support of widows and proper relations between preachers and members (1 Timothy 5 KJV). Preaching shaped attitudes about money (1 Timothy 6 KJV). What we must all admit is that preachers came preaching to shape and fashion the lives of those who called on the Lord Jesus.

The Preacher's Posterity

Finally, just as Timothy's parents contributed to his faith, just as Paul's preparation blessed Timothy, Timothy was to invest in others. Preaching did not end with Timothy or with his generation. Paul instructed Timothy, "And the things that thou hast heard of me among many witnesses, the same commit thou to faithful men, who shall be able to teach others also" (2 Timothy 2:2 KJV). Along with other instructions, Paul sought to make sure that no generation failed to understand that the preacher, evangelist, teacher must come preaching. He must accept that his work is as noble as Jesus demonstrated when the Lord himself came preaching.

> Dr. Jefferson R. Caruthers Jr. is a native of Anaheim, California. He is the son of a gospel preacher, Jefferson Caruthers Sr. Brother Caruthers began his work as preacher for the Carver Road church of Christ in July of 2005. He and his wife Felecia are the parents of seven children, one son in law, one daughter in law, and seven grandchildren.

HONORING PREACHING GIANTS FROM THE EAST COAST: STANDING ON THE SHOULDERS OF SOLDIERS OF THE CROSS

Introduction by Dr. James Michael Crusoe

"Every Paul needs a Timothy, and every Timothy needs a Paul." We are aware of the relationship Paul had with Timothy and Titus. They were his "sons in the gospel." Paul spoke highly of several preachers he considered to be co-laborers of the gospel of Christ: Epaphroditus and Tychicus in particular. Others who traveled with Paul in Acts 20:4 must have benefited from being in the presence of this globe-trotting evangelist.

Where would we be without "Fathers in the gospel" – older preachers who mentor younger preachers? Older, seasoned, mature preachers built churches from the ground, they sacrificed, sometimes preaching without pay or for meager salaries. Longevity seems to be the key to their successful ministry. An unparalleled work ethic that consisted of ministry, office administration, preaching, and simply blood, sweat, and tears are scars of these veteran preachers. They endured hardships as a good soldier of Christ Jesus. They paved the way, making pulpit ministry, contract negotiations, ministerial benefits, and minister appreciations acceptable in our brotherhood. These preaching giants are trailblazers and staunch guardians of the "ONE LORD, ONE FAITH, ONE BAPTISM." Their work continues until the Lord returns. We stand on their shoulders. We thank God for pouring their spirit into others and passing the baton in this

Christian race. Each of these men has influenced by ministry, and this book is a tribute to their legacy.

Dr. Eugene Lawton

I heard Dr. Eugene Lawton preach up close and personal in 1983 while a student at Abilene Christian University. He conducted a gospel meeting/revival for the Minda Street congregation. I was spellbound by his delivery, his style, and his charisma. His famous phrase, "Let Me Sound My Trumpet" became stapled in my mind. Dr. Lawton contributed to a graduate school project I was working on titled "Ethics in the Ministry." I remember being star-struck when I asked for his insight and participation. To my surprise, Dr. Lawton was genuinely approachable. Years later, he recommended me to my most successful work, which was in Hopewell, Virginia. He is a "tell it like it is; ain't going to take it back; straight shooter kind of preacher." I learned to dress like a preacher from him, and even tried to preach like him. Somewhere in the late 1990s I had a Sunday afternoon speaking spot at the National Lectureship held in New York City. Being a young preacher I wanted to impress this giant of a preacher. I can't count the number of "runs" during that sermon ("Am I right about it") I made to that national audience. Of course, "Let Me Sound My Trumpet" was off limits. I might have been young, but I sure wasn't brash enough to try to pull that off! Even though it was an after-lunch Sunday audience, it was well attended. After the sermon, I remember hearing people saying, "did you hear that young preacher who sounds like Dr. Lawton!" A few years later, Dr. Lawton invited me to preach the first of several gospel meetings at the Newark congregation where he labored. Anxious, on pins and needles, nervous, and at the same time wanting to impress him and afraid of the reprisal if I failed, I preached "Jesus Can Fix It." The Lord blessed that Sunday morning with 8 baptisms, finishing the week (Dr. Lawton is old-school, his meetings went Sunday to Friday) with 12 baptisms (I have to tell you the rest of the story, how we went from 8 to 12). Dr. Lawton felt comfortable to invite me as the keynote speaker to his 35th ministerial anniversary. I was honored that he was confident that I could honor him at such a prestigious event. What a preaching moment that was! It's been my privilege to share the same preaching platform with him on several occasions and, honestly, after forty years of ministry, I still find myself wanting him proud.

Joseph H. Brown

Joseph H. Brown is a great encourager and he often provided ministerial advice during my first tenure with the Arlington Road Church of Christ in Hopewell, Virginia. He encouraged and counseled me during my early years of ministry. He set the bar high in Richmond, establishing a school and erecting a beautiful edifice located on Sandy Lane in Richmond, Virginia. He is known in our brotherhood as the "Top Shelf" preacher. One of his famous phrases, "You ought to do yourself a favor and visit Richmond before going to heaven" still echoes today. I admire him for teaching the church to honor God with first class service.

Humphrey Foutz

Humphrey Foutz was a giant of a man in stature and in the gospel of Christ. God used the ministry of this giant to build the largest African-American congregation in Churches of Christ on the East Coast. When it came to church, the Central Church in Baltimore was the place to be! His style was without pretense, it was built on preaching "Christ and Him Crucified!" He held a meeting for me in Hopewell and I remember sharing with him my early anxieties of being in a small town with a small church. His words of wisdom were to plant my feet and go to work. I took his advice. Later, to my surprise, he invited me to conduct several gospel meetings at the Central Church, all resulting in double-digit baptisms. Now, not because of my preaching but, due to his teaching on discipleship, the harvest was ready. Of all the experiences with this great preacher, one that stands out is when he took me shopping and bought me a suit!

1 Corinthians 1:23-25 – *Preaching that Pleases God*

Dr. Eugene Lawton

Scripture Text:

> "*But we preach Christ crucified, unto the Jews a stumbling block, and unto the Greeks foolishness; but unto them which are called, both Jews and Greeks, Christ the power of God, and the wisdom of God. Because the foolishness of God is wiser than men; and the weakness of God is stronger than men*" (1 Cor. 1:23-25 KJV).

Man is a created being, not an evolving being, an exploded being, but rather, man was created by God and in the image of God (Genesis 1:26-27 KJV). Man is not a by-chance creature, a happy-go-lucky being to do whatever he wants to do on Planet Earth, but that same God who created man also sustains man. The Bible says that "in him we live, and move, and have our being" (Acts 17:28 KJV). Man was placed on Planet Earth for the exalted purpose to please God (Proverbs 16:7 KJV). Man's first purpose on earth is to please God; God is imperative and uncategorically number one, above all and over all. Time will not allow me to give you the galaxy of scriptural verses impacting this compelling thought.

Preaching is indispensable in the salvation of men and women. The Apostle Paul put it this way: "For after that in the wisdom of God the world by wisdom knew not God, it pleased God by the foolishness of preaching to save them that believe" (1 Corinthians 1:21 KJV).

This morning you are looking at a dying man preaching to dying men and women. I may not have another opportunity to preach to you again; time and circumstances may prevent us from meeting again; therefore, compulsion is in my bones, urgency is in my heart, fire is shut up in my soul to tell somebody about the love of Jesus. When the preacher-man preaches, he ought to preach to please God. When you preach to please God, you must preach the Word exactly as it is written.

The preacher-man is not to be . . .

a people-pleasing preacher,
a prominence-seeking preacher,
a popular preacher,
a watered-down, and don't hurt anybody's feelings preacher.

He ought to be . . .

a God-pleasing preacher,
a water-washed preacher,
a blood-bought preacher,
a Holy Spirit-filled preacher,
a Christ-exalting preacher, and
a true-to-the-Book gospel preacher.

Through the ages, God Almighty has chosen to make known His message of salvation through the process of preaching.

Noah was a preacher, 2 Peter 2:5 (KJV)
Abraham, the father of the faithful, was a preacher.
Moses, the great emancipator and lawgiver, was a preacher.
John the Baptist, the way-preparer of the Savior, was a preacher.
Jesus, God's only begotten Son, Mary's baby, was a preacher.
The twelve apostles that Jesus let loose on a hostile world, were preachers
Paul was a veteran preacher and a globetrotting preacher.
Timothy and Titus were young preachers.
Apollos was an eloquent preacher.

Thank God for the preacher-men. No wonder the Bible says, "How then shall they call on him in whom they have not believed? and how shall they believe in him of whom they have not heard? and how shall they hear without a preacher? And how shall they preach, except they be sent? as it is written, How beautiful are the feet of them that preach the gospel of peace, and bring glad tidings of good things!" (Romans 10:14-15 KJV).

Yes, preaching has always been, is now, and will always be God's method to save the lost in this old sinful world. That is why this subject is so very crucial and critical for us today. **Let me sound my trumpet, any kind of preacher will not do.** Can I preach a little? The right kind of preaching pleases God. Our text says, "Because the foolishness of God is wiser than men; and the weakness of God is stronger than men" (1 Corinthians 1:25 KJV).

Preaching That Pleases God Has
One Source Book – The Bible

To be able to please God, every preacher must understand that there is NO OTHER SOURCE BOOK, INSTRUCTIONAL MANUAL, BLUEPRINT, GUIDE, RULE, OR CANON THAN THE BIBLE from which we can learn the type of preaching that pleases God (2 Timothy 3:16-17 KJV; 2 Peter 1:3 KJV). The Bible is our guide from earth to glory, not the philosophy books, the psychology books, or Mama Lucy's book. When any preacher preaches salvation by faith only, he is not preaching from the Book. When a preacher preaches that the communion should be taken monthly, quarterly, annually, and neverly, he is not preaching from the Book. Any kind of preaching will not do; the right kind of preaching is to please God.

The preacher-man is obligated to be a defender of the faith against every man-pleaser, religious politician, professional crier, proclaimer of human doctrines, socializing counselor, charismatic orator, or human philosophical speculator of super-softness. The Bible teaches that preachers ought to "earnestly contend for the faith" (Jude 3 KJV); and "fight the good fight of faith" (1 Timothy 6:12 KJV). It is my cemented conviction and immovable position that regardless of the pressure of power, financial pressure or otherwise; in spite of some church leaders who fear the flock, indifferent, lukewarm attitudes, and comfortable attitudes of men; in spite of modern, affluent America trying to deify man and humanize God; in spite of historical awareness, hi-tech transportation, and communication, this Book, the Bible, is our only preaching source. Somebody says that we are educated; we live in condominiums and townhouses; we have high-paying jobs, influential friends, and business acquaintances; we own property; we have stocks and bonds; but **LET ME SOUND MY TRUMPET** – we have forgotten that our citizenship is in heaven and this earth is nothing more than an overnight motel. The voice of the people is not the voice of God (Jeremiah 10:23).

We are not to preach "ANOTHER GOSPEL" (Galatians 1:6-9 KJV). If we do, it will be a perverted gospel, and adulterated gospel, a twisted gospel. I think that I ought to tell you that preaching a perverted gospel will make the preacher accused, it will make the believers accused. His worship is in vain and his beliefs are in vain. Water is able to quench thirst, but with salt in it, it will create thirst. Water can save life, but when water is mixed with arsenic, it will destroy life. It does matter what a person believes and obeys. That is why the Bible is the only source of our preaching. Paul said, "Preach the word" (2 Timothy 4:2 KJV).

Preaching Is to Impact the Gospel, Not to Impress the People

Listen to Paul in Galatians 1:10 KJV, "For do I now persuade men, or God? or do I seek to please men? for if I yet pleased men, I should not be the servant of Christ." The preacher is not a comedian, a news reporter, a religious politician, a public relations man – but he is an evangelist making known the Good News about Jesus Christ and His glorious church.

The preacher-man is under a solemn charge. Listen to this solemn charge as was given to Timothy by the Apostle Paul:

> "I charge thee therefore before God, and the Lord Jesus Christ, who shall judge the quick and the dead at his appearing and his kingdom; preach the word; be instant in season, out of season; reprove, rebuke, exhort with all long suffering and doctrine. For the time will come when they will not endure sound doctrine; but after their own lusts shall they heap to themselves teachers, having itching ears; and they shall turn away their ears from the truth, and shall be turned unto fables. But watch thou in all things, endure afflictions, do the work of an evangelist, make full proof of thy ministry" (2 Timothy 4:1-5 KJV).

This solemn charge to the preacher is to please God; it is in the presence of God, the presence of Christ Jesus, and the coming judgment;

it is a charge from the superior commander, and his preaching will STIR those who will hear it, and provoke, stimulate, and arouse men and women to take action.

- Preach on God and you will stir the idolaters and the atheists.
- Preach on divine Creation and you will the stir the evolutionist.
- Preach on the one church and you will stir the denominational churches.
- Preach on the headship of Christ and you will stir the Catholic Church.
- Preach on modest apparel and you will stir the hot pants Jezebels.
- Preach on holiness and you will stir dancing church members, cocktail-sipping members, drug-using members, fornicating members, gambling members, and lottery-playing members.

But we have to preach!

- Preach boldly, and preach negatively.
- Preach to reprove and rebuke.
- Preach to the elders and preach to the members.
- Preach on specific sins.
- Preach on love and preach on hate.
- Preach when they like it and preach when they don't like it.
- Preach when they are shouting glad, and preach when they are fighting mad.
- Preach the plan and the Man.
- Preach the one Lord, the one faith, the one baptism, and the one church.

The gospel of Jesus Christ will cut through old sinful habits, expose sins, and present God's standard of righteousness. We have to dispel darkness with the light, spread purity in the world of immorality, convict sin in a world that loves sin, and protect the truth in a world of error and false doctrines. This kind of preacher has to give his allegiance to God and no other.

Preachers Should Preach the Whole Counsel of God

The Apostle Paul put it in these graphic words, "For I have not shunned to declare unto you all the counsel of God" (Acts 20:27 KJV). Paul did not preach ear-tickling sermons. Every gospel preacher should preach **THE WHOLE COUNSEL OF GOD**. A gospel preacher, to be pleasing to God in his preaching, must include in his gospel repertory the following:

- The negative as well as the positive (2 Timothy 4:1-5 KJV; Roman 13:9-10 KJV). When one preaches on the qualifications of elders, the preacher-man must preach all twenty-six qualifications; eighteen are positive and eight are negative.
- The law of God as well as the love of God (James 1:25 KJV; Romans 8:1 KJV)
- The two natures of God – His severity and His goodness (Romans 11:22 KJV)
- The sins of man as well as the salvation of man (1 John 3:4 KJV; 1 John 5:17 KJV)
- The fear we need as well as the faith we must have (2 Corinthians 5:11 KJV; Hebrews 10:31 KJV)
- The hell of the devil as well as the heaven of God. (Matthew 25:46 KJV; Revelation 20:10 KJV)
- The duty of man as well as the devotion of man to his Master. (Ecclesiastes 12:13 KJV; Luke 17:10 KJV)

There is no Bible subject on which a gospel preacher is not to preach. If anyone, including elders, tries to hinder him from preaching on any subject, he must remember to whom his allegiance belongs. The gospel preacher is under divine obligations to preach the whole counsel of God. He must preach . . .

on church discipline;
on marriage, divorce, and remarriage;
on pure Christian living and sinful habits;
on the one Lord, one faith, one baptism, and the one church;

that Jesus Christ is the Son of God and there is no other name by which man can be saved;
that the gospel is God's power to save this old sinful world;
devotional sermons as well as evangelistic sermons.

The world needs to hear the spiritual dynamite, the gospel, and it will turn the world upside down (Acts 17:1-6 KJV). **Let Me Sound My Trumpet,** unless the preacher-man is preaching true to the old path (Jeremiah 6:16 KJV), has a distinctive and clarion sound (1 Corinthians 14:8 KJV), makes known the faith, and lets people know that they are lost without the gospel, then our preaching is not pleasing to God and we ought to vacate the pulpit, resignation effective now, get a secular job, and stop misleading the souls of men. Is there a preacher in the house?

Is there anybody here who would like to become a child of God, get on the Lord's side, or be born again? The opportunity is yours this morning and I urge you not to put it off any longer. You come to the Lord by hearing the glorious gospel (Acts 15:7-8 KJV); believing the gospel (John 8:24 KJV); repenting of your sins (Luke 13:3 KJV); confessing that Jesus is the Christ, the Son of the living God (Acts 8:37 KJV) and being baptized for the remission of your sins (Acts 2:38 KJV). The Lord will add you to His church, the church of Christ. The Lord will bless you now and if you are faithful until the end, He will bless you forevermore.

> Dr. Eugene Lawton is an international evangelist, a defender of the faith, a veteran preacher, a radio and television evangelist, a successful writer of four books, and a great church builder. Dr. Lawton is a native of St. Petersburg, Florida. He was baptized into Christ by the late S. J. Dudley. He began preaching the glorious gospel while he was a student at Southwestern Christian College, Terrell, Texas.

2 SAMUEL 3:32-38 – *DEATH OF A BRILLIANT FOOL*

Joseph H. Brown

Scripture Text:

> *"And they buried Abner in Hebron: and the king lifted up his voice, and wept at the grave of Abner; and all the people wept. And the king lamented over Abner, and said, Died Abner as a fool dieth? Thy hands were not bound, nor thy feet put into fetters: as a man falleth before wicked men, so fellest thou. And all the people wept again over him. And when all the people came to cause David to eat meat while it was yet day, David sware, saying, So do God to me, and more also, if I taste bread, or ought else, till the sun be down. And all the people took notice of it, and it pleased them: as whatsoever the king did pleased all the people. For all the people and all Israel understood that day that it was not of the king to slay Abner the son of Ner. And the king said unto his servants, Know ye not that there is a prince and a great man fallen this day in Israel?"* (2 Samuel 3:32-38 KJV).

King David lamented (wept) over the death of Abner (read vs. 32, 33, and 38 KJV). This is the story of Abner – a great man, a wise man, a mighty man, a brilliant man. But he died heedlessly, he died mindlessly, he died foolishly, he died when he should not have died – he died "as a fool dieth" (2 Samuel 3:33 KJV).

That is what one of his closest friends, King David, said about him with tears running down his cheeks – that he should not have died in such a way. How foolish of

him – to allow himself to be slain in such a way.

How was Abner slain? – Let me give you some background for this passage of Scripture.

Chapter 2

Following Saul's death, his son Ishbosheth became king over Israel, over the army of the late King Saul. Abner was a warrior, in charge of the military. Abner sent word to David, who was king over Judah, that he would negotiate to bring Israel under his kingship (2 Samuel 2:12, 17-19 KJV).

Joab is a warrior in charge of King David's military. Joab has two brothers: Abishai and Asahel. Asahel could run like a deer. The two armies met one day in Gibeon by a pool (v. 12-13 KJV). Abner suggested some swordplay between the young men. Some of the young men died in the swordplay.

Afterwards, the two armies began to fight. Joab, the leader of King David's military, defeated Abner and King Ishbosheth's army.

2 Samuel 2:17-32 KJV

Asahel, is the brother of Joab and Abishai. Abishai began to chase after Abner. Abner does not want to fight with Asahel because he is a friend of Joab, his brother. But Azahel is itching for a fight. Azahel dies. Abner knows that Asahel's brothers will be chasing after him Joab and Abishai, Abner's brothers, began to chase after Abner to avenge their brother's blood. At nightfall, the chase is called off (vs. 26-28)

Abner knows that Joab is going to try to kill him because he is the kinsman redeemer, or the redeemer of his brother's blood. It was a law in the land that if you killed someone, that person's kin could kill you, unless you killed without malice and made it to one of the six cities of refuge.

The cities of refuge were ordained of God in Numbers 35:9-11, 13, 15:

> "⁹ And the LORD spake unto Moses, saying, ¹⁰ Speak unto the children of Israel, and say unto them, When ye be come over Jordan into the land of Canaan; ¹¹ Then ye shall appoint you cities to be cities of refuge for you; that the slayer may flee thither, which killeth any person at unawares. ¹³ And of these cities which ye shall give six cities shall ye have for refuge. ¹⁵ These six cities shall be a refuge, both for the children of Israel, and for the stranger, and for the sojourner among them: that every one that killeth any person unawares may flee thither." (KJV)

Joshua 20:7-9 gives the cities appointed by Joshua after they arrived in Canaan:

> "And they appointed Kedesh in Galilee in mount Naphtali, and Shechem in mount Ephraim, and Kirjatharba, which is Hebron, in the mountain of Judah. And on the other side Jordan by Jericho eastward, they assigned Bezer in the wilderness upon the plain out of the tribe of Reuben, and Ramoth in Gilead out of the tribe of Gad, and Golan in Bashan out of the tribe of Manasseh. These were the cities appointed for all the children of Israel, and for the stranger that sojourneth among them, that whosoever killeth any person at unawares might flee thither, and not die by the hand of the avenger of blood, until he stood before the congregation." (KJV)

Cities of Refuge: Ordained, Appointed by God for Refuge

Following the encounter with Joab and his army, a long war ensued between the house of Saul and the house of David (2 Samuel 3:1 KJV).

At some point, Abner is insulted by his king, King Ishbosheth. Abner visits with King David in Hebron, a city of refuge, and offers his services. He offers to negotiate to bring the two kingdoms together and David would be king over both. David gave him his blessings. Abner leaves Hebron on his mission.

Later that day, Joab returns to Hebron from a military victory (v. 22 KJV). He is informed that Abner has visited with King David and is now gone in peace. Joab is furious and informs the King that Abner is nothing more than a spy.

<u>Joab's cunning deception</u> (2 Samuel 3:26-27, 30 KJV)

> "26 And when Joab was come out from David, he sent messengers after Abner, which brought him again from the well of Sirah: but King David knew it not.
>
> 27 And when Abner was returned to Hebron, Joab took him aside in the gate to speak with him quietly quietly,

and smote him there under the fifth rib, that he died, for the blood of Asahel his brother. ³⁰ So Joab, and Abishai his brother slew Abner, because he had slain their brother Asahel at Gibeon in the battle."

It broke King David's heart because he died so foolishly, so heedlessly, so needlessly.

> "And David said to Joab, and to all the people that were with him, Rend your clothes, and gird you with sackcloth, and mourn before Abner. And king David himself followed the bier. And they buried Abner in Hebron: and the king lifted up his voice, and wept at the grave of Abner; and all the people wept. And the king lamented over Abner, and said, Died Abner as a fool dieth? Thy hands were not bound, nor thy feet put into fetters: as a man falleth before wicked men, so fellest thou. And all the people wept again over him [Abner]" (2 Samuel 3:31-34 KJV).

> "For all the people and all Israel understood that day that it was not of the king to slay Abner the son of Ner. And the king said unto his servants, Know ye not that there is a prince and a great man fallen this day in Israel?" (2 Samuel 3:37-38 KJV).

NOTICE:

Joab deceived Abner – he caused him to think he was his friend.

NOTE:

Abner's foolish choice could not be undone.
The king's tears could not bring Abner back.
The tears of his family and friends could not undo his foolish choice.
Abner abandoned God's divinely appointed place of safety.

CONCLUSION

What about you? Some of you are wise, you are intelligent; yet you have forsaken Jesus Christ as Lord of your life. Is He no longer first in your life?

> Joseph H. Brown, Evangelist and Elder Emeritus, faithfully served the Lord's Church in the Richmond area for over fifty years. He led the congregation through its growth from Chimborazo Blvd to Dill Avenue and Sandy Lane. He is married to Phyliss Brown, they have 3 sons, Hugh, Loren and Virgil.

2 CORINTHIANS 5:15-17 – *JESUS, THE REVOLUTIONARY*

Humphrey Foutz (deceased)

The word *revolutionary* is an action word and, to be sure, I realize that some may have trouble with it. But it is a good and fitting description of Jesus of Nazareth. The heart of the word revolution is *change* or *turn*. With its great intensity, it suggests a severe or drastic change. This word has no intrinsic morality. This must be determined by the direction of the turn and usually the self-interest of the moralist. Both George Washington and Che Guevara were revolutionaries. Your approval or disapproval will be determined primarily by your own self-interest. So, when we talk about Jesus, the Revolutionary, we are talking about the effect and thrust of His work and the radical difference He made in human society. Listen to Paul in 2 Corinthians 5:15-17:

> *"His purpose in dying for all was that men, while still in life, should cease to live for themselves, and should live for him who for their sake died and was raised to life. With us therefore worldly standards have ceased to count in our estimate of any man; even if once they counted in our understanding of Christ, they do so no longer. When anyone is united to Christ, there is a new world: the order has gone, and a new order has already begun"* (NEB).

Let us put aside all secular legends of Christ and as instructed by the Corinthian epistle lay aside worldly standards in our understanding of Christ. Let us renounce the well-behaved Jesus, innocent of scandal and controversy, the Jesus of superstition symbolized in dashboard statuettes and lucky charms, the fanciful, ineffectual innocuous Jesus of the cinema whom the multitudes found irresistibly attractive, the soft sentimental Jesus of Salman and other vulgar caricatures, and the Jesus of the fascist and rightist teaching democracy to primitive people before the French and American revolutions. Or the picture of Jesus teaching Marxism long before Karl Marx was a gleam in his father's eye.

Let us at the same time rid ourselves of some ideas of Christ in the religious world. Let us at least for this day expose and repudiate the fairy-tale concept of Jesus of the Sunday school story book: the ridiculously repulsive Jesus fashioned after the manner of the White Anglo-Saxon Protestant; the unapproachable Messiah captive in Cathedrals, as ascetic too esoteric for this world. "I longed to hear the voice of God. I climbed the topmost steeple. He said come down, come down. I dwell among the people."

Place this ascetic idea over against the statement of Jesus. "*Think not that I am come to send peace but a sword. For I am come to set a man at variance against his father, and the daughter-in-law against her mother-in-law. And a man's foes shall be they of his own household. He that loveth son or daughter more than me is not worthy of me. He that findest his life shall lose it and he that loseth his life for my sake shall find it*" (Matthew 10:34-39 KJV). These are not the words of a milque-toast, but a revolutionary in the highest sense of the word.

At first this may seem strange and in conflict with all that you have heard. The most glorious character that ever came to earth and here unabashedly He advocates change, and not just superficial change, but a change that creates conflicts and tensions. A change that goes so deeply into a man that Jesus called it a new birth (John 3:3 KJV), regeneration (Titus 3:5 KJV), a death and resurrection. Hence, Paul says, "*I am crucified with Christ, nevertheless I live, yet not I; Christ liveth in me*" (Galatians 2:20 KJV). This is profound change, revolutionary, plumbing the very depths of the soul.

Anyone acquainted with Christian thought during the past decade or so knows that at this point we are saying something that needs to be said. Many people have pretty much reduced their Christian commitment to admiration of Jesus – the Jesus of the distorted concept. This is an admiration taken for granted as easy and demanding nothing. Of course, we admire Jesus. This is an almost universal response. But there is another response – "I want nothing to do with your Christian ethic," says one. "I will have nothing to do with your Christian churches," says another. "But, of course, I admire Jesus the Lamb." Do you remember the nursery rhyme? "Charley had a little lamb; his fleece was white as snow. Everywhere that Charley went, he thought the lamb would go."

Many consent to that. They admire. They praise, and with all the eulogizing, that is about all the Christianity they have. But in these desperate days it is evident that this in not enough. We live in critical times. Look around you. Open your eyes and look at Jesus as He is. Realize this is no beautiful sunset of an outstanding painting about which we may say, "How lovely," and go back to business as usual. Such a Savior demands a response. The idea that Christ will do everything, and man should do nothing, is as untenable as the idea that man can do everything for himself. This is not Christianity, but superstition.

Then look at our generation. We are still taking the highest and noblest elements in human character and prostituting them to the bases causes. We produce Vietnams and are the most violent and warlike people on the face of the earth.

We take our science and its advancements that would be used to lift up mankind and use it to multiply ways to slaughter men. Ours is the generation that produced DDT to kill bugs, 24D to kill weeds, Formula 1018 to kill rats, and E Equal MC 2 to immolate or wipe out cities.

We take the virtues of loyalty, unselfishness, love of family, and make death fall from the skies and hurtle from ambush and burst out of subterranean caves and thousands are slaughtered.

We allow mercenaries to go into primitive cultures and blast fathers with superior arms and modern firepower while they starve children at home by blockades.

We are still encouraging racism in almost every phase and facet of American culture, with the churches leading the way. The eleven o'clock hour on Sunday morning is still the most segregated hour in the land. Christ is still being tied to *white middle-class America*. With this record, Jesus of Nazareth, believed in, is the most disturbing personality we can ever face. We do not instinctively turn to Him. Instinctively we try to escape Him. We flee into a world of clichés. "*Social Gospel, Social Gospel!*" as a leper crying, Unclean! Give Him His way and He will revolutionize our world. And as for our lives we cannot worship at the shrine of status quo. You may have Jesus. You cannot have both. And if we are to truly know Jesus of Nazareth, we must come to recognize that He was to the world an agitator, a revolutionary who drastically changed the Jewish culture of His time and, consequently, the world. Can we really relate to Christ without being imbued with a like Spirit?

The Revolutionary Spirit of Jesus upon the Individual

Jesus found a world much like the world in which we live, full of unpromising and ordinary people:

The Samaritan woman mishandling sex (John 4 KJV)
Zacchaeus mishandling a trust (Luke 19 KJV)
The rich man mishandling wealth (Luke 12 KJV)
The high court mishandling power, the Pharisees with race
prejudice, hating all Samaritans (Luke 10 KJV)
The rich, young ruler with the misplaced
emphasis in his life (Luke 18:18 KJV)

In each instance Jesus left them changed. Moreover, Jesus always took as a matter of course that such change was an integral part of living, so that, far from being strange, it was an expected occurrence. If this were intended to be strictly argumentative, I should contend today that this is psychologically correct. It is of the essence of life to change. Not only can personal life change, it cannot remain static.

At the center of personality is the power to direct change; the recognition of a chosen goal and working toward it. Then this is historically correct. The one thing most changeable is human life. And in the changing of human lives Jesus is the supreme personality of human history.

I understand the objection naturally raised to all of this. You Christians speak, they say, of changing people, but we are in an economic and social system that keeps many from getting out of themselves all that is there. On almost any Saturday evening in an eastern city someone is saying something like this: "You get up early every morning with roaches and rats running round your bed. You stumble over to your child's bed to make sure the rats ain't done bit his ears off. Then you make it through falling plaster to a leaky water closet to wash your face. You finally get the sleep out of your eyes and put on some clothes that you ain't finished paying for them yet. Then you go down in the garment district to meet the man."

This is the cry of those imprisoned in the ghettoes and in the tarpaper shacks in the hinterlands. Chronic unemployment, the threat of permanent unemployability, and seeing one's children embark for the same dead end by being consigned to decrepit, ill-equipped, overcrowded, and understaffed schools – while we Christians cry about bussing. You've bussed for years to segregate. There must be a change of the systems that produce this kind of misery. Do you say Christ can change people but not the establishment?

Can you conceive of the effect of Christ upon His contemporaries and the Jewish establishment?

— He changed the law that was the constitutions of Israel.
— He changed the Levitical priesthood (Hebrews 7:12 KJV)
— He changed the custom of animal sacrifices (Hebrews 9:12 KJV)
— He changed the observation of the holy days that were the heart and soul of a nation's culture (Colossians 2:14 KJV)
— He changed the peculiar relationship that Israel sustained to Jehovah, thus creating a new man, a new order the world calls Christian (Ephesians 2:12-15 KJV)

As a matter of fact, many of the characteristics of the modern, secular revolutionary are discernible in His relationship with the Twelve. The modern idea of a recruiter is paralleled in Christ. The ideology is akin to the gospel of Christ. This produced a company of committed men that today might be called a cell. These cells were to infiltrate the environment around them and shortly the entire then known world. Jesus tells them, *"Ye are the salt of the earth"* (Matthew 5:13 KJV). And in another place, *"The kingdom of heaven is like unto leaven, which a woman took and hid in three measures of meal till the whole was leavened"* (Matthew 13:33 KJV). In both of these stories the idea of infiltration is unmistakably present. So, now, we can understand the frequent injunctions to secrecy. At the preparation for the last meal: *"Behold, when you have entered the city, a man carrying a jar of water will meet you; follow him into the house which he enters and tell the householder, the Teacher says to you, where is the guest room?"* (Luke 22:10 RSV). Or, how do you explain the need to bribe Judas with a comparatively large sum to act as a counteragent and inform? Some of the operations of the group were public, but obviously others were not. Notice the infiltration in the epistles. *"There were saints in Caesar's household"* (Philippians 4:22 KJV).

How many persons does it take to change the existing order? I am convinced that hope does not lie solely in numbers. We must not be tempted to confuse deep commitment with "jumbo-ism." Dr. Elton Trueblood tells the story of a pivotal point in international communism. "Lenin barely won out in his struggle to limit the membership of their group to a small, disciplined and deeply committed body of men. If Lenin had not won at that point of history the world would undoubtedly have been very different. To this day the victories of militant communism are won, in every case, not by a majority, but by a highly disciplined, unyielding, and dedicated minority." It is the committed, the dedicated, those who are driven by an inner compulsion in a cause they consider more important than themselves, who will win the victory.

— Do you believe that all men are equal before God? (Acts 10:34 KJV)
— Do you believe that justice, mercy, and faithfulness are weightier matters and deserve to be so treated? (Matthew 23:23 KJV)
— Do you believe that the influence of Jesus should be felt in Town Hall, City Hall, County Seat, State House, or White House? (Matthew 5:13-14 KJV)
— Do you believe that systems designed to perpetuate injustice should be changed or abolished?

Then I do not suggest that we rise up, I say, *penetrate!* Penetrate the recalcitrant leadership in the church and leaven it with the influence of Christ. Penetrate the power centers in your communities and leaven it with the influence of Christ. Penetrate the political structure and work for reform and change. *Together! Yes, together!* We can hasten the day of which Amos spoke – when judgment will run down as waters and righteousness as a mighty stream (Amos 9:13 KJV).

"Humphrey Foutz died April 13, 2006. He was converted to the church from Catholicism and preached God's Word for 50 years in Texas and Maryland. He was instrumental in the development of the Central Church of Christ in Baltimore, MD. He preached in 34 states, was on the Herald of Truth TV series, and conducted gospel meetings across the country. He was a member of the board of directors at Southwestern Christian College in Terrell, Texas, and was a member of the advisory committee of the National Church Lectureship. He is survived by his wife, Annie Jewell Foutz. Interment was at the Woodlawn Cemetery, Baltimore, MD."

— *Gospel Advocate*, August 2006, p. 44

AUTHORIAL INTENT OF NEW TESTAMENT "SENDING"

Romans 10:15

Dr. James Michael Crusoe

> Romans 10:15 – *How will they preach unless they are sent?*
> *Just as it is written, "How beautiful are the feet of those who*
> *bring good news of good things!* (NASB 1995)

We hear a lot about being missional, fulfilling the Great Commission, and church planting in the 21st century. There was a time when evangelistic campaigns and gospel meetings were conducted with the intent of starting a congregation in an area where there was no church. Our pioneer preachers would conduct "tent meetings" that led to the establishment of churches that still exist today. I presently serve a congregation that was planted out of a tent revival in 1947. A Baptist preacher, along with 147 others from the Baptist Church he preached at, were converted during a month-long tent revival. Since 1947, several ministers were "sent" to this work (John R. Vaughner, Raymond Dunwood, John Smiley, Leurena Gilbert, and James Michael Crusoe). "Sending" from a New Testament perspective therefore involves "recommending" or "laying hands" on a qualified evangelist.

The New Testament concept of "sending" actually means to send away toward a designated goal or purpose. The word "sent" in Romans 10:15 means:

"to send away, dismiss:

a. to allow one to depart, that he may be in a state of liberty
b. to order one to depart, send off."[2]
c. "*to order* (one) *to go to a place appointed;* either persons sent with commissions, or things intended for someone."[3]

"In verse 13 Paul has affirmed that everyone who calls on the name of the Lord will be saved. For Paul the Lord is Jesus Christ, and it is clear to him that the Jewish nation as a whole has not called upon the name of the Lord. Throughout the remainder of this chapter Paul deals with the question as to why it is that the Jews have not called upon the Lord. He does this by constructing a logical chain with five links in order to see where the failure lies. These five links are expressed in reverse historical order by means of four questions (call to . . . believed . . . heard the message . . . proclaimed . . . sent out)."[4]

"The passive expression, if the message is not proclaimed, may be rendered as active, 'if someone does not proclaim the message to them.' Similarly, the passive expression if the messengers are not sent out may be rendered as 'if God does not send out the messengers' or 'if the churches do not send out the messengers.'

The scripture quotation in verse 15 comes from Isaiah 52:7 and is closer to the Hebrew than to the Septuagint. By rendering this as 'How wonderful is the coming of those who bring good news!'"[5]

---

[2] *Greek Dictionary* (Escondido, CA: Ephesians Four Group, 2001), 2.

[3] Joseph Henry Thayer, *A Greek-English Lexicon of the New Testament: Being Grimm's Wilke's Clavis Novi Testamenti* (New York: Harper & Brothers, 1889), 67.

[4] Barclay M. Newman Jr. and Eugene A. Nida, *A Handbook on Paul's Letter to the Romans* (New York: United Bible Societies, 1973), Logos.

[5] Newman and Nida, *A Handbook on Paul's Letter to the Romans.*

Churches start for various reasons: out of conflict, out of necessity, out of survival, or out of a vision for evangelism. Some well-established churches would organize evangelistic campaigns and support the new church plant financially and with strong families. Congregations were applauded for their vision of partnership to sustain the new church. The selection of the minister for the new church plant was critical and calculated. Older preachers have said, "you don't find a church for a preacher . . . you find the right preacher for the church." It was the belief of older preachers to be involved in the training and development of gospel preachers. So, Romans 10:15 was not an option, but a biblical mandate. The rhetorical question in Romans 10:15 deals with the authentication of the herald as one who has been "sent" by a higher authority.[6]

The following interview with Douglas Anthony Goodman is based on the success of the Central Church of Christ in Baltimore, Maryland, and their commitment to "sending" a qualified preacher to an area where there was no church.

---

[6] Robert Jewett and Roy David Kotansky, *Romans: A Commentary*, Hermeneia – A Critical and Historical Commentary on the Bible (Minneapolis: Fortress Press, 2006), 638.

EFFECTIVE CHURCH PLANTING: A PARADIGM THAT WORKS

Interview with Douglas Anthony Goodman

Q: Minister Goodman, tell us about your conversion experience.

A: I was blessed to grow up in the Central Church of Christ and baptized at age 11 under the teaching of Bro. Humphrey Foutz – growing up on the Bible School department; the teenage ministry. After my baptism, I had the privilege of being discipled and mentored by Talbert Gwynn and influenced by a number of other men, like Achaniel Lucas, Dr. Tyrone Adams, Michael Edison, Nate Hawkins, Dr. Steve Ozanne, Elmer Sembly Jr., and many others. I was blessed to be active in the church in various ministries, gaining experience and know-how.

Q: We can see how older men played a part in your development. You were blessed to have mentors. Tell us about your call to ministry.

A: I didn't plan on becoming a preacher at first. I was satisfied with winning souls and discipleship. I joined the church-planning ministry that campaigned seven times. It was Brother Foutz's dream to plant churches on the East Coast. So, he started a Timothy ministry for young men who were interested in preaching the gospel. Time was set aside on Friday nights to learn how to write sermons. This also gave opportunities to preach. At Central, evangelism and discipleship classes were available as well to equip us for ministry. The motto during that time was "only the strong survive." These classes, along with much fieldwork, had to be top priority in order to be successful in the ministry. I've been involved in seven church-planting campaigns within the Mid-Atlantic region and served as interim minister in preparation for the upcoming mission work in Annapolis. Like Timothy, I was recommended by the brethren to be one of the first to be sent out. That was 33 years ago. I'm still manning the post. I was trained, ordained, and earmarked for the work in the city of Annapolis in 1987.

Q: You are considered a "Son" of Bro. Humphrey Foutz. Describe your relationship with this giant of a preacher.

A: To me, he was friendly giant; a man who was willing to invest his life into young men that the gospel may live on even after he would be gone. He always encouraged us to be strong and preach the Word. I would always enjoy those special moments when we could talk shop, and whatever you discussed would go no further.

He encouraged me to be a reader. He was a good example of a preacher and a church builder. He told me once that it was hard to see the greatness of a mountain sitting at the foot of it, you had to step back to truly appreciate it. Every Timothy needs a Paul, and every Paul needs a Timothy. Even 33 years later in ministry, I think about what he taught me. I still go visit his grave to reminisce and to hope that in some small way I made him proud in fulfilling his dream. He trusted me and I felt like I owed him. I'm still where he left me.

Q: What do you attribute to the success of the ministry of Brother Humphrey Foutz?

A: First of all, I believe longevity was a key factor. He was like a father figure. He really loved people and had compassion for them. He was like the hub in the middle of the wheel; he was connected to everyone. He shared his vision, making sound financial decisions, keeping the Great Commission (Matthew 28), and he was always in the forefront of every ministry. Ministry to us wasn't about position, but more about service and commitment. He ran a loving, tight ship. His goal was to build a strong home base ministry, have community outreach, make disciples, raise up preachers, and establish congregations. Central was one of the largest African-American congregations on the East Coast, at one time 1,200 strong.

Q: How many churches did the Central Church of Christ plant?

A: We had a church-planning ministry that established four congregations and we helped to boost three congregations, so there were seven campaigns. Brother Foutz would select a city where there was no church. A scout would canvas the city – pick out a hotel, a restaurant, a meeting place for the church – and map out the city. Workers would take off two weeks to campaign the city. We would knock on doors all day, eat two meals together, and have worship at night. We would baptize people throughout the day. After two weeks, we would leave the church for the young preacher he had selected and trained. He would be supported for 3-4 years. Brother Foutz used to say that if you have what it takes, he could give you a map, a Bible, and a parachute, push you off the plane, come back in five years, and there would be a growing church, or that you would die from starvation!

Q: In what ways were you and the Capital Church of Christ accountable to Brother Foutz and the Central Church of Christ?

- Neither Bro. Foutz nor Central lorded over us like a mother church. They supported us in all our efforts.
- I would give a weekly progress report to Bro. Foutz.
- Brother Foutz would meet with all of his "sons" in the gospel every month. We would talk shop and eat chicken.
- Many times I would just go to share thoughts and goals and receive counseling and advice.
- I made sure to take members from Annapolis to Central's functions, so they may get to know them.
- I made sure Annapolis members understood that Central was the reason we were in existence.
- My father was the treasurer for many years, and he told me that Brother Foutz would reference Annapolis as a model for church plants.

Q: Walk us through some highs and lows of your church plant.

A: Well, let's start with the lows. I had to start from the ground. It's hard work, it takes time, but I believe you will be well-off down the road. When you lose some, you have to baptize some more. There will always be some problems, but there are some problems I don't experience because they are all my folk. I'm the only preacher they know since I've been with them from the beginning.

In the summer of 1987, after a two-week crusade took place in Annapolis, Maryland, the Capital Church of Christ was established with 26 members. Since 1987, the church purchased three acres of land and renovated a condemned school building and moved in 1992. The church had also purchased several school buses, and passenger and handicap vans for its ministry. Their commitment to Matthew 28:18-20, through evangelism and discipleship, had brought about an increase in church membership. In April 2000, a 325-seat auditorium was erected. Efforts such as gospel meetings, evangelistic campaigns, seminars, ladies days, youth rallies, 5th Sunday fellowships, VBS, and a variety of other activities were used to spread the Word in Annapolis and throughout Anne Arundel County. The church currently operates seventeen ministries and is supported by Christians committed to doing God's will. The church burned its mortgage in 2016 and is now debt-free. Since its inception, over 500 souls have been baptized into Christ.

Q: It is evident that Bro. Foutz was high on discipleship. Tell us how that (discipleship) works for your ministry today?

A: I believe every young preacher will most likely follow the pattern of the preacher who trained him or who had the most influence on him. In my experience, I learned and knew how to baptize people and disciple them. I knew how to establish ministries and do outreach in the communities. I did not have to rely upon transferees in order to build the church.

I've been blessed to work with five young men – three of them are preaching for congregations. As I watch them in their ministries, I see them mimicking some of the things they saw me do, which I saw my preacher do – things like loving the church, establishing ministries, solving problems, or just setting the tone for the church.

Q: What advice would you give someone with a desire to plant a church?

- Make sure you are planting a church for the right reason.
- Make sure you are going about it the right way.
- Take some classes from a Bible institution.
- Get some ministry training under an older minister.
- Get the approval of senior ministers.
- You may need financial support.
- Make sure that you don't split the church.
- Don't solicit members from other congregations.
- Have the support of local preachers.
- You want to be a full fellowship with area-wide congregations.

> Douglas Anthony Goodman was born in Raleigh, North Carolina, and raised in the inner city of Baltimore, Maryland. He preaches for the Capital Church of Christ in Annapolis, Maryland.

BEGINNING WITH EIGHT
Interview with Tradanius Beard

Q: Minister Beard, tell us about your conversion experience and call to ministry.

A: I am a native of Memphis, Tennessee. I obeyed the gospel of Christ in the summer of 1996 while visiting my grandmother in Ruleville, Mississippi. My cousin Debra Wardlow taught me the gospel of Christ. I started my Christian journey and vowed that I would tell others about Jesus Christ. That summer, I returned home and placed membership at the Norris Road Church of Christ in Memphis, Tennessee. I was only eleven years old, but yet excited about learning more about God. My parents weren't members of the Lord's church at the time, so someone picked me up every Lord's day for church. When I was 16 years old, I really began to study my Bible. The late Nokomis Yeldell Sr. took me under his wing. Minister Yeldell noticed how I would often set up one-on-one Bible classes and was baptizing those whom I had the privilege of teaching the gospel. I was invited into Minister Yeldell's Preacher's Training Class and that's when my call to ministry be.

Q: You are considered a "Son" of the late Nokomis Yeldell . . . describe your relationship with this legendary preacher.

A: Nokomis Yeldell Sr. was an amazing preacher. I thank God for the time that we shared together. Our relationship was for sure a mentor/mentee relationship. He was my teacher and I was his student. Bro. Yeldell had a way of disciplining you firmly as father, yet allowing you opportunity to learn from your mistakes. I am thankful for his wisdom and insight.

I can recall enrolling in a "school of preaching" in which he strongly discouraged me because of some concerns he had. However, I enrolled in the school anyway. Bro Yeldell simply told me, "Son, eat the fish, but spit out the bones." He never once condemned or ridiculed me. Let's just say I withdrew from the school in just two months after enrollment. Lol! My relationship with him is described as a coach and player relationship. Minister Yeldell was the coach and when he called the play, I ran the ball as the player. Our relationship taught me discipline, patience, and compassion. Bro. Yeldell's model of leadership was shown and exemplified by his interaction with other people. I believe because of that example I am the minister I am today.

Q: What are the memories of your mentor that stand out and have shaped your ministry in Southaven, Mississippi?

A: There are many memories that I have of Minister Yeldell. One of the memories that I have is when we were in our Preacher's Training Class on a Wednesday night. Bro. Yeldell was teaching hermeneutics. We (students) were interested in how to break down a text verse by verse. We were more interested in how to "wow" a crowd with our knowledge. Bro. Yeldell said something that has shaped my approach to ministry to this day. He said, "Don't be so interested in mastering the text, but let the text master you." In other words, live the Christian life because our lives preach better sermons. Another memory that stands out is a statement from Bro. Yeldell, "People will support what they help create." Northwest Church of Christ has been blessed because I have used this approach to empower people to use their gifts for the Kingdom.

Q: Walk us through some highs and lows of your church plant.

A: I planted the Northwest Church of Christ when I was 23 years old. It was exciting and yet challenging at the same time. The only thing I wanted to do was save souls and rebuild lives. I am thankful I still have the same passion. Some of the lows of church planting that I have experienced is not enough financial support. When I planted in 2008, only seven other people launched with me. We had a total of eight people, and out of the eight, six of them were women. Therefore, a lot of the teaching, training, and financial responsibility was on me. Church planting is different than going into an established work because usually all the work is not just done by one man. I did work a secular job. I would work from 7:00 a.m. to 3:00 p.m. and then get off work and have in-home Bible studies with those in our community. It was a toll on my physical body, but it was worth it. However, the highlight of church planting is that you don't have to fight a system that is not effective for church growth. I never had to worry about "leading brothers" who didn't honor the role of the evangelist. It's rewarding to set a vision for the church and then watch them catch what has been cast

Q: Could you speak to the passion and vision the Lord placed on your heart to plant a church, and what advice would you give someone with a desire to plant a church?

A: The reason I planted our church is not because I wanted to preach, teach, or be known by men. My heart's desire was/is that men and women who don't know Christ would come to Him by the preached Word. God gave me the gift of preaching and teaching so I desired to use the gift for the Kingdom. I went into an area that the gospel was not being preached intentionally among African-American. Therefore, the Northwest Church of Christ became the first African-American Church of Christ in Southaven, Mississippi. I would tell anyone who wanted to plant a church to make sure that they are doing it out of pure motives. When you are a church planter, soul-winning must be your number one priority.

> Tradanius Beard is a native of Memphis, Tennessee. He is currently the Ministering Evangelist at Northwest Church of Christ in Southaven, Mississippi. He is married to Dr. Darlisha Beard, they have a beautiful baby girl, Madison Grace.

PASSING THE BATON
Ministerial Transition #1
Interview with Dr. Lovell C. Hayes

Q: Tell us about your call to ministry, your mentors, and those you may have mentored that influenced your ministry.

A: Like Timothy, I had the influence of a godly mother. She was youth director at the Page Boulevard congregation while I was growing up. She made sure that I memorized Scripture and was active in youth activities at the church. One of the first passages that she had me memorize was 2 Timothy 4:1-8. Perhaps that admonition to "preach the word" rolled around in my head as I spent time with Bro. Roscoe Moore, our minister. His son, Will Roy, was close to my age and that led to me spending much time in Bro. Moore's home. At age 13, I made a decision to "preach the word." Again, my mother's influence was strong. She wrote my first couple of sermons and would be my "church" as I practiced delivering those sermons. She would often encourage me by saying, "put some gravy in it!"

Later on, Bro. Graham McGill came to St. Louis and was further encouragement. He drove me to Nashville Christian Institute when I decided to attend. While at NCI, I had the privilege of traveling with the renowned evangelist, Marshall Keeble.

Later in life, I believe that my sermon development was influenced by several peers. Among them are brothers David L. Lane and William Jones from whom I learned, through their modeling and motivation, to develop a more expository style and the outline of three major points. Then one of the greatest influences in my adult life in ministry has been Bro. Ralph

Smith. He has been an example, edifier, counselor, and adviser in the process of the day-to-day aspects of ministry and serving people.

Q: It has been said, "in order to speak on transitional leadership you have to have made it to the other side. There needs to be some years that go by to prove the success and health of that transition." How many years have transpired since your ministerial transition?

A: I was called to work with the East Jackson Church of Christ in Jackson, Tennessee, in 1994. Therefore, this transition occurred over 26 years ago. Bro. Walter Vance Sr. was a church builder and developer who was with this church for 30 years before I came and was a mentor and helper for a number of years after my arrival and before the Lord called him home. But I would have never accepted the work if I would have had to come right behind Bro. Vance. My observation is that coming into a church after a "legend" has been there is a difficult process for that first man who comes. I was blessed that Bro. John Marshall served here for three years after Vance retired. It was his tenure that made a great contribution to my ability and the congregation's ability to transition.

Q: What were your expectations coming in?

A: My initial expectations were high. I found a congregation of people who were strong in doctrine, but could grow in programs. They were ready to go to work and God blessed the works we were able to initiate in a mighty way.

Q: What were some of the initial challenges that you and the congregation faced early on?

A: One of the initial challenges was style of worship and sermon delivery. Bro. Vance was a great teacher and preacher whose "style" was to stand still and teach/preach. Bro. John Marshall, who followed him, was a great sermon organizer and teacher who was more animated that Bro. Vance, but less animated than I was. When I first arrived, there was only a microphone attached to the pulpit and no extension that allowed movement. The "protocol" for order of worship was strictly followed. My style was to close the sermon by "putting some gravy in it." It took awhile for the church to adjust. I believed that the adjustment was helped by my teaching and preaching good doctrinal lessons, along with attending to the other needs. My sense was that the church and leaders became far more comfortable with me as they could know that I was "doctrinally sound." I was used to a more "spirited" song service and we had to work to reach a happy medium over time. I came to understand what Dr. W. F. Washington was saying to me when I was looking to make this transition. His words were: "you know that Jackson is not Springfield, don't you?"

Another initial challenge was assessing if the right persons were sitting in the right seats from the aspect of church staff, church work, and church programs. Through leadership training and workshops, we were able to review our staff positions and make productive adjustments.

Q: What do you attribute to the success of your transition?

A: The contributions to "success" of this transition:

1. The support and camaraderie with Bro. Walter Vance. On my first Sunday there, he stood before the church and said that "this is the man who is going to lead us forward now." His endorsement at the beginning and all throughout the years he was alive was invaluable.
2. A leadership (elders) who (1) had been well taught in the respecting of the work of the evangelist – I have never felt like a "hireling" – and (2) who really had the best interests of the church at heart. With this as the focus, we were able to reach constant consensus and never had ill will between us.

The present challenge for me is that I have not been given the honor by God to take this congregation to the level that I envisioned 26 years ago. However, at my age and as my time of service gets closer to closing, I believe that, just like John Marshall's tenure opened some doors for me, my tenure will open even greater doors for the next ministering evangelist at this congregation.

Q: I'm aware of two books on ministerial transition. One is *Too Great a Temptation* by Joel Gregory, and the other is *Transition Plan* by Bob Russell. In the first book, someone from outside the congregation was brought in with the former minister remaining at the congregation. The baton was never passed, and the transition did not work. In the second book, the college minister worked with the senior minister for 18 years, mapping out a five-year strategy for passing the baton. After retirement, the former minister did not return for a worship service for a year. What was your situation like? Did the former minister stay or leave? How does one coming in as the new minister "honor the past" and "set vision for the future?"

A: Since I have already answered the first two questions in the above paragraphs, I will go to the third one. Some suggestions are:

1. Develop a relationship with the former minister if he is still there. If his role in the congregation has been positive, then his endorsement will be important.
2. Hopefully, the former minister has been someone whom the congregation appreciates and therefore you can often speak well of him before the church.
3. Be evaluative of changes and what "battles" you fight. Some things are more "sacred" to the congregation and its leadership. Some things can change now. Some things can change later. And, as hard as it is to accept, some things may not change (in my opinion).
4. Get people involved in finding ways to respect what is, and to work toward what can be.

Q: In a 21st century, African-American, small to medium size church context, what advice would you give to church leaders and preachers for a successful ministerial transition?

a. To leaders: understand that a change in ministerial leadership will lead to changes. Moses got Israel to a certain point and used some different tools given him by God that Joshua would employ.

b. Leaders and ministers: start with where your visions and processes intersect.

c. Ministers: teach, educate, teach. Teach the leaders and teach the members.

d. Patience and endurance. And then more patience and endurance.

MINISTERIAL TRANSITION #2

Interview with Dr. James Michael Crusoe

Q: Tell us about your call to ministry, your mentors, and those you may have mentored that influenced your ministry.

A: I'm a native of Dayton, Ohio, and grew up in churches of Christ. I was baptized at age seven. Ulysses Shields, Woodie Morrison, and Ivory James Jr. are the ministers who preached for my home church. My call to ministry came during my junior year in college.

I was away from church during age 16 to 20. It's a long story that involves "coming to myself" like the Prodigal Son in Luke 15 and being inspired by Ivory James Jr. to preach the gospel. After college I attended law school part-time, while working in a law office. Early on I was at a crossroads, pursue a law degree or go full time into ministry.

My mentors over the years have been Karlan Eugene Carter, John Lawson, Dr. Eugene Lawton, and Dr. David Jones, all preachers. In recent years, Herman Thompson (a retired elder) became a mentor and father figure in my life. My training under Karlan Carter was more "hands on," spending time with him every Sunday, having lunch after morning worship, and spending the afternoon visiting members and taking communion to sick. John Lawson taught a class for young ministers sharing his experiences in ministry, helping us with debate techniques and sermon preparation.

Q: It has been said, "in order to speak on transitional leadership, you have to have made it to the other side. There needs to be some years that go by to prove the success and health of that transition." How many years have transpired since your ministerial transition?

A: I've had two ministerial transition experiences. Although I was not aware at the time, my first church work was a ministerial transition. Dewayne Ester served a small congregation in Tucson, Arizona, that merged with another church. When he retired, John Lawson recommended me to the Southside congregation. I stayed two years and relocated due to finances.

My second ministerial transition led me to Memphis, Tennessee.

While serving a church in Virginia, I was asked by my predecessor to replace him. I remember it vividly. A message left on my voicemail by him that simply said, "This is Bro. Yeldell. I'm in the hospital, give me a call." I returned the call not having any idea what was on his mind. He was direct and simply said, "I'm retiring, I want you to come to Memphis." Prior to my coming, he had several health issues, cancer and a stroke, that led to his decision to retire. He and I worked together for six years until his death. I was able to serve that church for five more years after his death for a total of eleven years.

Q: What were your expectations coming in?

A: My expectations were high, positive, and optimistic. I had been offered three works before making the move to Memphis, each one with the predecessor intending to stay. While having a good ministry with the church I left in Virginia, the opportunity to do ministry with a kingdom agenda was a major factor that supported my decision to relocate. I wanted to serve a church that was evangelistic, progressive in community involvement, and had a heart for improving the quality of life by developing Christian schools, Senior Citizens' homes, and, of course, was doctrinally sound. I shared those expectations with the leadership and my predecessor. Before making the decision to accept the work, I asked in what direction he would like to see the church go. It was after getting his approval on my expectations that we decided to move to the South.

Q: What were some of the initial challenges that you and the congregation faced early on?

A: There were several challenges. First, there were third party interferences. The pressure of coming to a high profile congregation was a challenge. Before moving to Tennessee and even after arriving, I would learn of several sabotage tactics that one would expect in the corporate/business world, but not in the Lord's church.

Coming in, I was not aware of the huge shadow I would have to follow. My greatest challenge was succeeding a legendary preacher who retired after 40 years of successful tenure. My predecessor indicated that he planned to stay at the congregation, so I was in the shadows of a living legend. There were some awkward moments. One was determining the location of his office, and where mine would be. After learning my predecessor planned to remain active at the congregation, I insisted he keep his office. For several months, he and I shared an office. Later, I had two classrooms renovated into an office for myself, but the location was far away from administrative offices. It turned out to be a good study office for me, but did not send the signal that it was the minister's office.

I believe due to experiencing a number of losses in his life, my predecessor came every day to the church office. By loss, the stroke he suffered years prior to my arrival limited his walk, and a year after I arrived his wife passed away. He was also one of the elders of the congregation and not only attended, but for several years chaired the monthly business meetings. It was often uncomfortable in those meetings, especially when other leaders were not in agreement on important decisions. My personal challenge was being careful not to ever say or do anything that would give others the impression that the successor and predecessor were not on the same page.

Looking back, casting a vision for the church was difficult. Some leaders and members wanted change while other leaders were comfortable with just increasing the ministries already in place. The lack of a 10 to 20 year plan was a challenge. Along with that, church members sometimes were placed in positions of divided loyalties. For example, the annual holiday love offering that went to one preacher, was now a shared love offering, which was okay with me, but created some feelings when members began putting my name on checks.

Q: What do you attribute to the success/failure of your transition?

A: There were a number of successes during my ministry in Memphis. For at least eight years we hosted a national TV program on the largest African-American religious broadcasting network, "Word Network," we developed a separate 501c3 that received a HUD grant to build a retirement home, we ordained an elder and several deacons, and we initiated a Young Adult ministry. Our church building became available as a voting precinct and neighborhood watch meetings. My personal ministry goals of preaching in foreign countries were accomplished. When I left, our congregation had the highest attendance of all African-American churches in the city.

Unfortunately, my tenure did not end well. Looking back, part of the reason was the inability to honor the past and set a vision for the future. There are a number of things I would have done differently. One thing I would have done differently is come in as "co-minister" or as the official assistant minister. While given the title of senior minister, the actual role was more of a "hireling" or pulpit minister. That sent mixed messages to the congregation and to the leadership. Am I working with the predecessor, or am I leading this congregation? If I had a do-over, let me lead by assisting rather than be expected to lead but not being able to make full proof of my ministry and evangelistic charge.

I was not aware of Joel Gregory's book *Too Great a Temptation* or Bob Russell's book *Transition Plan* until after being there for a year or so. Russell's book *Transition Plan* outlines the process the Central Christian church in Louisville, Kentucky, took to replace the senior minister. They selected someone from within the congregation. There was buy-in with Russell's transition. In contrast, Gregory's book exposed a reluctance by the senior minister and behind the scenes tactics that hindered his success. My experience mirrored Gregory's situation.

Looking back, someone has to be the first to come behind a legend, but often ends up as the "sacrificial lamb." The statistics of being the "first one" to succeed a legend is not good at all. I think the success or failure has to do with "passing the baton." When the baton is passed, the success rate increases. When the baton is not passed, the rate of failure dramatically increases. The first man sometimes becomes the one who takes all the lumps, especially when the predecessor decides to stay. Those who could not "flex" their muscles with the former minister sometimes see the new minister as a door of opportunity to do what could not be done before. It takes time to transition, especially when the predecessor remains and is active. Both the successor and predecessor are human and have to deal with pride and the call of God in their lives. Both should have an attitude of "we will make this work."

Q: In a 21ˢᵗ century, African-American, small to medium size church context, what advice would you give to church leaders and preachers for a successful ministerial transition?

A: It has been said that "healthy things grow, and growing things change." It takes patience for healthy things to grow. Bringing someone in from the outside or grooming someone from within indicates that the congregation expects change. No two people are the same and much patience must be practiced by everyone involved. Allow the successor to be his own man, make his own mistakes, and grow from the experience. Preparation must be made prior to transition with the leadership and the membership.

There should be a "do no harm" policy in place when there is a ministerial transition. Why can't transitions in ministry mirror the marriage commitment? "For better or worse, richer or poorer, till death do us part" ought to be the mindset of everyone involved. Forced termination of a minister's tenure causes church splits, it damages reputations, and it sows seeds of bitterness.

I think it helps a congregation to heal, stabilize, and move forward when the former minister recommends his successor. It's easier for members to shift their allegiance knowing that the former minister has confidence in the new man. I've been able to do that in two congregations that I served. Also, it will bless the church when the successor, the former minister, and the present leadership publicly acknowledge each other's accomplishments. People in healthy families and relationships say "I love you" more than once.

Finally, churches must prepare financially for ministerial transitions. Only a few congregations can afford to provide financial support for two or more ministers, so an excellent retirement package should be in place.

MINISTERIAL TRANSITION #3
Interview with Ian Nickerson

Ian Nickerson is only the second ministering evangelist of the 41-year-old multicultural congregation, Minda Street Church of Christ in Abilene, Texas. He previously helped to lead the planting of a new work in Denver, Colorado, where 25% of the congregants were Spanish-speaking, first generational Christians. Ian is currently involved in mission work in the western region of Ghana, Africa. He serves on the Board of Directors for the Community Foundation of Abilene. As a Master of Divinity student, Ian was recently awarded the Stone-Campbell Journal Promising Scholar Award. His particular areas of interest are in church polity and the development of local congregations. Ian is married to his eighth-grade girlfriend Sherita (James), and they have three children.

Q: Tell us about your call to ministry, your mentors, and those you may have mentored that influenced your ministry.

A: I knew early on in life that I would one day become a preacher. I grew up in a house where it was mandatory that we go to church every time the doors were open. We went to the Baptist church where my father was a deacon, but before too long, my mother took me and my little sister to the churches of Christ, which is the faith tradition she was raised in. On June 15th of 1983, I was baptized into Christ at the Hawn Freeway congregation in Dallas, Texas. Kent Sutherland was the minister. He was a good and kind man and his preaching and teaching was appealing to me, even as a little boy. The Bible class teachers were influential as well. Sister Andrews planted the idea in my mind that I could one day serve during worship service. Some 37 years later, I still thank her for her encouragement back then.

I helped to lead a soul to Christ when I was eleven. Franklin Clay is his name. After he was added to the faith, I knew I wanted to be in ministry.

I preached my first sermon when I was sixteen at the Southern Hills congregation in Dallas. Bro. A. C. Chrisman Sr. gave me that opportunity in March of 1989, but it was my youth minister, Bro. Lawrence Branch, who worked to set that up. It was around that time that I met the man who would become my spiritual grandfather and influencer from afar, J. S. Winston. His work as an arbitrator and church developer was and is fascinating to me. Later in life, Dr. Tony Roach, the son in-law and spiritual son of J. S. Winston, became my spiritual father.

Dr. Roach is the person who has the most influence in my life as an evangelist. The training he received through Winston from G. P. Bowser, he passed on to me through the Sound Doctrine Training Program. I was in training under Bro. Roach's tutelage for some 25+ years before I succeeded him in ministry.

Q: It has been said, "in order to speak on transitional leadership you have to have made it to the other side. There needs to be some years that go by to prove the success and health of that transition." How many years have transpired since your ministerial transition?

A: October 2020 marked four years, officially. However, Dr. Roach was proactive in conditioning the church for the transition for multiple years before the actual event.

Q: What were your expectations coming in?

A: I was already "in" the congregation, but stepping into the role was not going to be a big shift, initially. I did not expect anything significant to change. I knew I would preach much more, but not all of the time. Bro. Roach preached once a month for the first year of the transition. I expected the influence of Bro. Roach to be superior than my own. I expected people to make flattering comments about my style of preaching and leadership, but I knew I would only carry positional responsibilities and not influential power.

Q: What were some of the initial challenges that you and the congregation faced early on?

A: The challenges (if you want to call them that) had to do with:

1. Leadership style – Bro. Roach and I are at times on the opposite ends of the spectrum when it comes to our personality. Our

personality affects our style of leadership. It took some time for the leaders of our congregation to adapt to me and for me to adapt to them.

2. Communication – This might fall within the leadership style category, but I had to learn how to over-communicate. There were a couple of occasions early on where I thought the elders and I were on the same page and ready to move forward. I soon realized that was not the case.

3. Unrealized expectations – When change occurs, a few things can be expected. One, somebody is going to get more responsibilities, and they might or might not appreciate that. Two, somebody is going to get fewer responsibilities and they might or might not appreciate that. And, three, change will occur and some people will not be affected by the change at all. During our transition, there were a few members who were looking for major changes in some cases, while others were looking for quick changes in other areas. Most of these people were disappointed because I was not looking to make any changes during my first year or so of my new role.

Q: What do you attribute to the success of your transition?

A: 1. Following the leading of Holy Spirit – this is primary.
2. Maintaining my kingdom relationship with Bro. Roach. Kingdom relationships are based upon HONOR, LOYALTY, and TRUST – that was/is key.
3. Believing that I am chosen by God to do what I do – this allows me to be comfortable in my own skin; and in my own gifts, talents, and abilities. This helps me to avoid the challenges of people comparing me to my predecessor – that is ongoing.

Q: I'm aware of two books on ministerial transition. One is *Too Great a Temptation* by Joel Gregory, and the other is *Transition Plan* by Bob Russell. In the first book, someone from outside the congregation was brought in with the former minister remaining at the congregation. The baton was never passed, and the transition did not work. In the second book, the college minister worked with the senior minister for 18 years, mapping out a five-year strategy for passing the baton. After retirement, the former minister did not return for a worship service for a year. What was your situation like?

A: This question made me chuckle. Our situation was like the first example. He did not leave for over a year, and when he left, he did not leave. The transition was slow and intentional. He did not rush and I did not push. It took three years before he relinquished his office over to me. I never asked for it. I never brought it up. I understood (as best I could) the emotional attachment. Even after I entered the office, I intentionally did not make any immediate changes. I honored him in that way.

Q: Did the former minister stay or leave?

A: He moved out of the city after a couple of years, but maintains a pretty healthy relationship with the congregation as minister emeritus. He preaches and joins in leadership meetings when asked or when he feels a strong need to be present.

Q: How does one coming in as the new minister "honor the past" and "set vision for the future?"

A: Every year, we tell our story. We speak of the ways God has blessed over the years and give honor to those through whom God has worked. Psalm 78:4ff gives an example of honoring the past. When we honor the past, we immediately cast vision for the coming year or years. In doing that, we continue to connect our future to our past. The past and the future are not two separate realities; they are two ends of God's purpose for our ministry.

Q: In a 21ˢᵗ century, African-American, small to medium size church context, what advice would you give to church leaders and preachers for a successful ministerial transition?

A: 1. Be intentional. Acknowledge, inquire of, and abide with the Holy Spirit from start to finish.

2. Train ministers within your congregation. That's part of the evangelist role. One of them could or should become the minister to receive the baton. Do not take this for granted.

3. Plan ahead. Many ministers do not. They preach until they cannot. Or they are forced out due to nefarious activity. Some continue to preach until they die. That's not a transition, that is a vacant role.

4. Train the church on the Biblical Model of the Government, Organization, and Development of the Local Church. This information will help the congregation to become or remain a healthy congregation. They will have a greater appreciation for church organization and the role of both the members and the leaders.

5. Have a financial package for the outgoing minister (if he is retiring). Some preachers cannot afford to leave the pulpit. This might help the transition to occur sooner rather than later, in some cases. The training mentioned above in #4 can speak to this issue.

THE MAN OF GOD AND CHURCH HURT

Dr. James Michael Crusoe

> 1 Timothy 6:11: *But flee from these things, you man of God, and pursue righteousness, godliness, faith, love, perseverance and gentleness* (NASB 1995).

> 2 Timothy 3:16-17: *All Scripture is inspired by God and profitable for teaching, for reproof, for correction, for training in righteousness; so that the man of God may be adequate, equipped for every good work* (NASB 1995).

The preaching ministry became so difficult that the prophet Jeremiah did not want to preach, and is called "the weeping prophet." Elijah, after a successful battle at Mt. Caramel, later had a change of heart at Mt. Horeb and asked the Lord to take his life. The Apostle Paul shared "church hurts" that included persecutions, afflictions, sleepless nights, encounters with false brethren, abandonment, and the daily care of the church. Jesus Christ came preaching the gospel of the kingdom . . . and was nailed to a Cross. Without a doubt, the Man of God, the preacher, the minister, the evangelist, the mouthpiece of God has a unique calling. I've learned that through it all, ONLY THE STRONG SURVIVE.

Who is this Man of God? The Man of God is not just another brother in the church! The late pioneer preacher J. S. Winston stated, "the preacher is a special servant of the Lord, with delegated responsibility." He is not a hired servant at the members' beck and call. He is not one who timidly straddles the fence to avoid unemployment.

The Man of God is a gift to the church with spiritual entitlements and delegated authority. Dr. Luis R. Lugo Sr. describes this gift in his book, The *Five Fold Work of the Evangelist*. He, the Man of God, is a Proclaimer, Teacher, Organizer, Defender, and Discipliner. Lugo encourages preachers for the task ahead:

> "To those who aspire to proclaim the gospel, remember [that] to be an evangelist, a successful evangelist, you must know what the work is. There must be the resolve to see that work through. There are hardships to endure, difficulties encountered and more than likely the storm and wrath of those who are worldly-minded, both within the church and out of the church. . . . Success is measured in the free course of God's word in the lives of people, and that he [The Man of God] can proclaim the word freely and without doubt or fear of mankind."

The attitude that "we hired you, we can fire you" is carnal, unbiblical, and borderline evil. How one treats the church and the gifts given to the church is a reflection on how one feels about the head of the church – Jesus Christ. We could learn from Jesus. When Judas betrayed him, Jesus did not call him a traitor. Jesus did not call Judas a backstabber. Jesus did not accuse Judas of sowing discord. Jesus did not attempt to ruin Judas's reputation. Jesus called him "friend."

Over the course of ministry (now 40 years), I've vicariously lived the life of several Bible characters: Joseph (put in a pit and sold by brothers; encountered false accusations); Jacob and Esau (deceived, backstabbed, and the brotherhood political cover-up to hide the deception is worthy of another book itself), and the Apostle Paul (misrepresented and abandoned). The horror stories of brotherhood politics, leadership power struggles, forced resignation, changing the locks of the preacher's office, armed guards to prevent The Man of God from entering the sanctuary, police being called, intimidation tactics, along with cowardly anonymous letters became a reality.

"Crucify him, crucify him" is what the crowd shouted toward the Roman government regarding Jesus, the Son of God. Unfortunately, The

Man of God faces similar hostile audiences hiding behind the veneer of protecting the church, when in reality it's about protecting self-imposed territory. Members applauding and celebrating they got rid of a preacher. If he is wrong, rebuke and restore The Man of God, because right or wrong, he is still "the Lord's Anointed." The Man of God, if loyal to his calling, will continue, even though he may be bruised, beaten, and broken; all the while hoping, praying for forgiveness, restoration, and true reconciliation to occur in the Lord's church. Preachers know that loneliness and isolation are real burdens in the ministry. We wonder, does anyone care . . . where's the grace we preach about? The Man of God will bleed when cut, will bruise when hit by rocks. The meager offer of three months' severance pay does not mitigate the stress of relocation and starting over again. If married, the emotional toil affects his wife and children. They hurt while living in a proverbial glass house.

The Man of God presses on, bruised but not bitter, preaching through pain, dedicated to leading folk who don't want to follow. The late evangelist Nokomis Yeldell, (who I succeeded and worked with for six years before his death) wrote about the preacher/ elder relationship:

> "It appears that those involved wanted the preachers to know who the BOSSES were in the congregation. The teaching was and is saying to the preacher, you are just another member in the congregation. We want members to be sure to look to the elders and never to the preacher for your information, especially official information."

What makes the "Man of God" uniquely different in his calling? Bro. Yeldell also said, "the minister, because of his training and leadership, and soundness in the faith is approved by God and sent by the church to set things in order (organize) teach, train, develop men in the different congregations." This wise preacher emphasized that church leaders:

> "should not act so insecure with the minister, as many do. So much of the moving preachers around the country is because elders say in some cases that it is not good for the preacher to stay too long and gain too much influence.

Members will begin to think he is the pastor of the congregation."

Looking back over unresolved conflicts I've experienced, the common denominator has been a carnal, corporate business attitude of "bossing the preacher" instead of lifting up the hands of The Man of God. How I wish church leaderships would take a theocratic approach to interpersonal and functional relationships in the Lord's body.

The late, legendary preacher Humphrey Foutz preached a sermon, "Come before Winter" recorded in his book *Preaching to a Decision*. I've attempted to preach from that text, 2 Timothy 4:9-22, on numerous occasions. Any preacher, after close to 40 years of ministry, can relate to the loneliness from the pen of the Apostle Paul in the text: "only Luke is with me; pick up Mark and bring him with you, for he is 'useful' to me for service; Alexander the coppersmith did me much evil . . . at my first defense, no one supported me, but all deserted me . . . make every effort to come before winter." The pathos of Paul's pain comes after what we call "The Minister's Charge." Paul, the preacher, was run out of Corinth and fought the "beasts of Ephesus," but now needed support from fellow laborers of the gospel. Defenders of the faith today also need support as they face 21st century challenges. Where are the Luke's, the John Mark's, the Barnabas's who seek to restore or come to a preacher's rescue? Where is the "Jerusalem Council" that will address the trends facing us? What we can appreciate about the pioneers and legends in our fellowship is their public and private support of their peer group – we can appreciate their united front regarding core beliefs and our identifying marks. Men of God, fellow preachers, stop throwing shade, stop the backstabbing, stop the mudslinging, stop the political agendas, stop disrespecting each other. Men of God have to support each other!

The Man of God may have counseling skills, be able to provide therapeutic insight, be scholarly, be a charismatic orator, and may be a cutting edge creator, but first and foremost, The Man of God is a spiritual leader. *"Be thou an example of the believers"* is the encouragement given. *"Make full proof of your ministry . . . do the work of an evangelist . . . preach the word"* is the charge. Yes, The Man of God is God's special servant charged, in the words of Steven Lawson, to be one who "preaches to change culture." Even when there is a famine in the land for hearing the words of the Lord (Amos 8:11), The Man of God is called by God to preach without compromise. Help The Man of God. Lift up the hands of The Man of God. Pray for The Man of God. Support the ministry of The Man of God.

Remember your calling, Man of God. Forty years of ministry has been tough, but not once did I stop loving the church . . . not once did I question the faith once delivered . . . not once did I consider stopping preaching . . . this preaching ministry has its good, bad, and ugly . . . it's more than a career, it's a calling . . . through it all I've learned, "only the strong survive." Preachers, hold on when you grow weary. Remember Jeremiah, the weeping prophet, was disillusioned but had a fire shut up in his bones! Elijah wanted his life to end, but was reminded there were seven thousand in Israel who had not bowed to Baal. Facing the chilly hands of death, the Apostle Paul was ready to die for the name of the Lord. Preaching is not easy, but ONLY THE STRONG SURVIVE!

WHY EXPOSITORY PREACHING?
David Wilson

> *"So they read distinctly from the book, in the Law of God; and they gave the sense, and helped them to understand the reading"* (Nehemiah 8:8 NKJV).

This is one of the high points in the history of God's people. It is a grand example of faith, repentance, and renewal, culminating in joy with righteous resolve. This is also a clear demonstration of the need and efficacy of expository preaching.

It began with an awesome request: *"and they told Ezra the scribe to bring the Book of the Law of Moses, which the LORD had commanded Israel"* (Nehemiah 8:1). This great revival began with a call for the Word, and expository preaching met the need to the full. When people ask the leaders for the Word, something fantastic is about to happen. We of this time are unfortunately used to the exact opposite.

Picture it. These Israelites, wearied from decades of national displacement, exhausted by months of embattled rebuilding, were determined to get things right with God. They understood that the city's walls were not broken due to faulty engineering. They knew that the Temple was not demolished because of the ferocity of their adversaries. They knew that something more than hewn stones, mixed mortar, and resinous pitch was necessary for national security. They needed God. They needed His presence, favor, mercy, and holiness. So they met at the Water Gate during Trumpet Feast Day and requested the Book of the Law of Moses.

Ezra delivered what was needed. He did not come forward with a touching poem, a heart-wrenching story, or a colorful robe ensemble. He did not rehearse the pain and suffering of Jewish years in captivity, being handed over from one megalomaniacal despot to the next. He did not come with a three-year plan for rebirth, regrowth, and renewal. Nor did he come leading them in psalms, hymns, and spiritual songs. He brought the Word.

How did he bring it? This is a great question as it reveals the essence and effectiveness of expository preaching.

- He read it distinctly – Observation
- He gave the sense – Interpretation
- And he helped them understand – Application

While these are familiar terms for those affiliated with biblical studies, they are nonetheless important factors in Expository Preaching (EP). Ezra demonstrated the craft by 'clearly reading' the Law written in Hebrew to people who spoke Chaldee (Babylon). 'Giving the sense' meant to explain the meaning of what was read. 'Helping them understand' is actually pointing them to action, telling them what to do. He told them what the Word said, told them what it meant, and told them what to do. That's how the book got brought!

Perhaps a few well-articulated definitions will help. Theologian and author John Stott wrote, "All true Christian preaching is expository preaching. . . . The expositor prizes open what appears to be closed, makes plain what is obscure, unravels what is knotted, and unfolds what is tightly packed (*Between Two Worlds*, pages 91-92). Professor and author Richard Mayhue wrote that an expositor is "one who explains Scripture by laying open the text to public view in order to set forth its meaning, explain what is difficult to understand, and make appropriate application" (*Rediscovering Expository Preaching*). And, finally, in *Biblical Preaching*, Haddon Robinson wrote, "Expository preaching is the communication of a biblical concept, derived from and transmitted through a historical, grammatical, and literary study of a passage in its context, which the Holy Spirit first applies to the personality and experience of the preacher, then through the preacher, applies to the hearer."

Among these famous scholars, I humbly submit my own definition.

- EP is the explanation of concepts, relaying of directions, and encouragement of the soul from the Word of God with passionate and practical appeal.

- Expository preaching is the unpacking of scriptural text to expose meaning and to lift godly principles, while directing the listener to reflective, contemporary action.
- EP is a revealing of the text, using the historical-cultural context, word meanings, and literary structures, to inspire biblical faith in the learner.

I think it is also helpful to say what EP is not in order to furthermore shape the concept.

- EP is not presenting one's study in a 3- or 4-point format.
- EP is not a discussion of word meanings, Greek pronunciations, or immersion into the culture surrounding the text.
- EP is not preaching extemporaneously, nor is it from an alliterated outline.
- EP is not sounding deep and mysterious as you hold the audience captive until a final big revealing point.
- EP is not preaching with a heart-warming story or unforgettable illustration.

While all of these may be used in EP, they do not encapsulate the essence of EP. If the 'book isn't brought,' explained, and applied, none of the aforementioned tactics or characteristics matter. In fact, while EP is often referred to as a style, it is really about substance, the Word! Scripture-based, historically accurate, culturally sensitive, contextually defined with contemporary application is what Expository Preaching is all about.

Here are three qualities of properly achieving Expository Preaching that argues its merit and persuades your consideration: It is honest, it is easy to grasp, and it lifts principles for life.

It Is Honest

Paul argued the validity of his apostleship by saying, *"But we have renounced the hidden things of shame, not walking in craftiness nor _handling the word of God deceitfully_"* (2 Corinthians 4:2 NKJV). To preach contrary to the meaning of the text is deceitful, even if for good intentions. A classic example is the preacher looking at a small crowd on the opening of a gospel meeting and saying, "Well, the Lord said, 'where two or three are gathered in my name.'" Or looking at the story of Jesus calming the storm and allegorizing the historical and phenomenal Christological event with, "We all go through different storms in our lives." Or "You don't have to worry about who's talking about you or hating on you because God said, 'No weapon formed against you.'" These may be emotional, sermonical, powerful, and even spiritual, but they lack integrity. These examples create celebration and invite faith based on irresponsible exegesis. They express a truth, but not the truth represented by the individual texts. All of Scripture has a message revealed in its original context and culture that will relay principles and instructions for contemporary application. Preaching the Word requires the dedication and discipline to find the meaning and bring it to the people. "Bring us the book!"

It Is Easy to Grasp

EP tends to focus on a passage or verse of Scripture. Whether a biblical narrative, ecclesiological mandate, or Christological concept, EP is best at narrowing the lesson's scope down to a specific portion of Scripture instead of multiple passages. I contend that people will more readily understand the Supremacy of Christ from Hebrews 1:1-4 than quoting or reading the many passages that reflect the same. To show the concept in the housing of its original context is immeasurably more attainable than fifteen scripture passages given without context or explanation. It is like the difference in someone telling you about twelve waterfalls versus taking you to a waterfall. Hearing the thunderous flow, feeling the mist on your skin, and smelling the wet gravel impacts the memory in a way that reporting cannot. EP does not want to tell you about the text (proof-text), but wants to bring the listener into the passage. Once they leave our religious freedom and travel back to the original recipients; once they leave the cushioned pews of an air-conditioned auditorium and sit by a fire in the woods with Saints worshipping in fear; once they feel the dismay of the original audience being persecuted to go back to Judaism, the high description of Jesus in the passage and the imperative to listen to Him will make sense like never before.

It Lifts Principles for Life

EP is not just a reading and explanation of the text; rather, it gives a charge or call to action. As the Bible is the Word of God, when God speaks, something has to change. The expositor's task is not to lead in a discussion or 'lift a nugget for our consideration,' but rather to reveal the will of God with the purpose of issuing the prophetic call to repentance and compliance. Every sermon should have at its base the great question, What does God want us to do with this Word? What is the desired result of this message? If the preacher is not clear on the purpose, we can be sure the audience will not be clear on the purpose at all. I have found that the more directive or purposeful the sermon, the more people engage to listen. They know something significant is required from the lesson, rather than their delight in the preacher's performance.

The benefit of EP is that every passage has principles that can be applied to every age and stage of the listener. As the expositor lifts those principles, or unpacks truth from the text, he or she can call the listener to new or better behavior. This is what Henry A. Virkler called 'principlizing' rather than allegorizing the text. He wrote, "*Principlizing* is an attempt to discover in a narrative the spiritual, moral, and/or theological principles that have relevance for the contemporary believer (*Hermeneutics: Principles and Processes of Biblical Interpretation*, page 194). Rather than allegorizing the text with unverifiable and imaginative equations, EP lifts clear truths for application. Ultimately, the listener begins to rely on the substance of God's Word as a relevant guide for life and not the finesse or creativity of the preacher. This alone is a great goal of biblical preaching.

"Preach the Word!"

> David Wilson is the Senior Minister of the Kings Church of Christ in Brooklyn, New York. Minister Wilson leads a progressive ministry in the neighborhoods of Brooklyn. David is supported by his loving wife Cathi, and their children: David Jr, Dyahnah, and Dominic.

THE CHALLENGE OF EXPOSITORY PREACHING IN AFRICAN-AMERICAN CHURCHES OF CHRIST

John Davis Marshall

Somebody must come preaching. Somebody must come preaching expository sermons. Somebody must come preaching expository sermons in the African-American Churches. But there indeed is a challenge of expository preaching in African-American churches. In actuality, there is a challenge of expository preaching in all churches. Expository preaching would have eliminated and even now will eliminate some of the unhealthy division and foster a more perfect unity in the body of Christ. But what really is the challenge of expository preaching?

First, there is the challenge to extract the expository concept, that one principle that is always true under all circumstances, from within the passage of Scripture. Therefore, the challenge of expository learning (studying) lodges itself and looms large before we get to the preaching. Yes, before there can be expository preaching there must be expository learning. You must learn to master the art of expository study and you must study to master the art of expository learning.

The expository study leads one to accurately extract contextual answers from the immediate pericope under consideration. Therein, one must work to see the main points of the proposition and how to derive them from the verses being studied.

Unfortunately, for too long, a "too highly allegorized" view of the biblical text has satisfied the thirst within African-American churches. For example, let's consider the story of the prodigal son (Luke 15:3-42 NKJV).

What have you heard preached from this story? I heard that one preacher said, "A father should always have something to give his boys," another preacher said, "When your sons think they are grown and desire to leave, let them leave," while still another preacher said, "God was always dividing people into two categories." All of these assessments miss the expository concept therein.

Expository studying leads you to the one concept that is always true and mandated by the mind of God. Though there may be some peripheral truths to the aforementioned propositions, none of these are always true nor mandated by God. The expository concept is this, when that which is lost is found we ought to celebrate. The older brother was out of order. He was unwilling to celebrate when his brother, who had been lost, was found. A sheep had been lost and had been found. When it was found, earth celebrated (Luke 15:6 NKJV). A coin had been lost and had been found. When it was found, earth celebrated (Luke 15:9 NKJV). These two truths illustrate how heaven celebrates when a sinner repents and becomes found (Luke 15:7, 11 NKJV). Now, then, a son had been lost and had been found. Heaven was celebrating and a portion of earth was celebrating. Unfortunately, the older brother refused to celebrate. He was out of step with heaven and earth.

The younger brother could represent the gentiles who had wandered away from the Lord while the older brother could represent Israel who thought they had never been lost. Nevertheless, when that which is lost is found, we ought to celebrate. Any preaching from this text that fails to announce and champion that "always true" principle fails miserably as expository preaching.

Expository preaching sits on the foundation of a true-to-the-text understanding of the verses of Scripture. Meditate upon the text until you are sure that you see an accurate meaning. The meaning of a biblical text must be derived from a healthy extraction through a historical-grammatical and literary study of a passage. The meaning sets on the sole source of Scripture. Carefully exegete the Scripture so that you can extract the accurate meaning. The meaning comes when you correctly interpret Scripture within its context. The meaning is what God originally intended to convey.

For how long have those who preached in African-American churches been taught expository study? How well have they been taught expository study? Therein may lie the answers to the root that grows into the major challenge of expository preaching in African-American churches.

Second, there is the challenge to expose the message. Most African-American churches have not been treated to expository preaching. Therefore, their appetite may immediately reject it. The listener needs to study to train his mind to begin to think in an expositional manner.

In October 1983, I announced to the congregation where I served as minister that I would begin preaching expository sermons through the book of 2 Corinthians. After several sermons, one member came to me and said, "When you announced that you would be preaching through a book of the Bible, I thought how boring will this be." Yet, she went on to say, "But fortunately this has been the most interesting and informative sermons through a book of the Bible that I have ever heard." Notice that her mind was predisposed not to listen to expositional messages. Part of the challenge is overcoming these unhealthy notions of disinterest.

In the African-American church, the preacher must work even harder to expound Scripture and bring out of the text what is there and expose it to the receptive view of the hearer. Therein lies another enormous component of the challenge: Not only must the preacher come to understand the Bible for himself, he must also now consider how to make the theological truth relevant to his audience. There is no one simple and easy way to succeed. Nevertheless, we must unfold the text in such a way that makes contact with the listeners' world. Yet, we must not divorce our message from the inherent demand that all preaching must exalt Christ and confront the need to conform to the preached message.

African-Americans are often labeled as very emotive, jubilant, and celebrative people. That expressiveness permeates our worship experience. Often, the listeners expect and anticipate for the worship climate to cater to their expressive perspective. The preacher, the major catalyst, must set the stage and create the cadence that makes the entire service palatable. Therefore, he must craft sermons that champion this climate. Topical, narrative, and storytelling can easily be designed to satisfy these expectations. Expository sermons may be, or at least perceived to be, the most difficult to fashion excitedly enough to meet the expectations of the high energy appeal. For that reason, those who have preached in African-American church may have shied away from expository preaching.

But now the time has come. I challenge every messenger of God to develop the skill of expository study so that you can master the art of expository preaching. What a blessing for the world when we do.

John Davis Marshall is an author, counselor, editor, life coach, minister, and relationship consultant. John is the grandson of a former slave. He was born and raised in Medon, Tennessee. He is married to the former Priscilla Jackson of Blytheville, Arkansas. They have four children and thirteen grandchildren.

EXPOSITIONAL
SERMONS

PENTATEUCH
Exodus 12:40-51 – *Oh, What a Night: The Passover Lamb*
Dr. Harold Redd

Using Exodus 12-13 and John 19, this message helps Christians think about God! The sermon explores the most tragic night in Egyptian history, connects to the most memorable day in Christian history, and highlights three practical applications.

Scripture Text:

"Now the sojourn of the children of Israel who lived in Egypt was four hundred and thirty years. And it came to pass at the end of the four hundred and thirty years – on that very same day – it came to pass that all the armies of the LORD went out from the land of Egypt. It is a night of solemn observance to the LORD for bringing them out of the land of Egypt. **This is that night of the LORD, a solemn observance for all the children of Israel throughout their generations.** And the LORD said to Moses and Aaron, 'This is the ordinance of the Passover: No foreigner shall eat it. But every man's servant who is bought for money, when you have circumcised him, then he may eat it. A sojourner and a hired servant shall not eat it. In one house it shall be eaten; you shall not carry any of the flesh outside the house, nor shall you break one of its bones. All the congregation of Israel shall keep it. And when a stranger dwells with you and wants to keep the Passover to the LORD, let all his males be circumcised, and then let him come near and keep it; and he shall be as a native of the land. For no uncircumcised person shall eat it. One law shall be for the native-born and for the stranger who dwells among you.' Thus all the children of Israel did; as the LORD commanded Moses and Aaron, so they did. And it came to pass, on that very same day, that the Lord brought the children of Israel out of the land of Egypt according to their armies" (Exodus 12:40-51 NKJV).

Passover was an annual feast that reminded Israel of the night God delivered them from Egyptian slavery. Moses wrote about that night:

> "And it came to pass at midnight that the Lord struck all the firstborn in the land of Egypt, from the firstborn of Pharaoh who sat on his throne to the firstborn of the captive who was in the dungeon, and all the firstborn of livestock. So Pharaoh rose in the night, he, all his servants, and all the Egyptians; and there was a great cry in Egypt, for there was not a house where there was not one dead" (Exodus 12:29-30 NKJV).

What a night! Pharaoh had arrogantly said, "I do not know the Lord, nor will I let Israel go" (Exodus 5:2 NKJV). However, *on that night*, "he called for Moses and Aaron . . . and said, 'Rise, go out from among my people, both you and the children of Israel. And go, serve the Lord as you have said. Also take your flocks and your herds, as you have said, and be gone; and bless me also'" (Exodus 12:31 NKJV).

The Firstborn

God gave Israel two significant memory practices so they would never forget that great deliverance. One, He commanded them to give their firstborn males back to Him: "the Lord spoke to Moses, saying, 'Consecrate to Me all the firstborn, whatever opens the womb among the children of Israel, both of man and beast; it is Mine'" (Exodus 13:1-2 NKJV). God's command was reasonable since He had forewarned the Israelites to:

> "take a bunch of hyssop, dip it in the blood that is in the basin, and strike the lintel and the two doorposts with the blood that is in the basin. . . . For the Lord will pass through to strike the Egyptians; and when He sees the

blood on the lintel and on the two doorposts, the LORD will pass over the door and not allow the destroyer to come into your houses to strike you" (Exodus 12:22-23 NKJV).

Without that warning, the Israelites' firstborn could have been just as dead as the Egyptians' firstborn. So, God spared Israel's firstborn, then commanded them to give their firstborn males back to Him. Exodus 13:11-16 (NKJV) contains additional instructions about offering the firstborn:

"[Y]ou shall set apart to the LORD all that open the womb, that is, every firstborn that comes from an animal which you have; the males shall be the LORD's. 13 But every firstborn of a donkey you shall redeem with a lamb; and if you will not redeem it, then you shall break its neck. And all the firstborn of man among your sons you shall redeem" (Exodus 13:12-13 NKJV).

Notice, all firstborn males belonged to the Lord. Children and unclean animals were typically redeemed. However, if one decided *not* to redeem an unclean animal, that person must break its neck. This implies that God's people should refrain from withholding what rightfully belongs to the Lord for personal use. Noticeably, the command also involved future generations. Moses wrote:

"So it shall be when your son asks you in time to come, saying, 'What is this?' that you shall say to him, 'By strength of hand the LORD brought us out of Egypt, out of the house of bondage. And it came to pass, when Pharaoh was stubborn about letting us go, that the LORD killed all the firstborn in the land of Egypt, both the firstborn of man, and the firstborn of beast. Therefore I sacrifice to the LORD all males that open the womb, but all the firstborn of my sons I redeem. It shall be as a sign on your hand, and as frontlets between your eyes, for by strength of hand the LORD brought us out of Egypt" (Exodus 13:14-16 NKJV).

The Feast of Passover

The second reminder of that night was the Passover feast:

> "And Moses said to the people: 'Remember this day in which you went out of Egypt. . . . Seven days you shall eat unleavened bread, and on the seventh day there shall be a feast to the LORD. Unleavened bread shall be eaten seven days. And no leavened bread shall be seen among you, nor shall leaven be seen among you in all your quarters. And you shall tell your son in that day, saying, "This is done because of what the LORD did for me when I came up from Egypt." It shall be as a sign to you on your hand and as a memorial between your eyes, that the LORD's law may be in your mouth; for with a strong hand the LORD has brought you out of Egypt. You shall therefore keep this ordinance in its season from year to year'" (Exodus 13:3, 6-10 NKJV).

Exodus 12:43-49 contains additional Passover regulations:

> "And the LORD said to Moses and Aaron, 'This is the ordinance of the Passover: **No foreigner shall eat it.** But every man's servant who is bought for money, when you have circumcised him, then he may eat it. A sojourner and a hired servant shall not eat it. In one house it shall be eaten; you shall not carry any of the flesh outside the house, **nor shall you break one of its bones.** All the congregation of Israel shall keep it. And when a stranger dwells with you and wants to keep the Passover to the LORD, let all his males be circumcised, and then let him come near and keep it; and he shall be as a native of the land. For no uncircumcised person shall eat it. **One law shall be for the native-born and for the stranger who dwells among you.**'" (NKJV)

Israel left Egypt with two specific ways to remember God and that wonderful, horrific night!

Three Related Factors

In Exodus 13:17-22 (NKJV), Moses wrote about three other factors that apply to this sermon: (1) God led Israel a longer way because He knew they were not spiritually strong despite such powerful testimony, (2) Moses took Joseph's bones, and (3) God led them with a pillar of cloud by day and a pillar of fire by night. All three factors indicated God's love and presence.

In summary, God delivered His people! Repeatedly, Moses highlighted, "by strength of hand the Lord brought Israel out of Egypt" (Exodus 13:3, 9, 14, and 16 NKJV). Since it was a night to be remembered, God established two specific memory practices. Finally, God gave them three good reasons to believe He was with them! For generations after the original deliverance, the Israelites were offering their firstborn and observing the Passover.

New Testament Perspective

Now, we shall study New Testament perspectives, considering the Old Testament information above. In John 19, Jesus was en route to the cross. Scripture says:

> "From then on Pilate sought to release Him, but the Jews cried out, saying, 'If you let this Man go, you are not Caesar's friend. Whoever makes himself a king speaks against Caesar.' When Pilate therefore heard that saying, he brought Jesus out and sat down in the judgment seat in a place that is called The Pavement, but in Hebrew, Gabbatha. Now it was the Preparation Day of the Passover, and about the sixth hour. And he said to the Jews, 'Behold your King!' But they cried out, 'Away with Him, away with Him! Crucify Him!' Pilate said to them, 'Shall I crucify your King?' The chief priests answered, 'We have no king but Caesar!' Then he delivered Him to them to be crucified. Then they took Jesus and led Him away" (John 19:12-16 NKJV).

It simply cannot be coincidental that during a Jewish Passover feast, the real **Lamb of God** was crucified! John the Baptist saw Jesus and declared, "Behold, the lamb of God that taketh away the sin of the world" (John 1:29 NKJV). The Jews had remembered *that Passover night* since Exodus 12!

That Scripture Might Be Fulfilled

Passover foreshadowed the cross and crucifixion so that Scripture might be fulfilled. Scripture was being fulfilled when, "Then they took Jesus and led Him away" (John 19:16). Isaiah prophesied, *"He was led as a lamb to the slaughter, and as a sheep before its shearers is silent, so He opened not His mouth"* (Isaiah 53:7). So much of what Jesus experienced happened that Scripture might be fulfilled. Consider additional texts.

The soldiers who crucified Him fulfilled Psalm 22:18:

> "Then the soldiers . . . took His garments and made four parts. . . . They said therefore among themselves, 'Let us not tear it, but cast lots for it, whose it shall be,' that the Scripture might be fulfilled which says: 'They divided My garments among them, and for My clothing they cast lots'" (John 19:23-24 NKJV).

According to John 19:28, "Jesus, knowing all things were now accomplished, **that Scripture might be fulfilled**, said, "I thirst." Then, according to John 19:31-37, the Bible reads:

> "Therefore, because it was the Preparation Day, that the bodies should not remain on the cross on the Sabbath (for that Sabbath was a high day), the Jews asked Pilate that their legs might be broken, and that they might be taken away. Then the soldiers came and broke the legs of the first and of the other who was crucified with Him. But when they came to Jesus and saw that He was already dead, they did not break His legs. But one of the soldiers pierced His side with a spear, and immediately blood and water came out. And he who has seen has testified, and

his testimony is true; and he knows that he is telling the truth, so that you may believe. **For these things were done that the Scripture should be fulfilled**, 'Not one of His bones shall be broken.' **And again another Scripture says**, 'They shall look on Him whom they pierced'" (John 19:31-37 NKJV).

They crucified Him between two thieves, but they buried Him in Joseph's new tomb. Isaiah prophesied, "They made His grave with the wicked – but with the rich at His death because He had done no violence, nor was any deceit in His mouth" (Isaiah 53:9NKJV).

A most unforgettable sight was Jesus' mother, his mother's sister, Mary the wife of Cleophas, and Mary Magdalene standing at the foot of the cross – there hung Mary's **firstborn** son! There hung the **Real Passover Lamb!** There hung **the fulfillment of Scripture – that Scripture might be fulfilled.** Therefore, when He was risen from the dead, the disciples remembered how these things were foretold. They confessed Him and declared Him to be the Christ, the son of the living God!

Practical Lessons

We can use the stories about the Passover and the real Passover Lamb to think about God. More than weekly communion, Christians should have periodic times when they **meditate** about what God did through previous generations; when they **contemplate** what God has done since their deliverance; and when they **anticipate** His eternal presence. There should be times when such collected thoughts merge into worship and stimulate praise! The following paragraphs discuss these three parameters.

First, Christians should reflect through previous generations and meditate from where God has brought them. Every year the Israelites gathered for Passover to remember how God brought them out of slavery. It was not a time to deny that bondage happened; it was a time to remember how God brought them out. Christians gather weekly to remember how God brought them out of the bondage of sin! They are not in denial and often think about how God delivered them.

They think about their parents, grandparents, great-grandparents, and other people who guided them from birth and helped correct and shape therm. Many of those people have gone to their eternal reward. Their service merged into our journey and became a part of how and from where God brought us.

Do you think about your deliverance and where God has since brought you? Do you remember when you were baptized, and God washed your sins away? Do you remember the joy? Can you recall the peace you slept with that night?

Some have been Christians for years now and often reflect on what God has done since their deliverance. He guided them through the wilderness and around danger. He provided for them in ways they did not know existed and would never have imagined. Christians personal examples vary, but their testimony is consistent – God is good and He brought us from a mighty long way!

Second, Christians should <u>contemplate</u> God's abiding presence! He is still with us! God did not bring us to this point to leave us. God delivered Israel but stayed with them, even for the longer distance. He guided them with a pillar of cloud by day and a pillar of fire by night. He protected them beyond their understanding. He ***did not*** deliver them and leave them.

There is an illustrative story in Judges about the birth of Samson. The angel of the LORD appeared first to Manoah's wife, then later to both of them. The Bible says:

> "And Manoah said to his wife, 'We shall surely die, because we have seen God!' **But his wife said to him, 'If the LORD had desired to kill us, He would not have accepted a burnt offering and a grain offering from our hands, nor would He have shown us all these things, nor would He have told us such things as these at this time.'** So the woman bore a son and called his name Samson; and the child grew, and the LORD blessed him" (Judges 13:22-24 NKJV).

Manoah's wife reasoned that God did not intend to kill them because He gave them the instructions for raising Samson and accepted their offerings. God was with them and planning to use them. God is with us like He was with the Israelites and Samson's parents. If He intended to leave or kill us, He would not have brought us to this point. He is still planning to use us.

Christians might reason and ask, "Israel knew God was with them because they saw the pillar of cloud and the pillar of fire. But modern Christians do not see the pillar of cloud and pillar of fire. So how can we know God is with us?" The Christian's answer would be the cross. Paul reasoned: "What then shall we say to these things? If God is for us, who can be against us? He who did not spare His own Son, but delivered Him up for us all, how shall he not with Him also freely give us all things" (Romans 8:31-32). God gave us Jesus and we should expect Him to freely give us all things. Christians must keep their eyes fixed on the cross.

Some might say, "I lost a loved one." Others, "I went through a divorce." Still others, "I filed bankruptcy." Complete the list of what God already knows. But, think about it. You are still here and God did not bring you to this point to leave you. There is something ahead and God is present! Despite everything, "we are more than conquerors through Him who loved us" (Romans 8:37 NKJV).

Third, Christians should <u>anticipate</u> God's eternal presence. Their practices and teachings are designed to perpetuate their faith. Moses told Israel:

> "And you shall observe this thing as an ordinance **for you and your sons forever**. It will come to pass when you come to the land which the LORD will give you, just as He promised, that you shall keep this service. And it shall be, **when your children say to you, 'What do you mean by this service?' that you shall say, 'It is the Passover sacrifice of the LORD, who passed over the houses of the children of Israel in Egypt when He struck the Egyptians and delivered our households.'**

So the people bowed their heads and worshiped"
(Exodus 12:24-27 NKJV).

God knew children would observe their parents giving or redeeming a firstborn and inquire. So, He said:

> "when your son asks you in time to come, saying, 'What is this mean?' that you shall say to him, 'By strength of hand the LORD brought us out of Egypt, out of the house of bondage. And it came to pass, when Pharaoh was stubborn about letting us go, that the LORD killed all the firstborn in the land of Egypt, both the firstborn of man and the firstborn of beast. Therefore I sacrifice to the LORD all males that open the womb, but all the firstborn of my sons I redeem'" (Exodus 13:14-15 NKJV).

If Christians observe the Lord's Supper regularly, their children will eventually ask, "Why do you continue to do this?" Those are good times to explain, "I do it because of what God has done for us. Your question is a part of the design. Let me teach you what God has done for us."

Joseph's bones illustrate how the God of our ancestors will be with our descendants. Moses took Joseph's bones when they left Egypt. Before Joseph died, he called his relatives together, and he said: "I am dying. . . . Then Joseph took an oath from the children of Israel, saying, 'God will surely visit you, and you shall carry up my bones from here.' So Joseph died, being one hundred and ten years old" (Genesis 50:24-26). Joseph was just that sure that God, who had been with Abraham, Isaac, and Jacob, would also be with his descendants.

Have you considered what you might say to your children at your death? Would you talk about carnal things? Or could you say with courage, "I'm going the way of all the earth. God will be with you!" Are you as sure about that as Joseph was? You have nothing better to leave this world than God! I know about inheritances, but God forbid that we make wills to leave material things with people who are not saved. Leave them God! God brought us to this point, He has been with us, and He will be with us in eternity.

Conclusion

Finally, the Passover stories can be used to explain God's plan for salvation. They came to break Jesus' bones, but He was already dead because you never break the bones of the Passover lamb. A soldier pierced His side and blood and water came out. The same elements that God used to deliver the Israelites, He used to deliver post-cross people from the bondage of sin. Israel put lambs' blood on their doorposts, but still had to pass through the water (Red Sea). Paul wrote, "all were baptized into Moses in the cloud and in the sea" (1 Corinthians 10:2). In like manner, the blood of Jesus has been shed. However, candidates for salvation must pass through the water! Jesus commanded the apostles, "Go into all the world and preach the gospel to every creature. He who believes and is baptized will be saved; but he who does not believe will be condemned" (Mark 16:15-16).

Dr. Harold Redd is a native of Meeker, Oklahoma. He began preaching as a young man. He currently preaches for the Midtown and Raleigh Springs congregations in Memphis. He has been married to Joyce Ann Redd for nearly forty-one years and they have nine children and six grandchildren.

HISTORICAL OLD TESTAMENT
Ruth 3:1-6 – *A Mother-in-Law Who Mentors*

Dr. James Michael Crusoe

I see an old school mother in Naomi, who developed a mentoring relationship with her daughter-in-law Ruth. Their story is an example of two generations bridging a gap – an older woman giving advice to a younger woman and a younger woman dedicated to serving an older woman. Their story is unique because these women also crossed racial and cultural barriers. Naomi was Jewish, from Bethlehem, and Ruth was from Moab.

Naomi, with her husband and their two sons, moved to Moab due to a famine in their homeland. After moving to Moab, their two sons married girls from Moab. Tragedy set in not long after the move. Naomi's husband died, and her two sons died. Three women were now widows, and Naomi decided to return to Bethlehem. There she had a rich relative, Boaz, to whom Ruth was eventually married. Ruth would become the mother of Obed, the grandfather of David. Thus, Ruth, a Gentile, is among the maternal progenitors of our Lord (Matthew 1:5).

I believe that Ruth was a young adult for the following reasons. The total time Naomi was in Moab was about ten years (Ruth 1:4). Ruth's approximate age can be surmised from this timing. The earliest she would have been married would have been age 14 (which would not be unusual for the Moabites); otherwise, due to promiscuity, the girl would often not have been a virgin at the time of marriage. If the family were in Moab five years before Machlon married Ruth, then Ruth would have been 19 at the time. It is probably reasonable to assume that she was 19 to 24 at the time of the return to Bethlehem.

In this sermon, I want to focus on the special relationship between Naomi and Ruth. It was a mentoring relationship worth modeling. It has been established that young adults desire a nurturing relationship. It has been established that young adults need counsel and guidance from older adults. The body of Christ is a living organism of members mutually dependent upon each other. "Generation X" and the "Peacekeeping Generation" need each other. "Baby Boomers" need "Millennials." We can't make it by ourselves!

Mentoring can be done in various ways. It can be intentional, formal, informal, shadowing, or reverse mentoring. A good mentor is transparent, faithful, and knowledgeable concerning God's Word. A mentee should also be transparent, as well as loyal and teachable. We find these qualities in Ruth and Naomi. I want to share the following points in this lesson today: A mentor will challenge others to have "GOALS BEYOND GLEANING"; a mentor recognizes that "GIRLS NEED GUIDANCE"; and when the mentor/mentoree relationship works, both parties receive "GRACE FROM THE "GO'EL."

Goals beyond Gleaning . . . Ruth Need a Plan (Ruth 3:1)

Life was difficult for Naomi and Ruth. They were two widows and Ruth was forced to work for a living, threshing grain in the fields (like picking cotton). The sovereignty of God is at work in the life of Ruth. Ruth understood the rights of the poor in Israel who gathered grain in a field after the harvesters had passed through. The corners of the field were to be left for the poor to reap (Leviticus 19:9-10; 23:22). Some generous landowners were known to have left as much as one-fourth of their crop for the needy and aliens.[7] While working in the fields, Ruth found favor with Boaz and was given special treatment.

The barley harvest was about to end. Naomi was concerned about the welfare of Ruth and sought to secure the future of her daughter-in-law. She then posed a rhetorical question: Was it not up to her to secure Ruth's future? As her mother-in-law, Naomi asked if she should provide "rest"

---

[7] John W. Reed, *Ruth*, The Bible Knowledge Commentary: An Exposition of the Scriptures, vol. 1, ed. J. F. Walvoord and R. B. Zuck (Wheaton, IL: Victor Books, 1985), 422.

(NIV "home") for her daughter-in-law. The word *mānôaḥ*, "place of rest," derives from the same root as *měnûḥâ* in 1:9 and speaks of the security and tranquility that a woman in Israel longed for and expected to find in the home of a loving husband.

In the story of "the gleaner," Ruth illustrates a number of things:

1. The friendly relations between the good Boaz and his reapers.
2. The Jewish land system, the method of transferring property from one person to another.
3. The working of the Mosaic law for the relief of distressed and ruined families; but, above all, handing down the unselfishness, the brave love, the unshaken trustfulness of her who, though not of the chosen race, was privileged to become the ancestress of David, and so of 'great David's greater Son' (Ruth 4:18-22).[8]

Ruth was poor, but she was willing to work. Naomi saw something special in her and suggested a plan for Ruth to rise above the poverty level. Sometimes we need someone to light the fuse or give us a boost. Naomi looked into the future and realized that Ruth had the potential to go from a gleaner to an owner.

We Have More Potential Than We Realize

Our girls need to set goals early in life. It's quite acceptable to have a "Plan A" and a "Plan B." It is also fine to have a "back-up plan," and I want to suggest that it's wise to have a "just in case" plan! Plans are like the following: Just-in-case you do not meet a "knight in shining armor"; just-in-case your prince charming turns out to be a poor choice; just-in-case after you "kissed the frog" he stayed a frog instead of turning into a prince; just-in-case you don't get the picket fence, the two-car garage, the 2.5 children, big back yard, and doghouse; and "just-in-case" you don't have money in the bank – it's alright to have a "Plan B." Someone ought to teach our girls to have goals beyond gleaning. It's good to have a man, but don't position yourself to be totally dependent on a man.

---

[8] M. G. Easton, *Easton's Bible Dictionary* (New York: Harper & Brothers, 1893).

Girls Need Guidance . . . Ruth Needs Preparation (Ruth 3:2-4)

Without telling Ruth specifically that she had her marriage to Boaz in mind, Naomi gave her daughter-in-law detailed instructions on how to take advantage of the situation. Of course, all of these actions were designed to make Ruth as attractive to Boaz as possible and to break down resistance. The steps may be summarized briefly.

First, Ruth was to take a bath (*rāḥaṣ*, "to wash"), a normal first step in preparation for a sexual encounter and/or marriage. Second, she was to apply perfume. The verb *sûk* means "to anoint." Here, it refers to the application of perfumed olive oil. The need for perfume was heightened by the hot climate and the lack of modern-style deodorants to combat body odors. Third, Ruth was to put on her dress. The word used for "dress" is *śimlâ*, which normally refers to the outer garment that covers virtually the entire body except the head. The word designated garments to be worn by both men and women, though Deuteronomy 22:5 suggests they were distinguished.[9]

Naomi was a wise woman. She realized the journey in life is filled with slippery slopes. It's a journey when girls go from "pigtails to ponytails"; from "dolls to dishes"; from "diapers to Daisy's Dukes." A good mentor will help young girls understand the difference between "face powder" and "baking powder." Even as young adults, our girls need help with what to wear, how to dress, what to say, and what not to say, especially if the young lady wants to "be found." The Bible does say, "Whoever finds a wife, finds a good thing" (Proverbs 18:22). Naomi helped Ruth to be found by Boaz. Sometimes it's about being in the right place at the right time.

Grace from the Go'el . . . Ruth Needs a Protector (Ruth 3:5-6)

There is a concept in the Bible called the Kinsmen Redeemer – a relative that has the right of redemption over a deceased relative's household. A Kinsmen Redeemer is a man eligible to marry and provide an offspring for the dead husband. The concept has much to do with God assigning each family of each tribe a section of the Promised Land to inhabit. This

---

[9] Daniel I. Block, *Judges, Ruth*, The New American Commentary, vol. 6 (Nashville: Broadman & Holman, 1999), 683.

land was very important to God and the Israelites. So, to make sure that it stayed in the family, the kinsman-redeemer law was instituted.

If a man died and left land and a widow who bore no sons, his nearest kinsman would be given the opportunity to buy his land and to marry his widow and have sons to carry on the deceased's name. If he wouldn't, then the next closest kin could redeem.

But now here was the catch. The kinsman-redeemer couldn't make the decision to redeem. He had to be asked by the widow to redeem her husband's land.

Go about It the Right Way . . . Go to the Right Place

The uncovering of the **feet** was a ceremonial act that was completely proper. Probably the scene took place in the dark so that Boaz had the opportunity to reject the proposal without the whole town knowing about it. Ruth is to "lift the covers." What this means in Hebrew literally is to "uncover the place of his feet." The purpose of what Ruth did was essentially to ask for Boaz's protection.

What did Boaz do? He was so sensitive and faultless. He started heaping compliments on Ruth – expressing flattery that such a beautiful young woman would be interested in having him as her redeemer. HE WAS HONEST! But he said, "There is one problem: I'm not really the first in line to redeem you. There is one other relative that is closer. So let me see what I can work out" (Ruth 3:12).

He gave her another load of grain to take home. And just before the sun rose, he sent her back to Naomi in a stealth fashion. But as soon as things started to wake up in the little town of Bethlehem, Boaz took his place at the city gates to wait for the other relative.

Boaz represents a picture of God. He was not God, but he was an illustration of what God is like and what God is doing. What were some things in Boaz's life that were Godlike? Mercy, Generosity, Righteousness, and, most of all – REDEEMER. Don't we all need protection? Psalms 121:1-2 says, "MY HELP COMES FROM THE LORD"!

Had it not been for Naomi, there would be no Ruth and Boaz. If there were no Ruth and Boaz, there was no Obed. If there was no Obed, there was no Jesse. If there was no Jesse, there was no David the King. You know the genealogy in Matthew, chapter 1, don't you? The bloodline of Boaz can be traced to Joseph, the husband of Mary, to whom Jesus was born, who is called the Messiah (Matthew 1:5-16).

I feel like singing a song. The Lord is my light and my salvation!

"The Lord Is My Light"
Frances Allitsen (1897) Boosey & Company, London

The Lord is my light and my Salvation
The Lord is my light and my Salvation
The Lord is my light and my Salvation
Whom shall I fear, whom shall I fear, whom shall I fear
The Lord is the strength of my life, whom shall I fear.

In the time of trouble, He shall hide me
O in the time of trouble, He shall hide me

> Dr. James Michael Crusoe is minister of Arlington Road Church of Christ, Hopewell, VA. He and his wife Debra are the parents of three children and one grandchild.
>
> This sermon was preached at East End Church of Christ in Memphis, Tennessee, as a dissertation requirement: "Developing a Young Adult Ministry at East End Church of Christ, Memphis, Tennessee."

2 SAMUEL 18:18-29

A Biblical Response to Social Injustice – Are the Young Men Safe?

Dr. James Michael Crusoe

I'm concerned about the riot that took place in Baltimore. Each of us should be concerned about the riot in Baltimore because what happened there could happen in Memphis. I'm really concerned about what happened in Baltimore and I want to spend the whole day talking about it. We would take social injustice personally if tragedy happened to someone in your family.

I'm concerned about what happened in Baltimore. After experiencing the tragic death of my blood brother who died at 16 years old (black on black crime), I'm very concerned. I have a son, and we have young men here who could just be walking down the street and become a victim of police brutality. It could be one of our young men. I see Dylan in the audience, and I see other young men, so we all should be concerned. Are they safe walking down the streets of Memphis, Tennessee? That's the question on the floor this morning: are the young men safe? Are they safe if they walk down the street with a Hoodie? Are they safe because their skin is black, and their hair is nappy? Are they safe when their pants are hanging low? Are they safe when pulled over for a routine traffic stop?

The relationship between poverty and race in Memphis is alarming. The poor in Memphis tend to be minorities. The poverty rates for Blacks and Latino are higher than the overall poverty rate, and poverty rates for minorities are higher in every age category than poverty rates for non-Hispanic Whites. Moreover, poverty rates for non-Hispanic Whites are lower in Memphis and Shelby County than in Tennessee as a whole or the United States in every age category.

Aren't you tired of the sarcastic criticisms the city of Memphis receives for being broadcast on the crime show, "The First 48 Hours?" However, statistics do not reflect our city in a good light. The Memphis Police Department investigated 168 murders in 2014, according to a news release issued by a department spokesperson. Out of 168 homicides, police said 24 of the killings were justifiable. Recently, I sat in a courtroom and witnessed young person after young person charged and arraigned. I witnessed court dates and hearings, and heard probation officers give reports. I looked on the faces of those handcuffed and saw the hopelessness and despair. The cry of David in 2 Samuel 18 is a relevant cry today – "Is the young man safe?"

Baltimore is not the only place where police brutality has occurred. Baltimore is not the only place where social injustice has occurred. Trey Vaughn Martin was killed in Florida. His killer was put on trial and acquitted, which resulted in protests. And then Michael Brown in Ferguson, Missouri was a victim of social injustice. The killing of Botham Jean in Dallas, Breanna Taylor in Louisville, George Floyd in Minneapolis, Atatiana Jefferson in Fort Worth, along with Eric Garner, Tamir Rice, and John Crawford are just a few "high profile" cases of police brutality. What about the names of black men and women who do not make national news?

Let's wake up and smell the coffee, African-Americans do not receive the same treatment as others. We do not live in the 1960s, but in some cases things are still the same. We have to admit that racism still exists in our country. White privilege still exists in our country. We may not live under Jim Crow laws as we did years ago, but there is still a class system in the United States of America. It is unfair, unjust, and evil when African-Americans make up 13% of the population "but are killed by police at more than twice the rate of white Americans." The honest truth is people of color are treated differently.

There is very little press coverage when white liberal arts college students burn down buildings after a ballgame. But when people of color burn something, it is shown all over the country making us look like savages. We have to realize that young black men are thrown in jail for carrying a small amount of "weed" in their car, while a majority race will get a "slap" on the wrist for possession of cocaine. Racial profiling and police homicide is a reality that must be addressed, given the fact that during 2004 to 2012 there were 4.4 million random stop-and-frisks in New York City. This may mean nothing until it hits home. What if it was your son or nephew, your grandchild, or your brother? My concern today is that church members ought to have something to say!

In our text this morning, David is asking a relevant question. His question is about his son Absalom. In this text, David was concerned about the welfare of his son Absalom. In order to understand this text, it would be helpful to understand David's punishment due to his indiscretion with Bathsheba. Most of us are familiar with the story of the adulterous relationship between David and Bathsheba. We are aware that Bathsheba became pregnant as a result of this relationship. In an attempt to cover up the pregnancy, David arranged for her husband, Uriah, to come home from battle and spend time with his wife, Bathsheba. However, Uriah refused to sleep with his wife while his fellow soldiers were in battle. David countered by having Uriah sent to forefront of battle, insuring sudden death. After Uriah died in battle, David took Bathsheba as his wife.

Of course, this sin displeased God and the prophet Nathan declared that the sword would never leave the house of David. From this point on, there was conflict and dysfunction in the house of David. There was so much dysfunction that Amnon, a son of David, raped his half-sister Tamar. Tamar, a virgin, pleaded with Amnon not to force himself on her, but being the king's son, he could ask for her hand in marriage. Amnon refused her wise counsel, had his way with her, and afterwards hated her.

There are a number of lessons that need to be shared. There are fellas out there who want to have their way with our daughters and then kick them to the curb. The question must be asked, "Are the young women safe?" Can our young ladies go to the mall without being "hit on?" Can they go to school or even come to church without being "hit on?" Are our young women viewed only as trophies? We need to teach our young men manners. Someone ought to tell our young men to "keep their hands in their pockets and their eyeballs in their sockets." We must remind our young ladies there is nothing wrong with saying no to sex before marriage. Virginity is pleasing in the sight of God!

David's indiscretion with Bathsheba has catastrophic consequences that affected his other children. Absalom, the older brother of Tamar, is angry that their father David does not avenge the wrong that Amnon committed. Absalom vowed to avenge the deed for his sister. I think it is good if there are big brothers who look out for their sisters. Absalom was attractive, charismatic, and influential, and had led a failed revolt to take the throne from his father. David and Absalom are in battle. At Mahanaim David numbered and organized his forces. He appointed three commanders, each in charge of one third of the force: Joab, his brother Abishai, and Ittai. David intended to lead the army, but his troops vetoed this idea. His presence on the battlefield would become the focal point of the enemy attack. It would be better if David remain in the safety of the city with whatever reserve forces there may have been. The king reluctantly agreed. So David stood by the gate and reviewed his troops before the battle. In the hearing of the entire army, David charged his three commanders for his sake to deal gently with his son Absalom.

The two armies met in the forest of Ephraim. David's troops gained the advantage almost immediately. In the wide-ranging battle, the forest proved a formidable obstacle for Absalom's less skilled partisans. In all, Absalom lost twenty thousand troops that day, a good portion to the pits and perils of the forest (2 Samuel 18:6-8). As Absalom tried to escape the battle, his head became lodged in a low-hanging tree. He was jerked from the back of his mule and left dangling in midair. His predicament was reported to Joab. David's close friend Ahimaaz wished to carry the news of the battle to David. For some reason unexplained in the text, Joab denied the request of Ahimaaz. He dispatched instead a Cushite (Ethiopian black man) runner. Still, Ahimaaz pressed Joab for permission to carry the news to David. Perhaps he felt that the Cushite would not present the news of Absalom's death in a sympathetic manner. Joab finally consented to dispatch Ahimaaz. Taking a longer but quicker route, Ahimaaz outran the Cushite (18:19-23).

David waited anxiously "between the two gates" of Mahanaim for news from the battle. At last, a watchman caught sight of a man running alone. David reasoned that the news must be good else the watchman would have seen many men fleeing in all directions from the battlefront back to the safety of the city. Then the watchman spotted the second runner. Again, David consoled himself with the assessment that the news must be good. As the runners drew nearer, the watchman thought he recognized the unique running style of Ahimaaz. David was convinced now. Ahimaaz was a good man. He would surely be bringing good news (18:24-27).

Ahimaaz approached his king and breathlessly blurted out the message, "All is well." He then prostrated himself and praised Yahweh who had delivered up all those who had lifted their hands against the king. David anxiously inquired about the well-being of Absalom. In spite of all that had happened, David still loved that rebellious son (18:1-5). David is still concerned about the welfare of his son, and asked the question, "Is the young man safe?" David's paternal instincts may have been motivated by guilt and remorse. The question he asked is relevant today.

I want to ask the question, are our young men in Memphis, Baltimore, and across the nation safe? The incarceration rate for young black males is higher than young white males. Why are there more black males in prison than graduate from college? The poverty rate in Baltimore among Blacks is 30%, when the national poverty rate is only 14%. The unemployment rate for Blacks in Baltimore is 21%, but the national unemployment rate is only 5.5%. In Baltimore, per 100,000 people, the incarceration rate is 3,074, while the national average is only 455. Young black males are prime to be arrested. In Baltimore alone, when it comes to teen births, the female age range for those 15-19 per 1,000 people is 108, but the national rate is only 26. The infant mortality rate in Baltimore is 21.2%, but the national rate is 6%. That means that proper medical care is not being provided.

What is really going on? Young adults in Baltimore are fed up, frustrated, and angry. There is a rage inside of them without a way of venting properly. Whenever a group has been held hostage, oppressed, or ostracized, eventually that frustration is going to be released. It was the young people that led the protests in Baltimore. Millennials are challenged today to lead the charge of addressing social change. Millennials are the foot soldiers and leaders of today who can make the world a better place.

Conclusion

Why is it that for the most part churches of Christ are not progressive when it comes to responding to race, religion, and responsibility? I'm concerned when members of churches of Christ are not visible and speaking out against social injustice. I am not suggesting that we use injustice as a platform to speak on or ignore doctrinal and salvific matters. I am suggesting that we ought to have a voice and let the community know that the churches of Christ members care about the plight of social injustice. I am more than a little bothered that while we claim our religious neighbors have missed the mark on doctrine, we bury our heads in the sand when it comes to social injustice. There is a balance between preaching the gospel to save souls and preaching the gospel so that the world looks more like heaven.

I want to suggest some preventive things we should do. It may be too late once the police arrest our children. What can we do to prevent our boys from being arrested? The casualty list is piling up – Ahmaud Arbery in Georgia and, most recently, Jonathan Price in Wolfe City, Texas. My question today is, are the young men safe? Have they ever been safe? What can be done to ensure Black Americans, especially young Black Americans, are safe?

We need to remind our young people that Romans 13 teaches that there are God-ordained servants that are to be respected. Be respectful if you are pulled over by the police. Don't be smart with the police, talking back or agitating the police. Yes, you have rights, but don't instigate. There is a right way to conduct ourselves. The church should support peaceful protests. We cannot forget who we are. We are children of God. Jesus taught, "Blessed are the peacemakers." We have to teach our young people how to conduct themselves out in public. We need men to mentor younger men. Talk to our boys, teach them how to talk, how to dress, how to interview for a job. We need older men and older women to step up and model Titus 2:1-9. Older men and older women have to take time to teach.

Parents have to discipline their children. Do you remember the mother whose actions went viral during the Baltimore riot? She was shown slapping her boy for being in the wrong place at the wrong time. She was criticized and complimented; yet the good thing is that she was visible. She went where he was. We need "old school" parents. Old school parents know where their children are. Old school parents start early pointing their children in the right direction. Old school parents make sure their young men and young women are safe.

Older adults must model for young adults. Modeling involves setting the right example when it comes to spiritual faithfulness . . . yes, church attendance and commitment is important. Young adults learn by observation and it is important that they see the older generation faithful in attendance and fruitful in ministry. I must echo that there is a need for older men to mentor younger men. The school system needs mentors. The court system needs mentors. The business world needs mentors. The home needs mentors. The church needs mentors. We need mentors at East End Church of Christ!

This sermon comprises two sermons from a sermon series submitted as a requirement for his D.Min dissertation while he was preaching for the East End Church of Christ in Memphis, Tennessee: "A Biblical Response to Baltimore – Are the Young Men Safe" and "A Biblical Response to Baltimore – Don't Remove the Hedge (Job 1:1-12)." Both sermons were written in response to the 2015 riots in Baltimore after the death of Freddie Gray. For this book of expositions, he has taken the major portion from "Are the Young Men Safe" and portions of "Don't Remove the Hedge" and retitled this sermon: "A Biblical Response to Social Injustice – Are the Young Men Safe" and contemporized this sermon.

WISDOM LITERATURE
Job 23:1-12
When He Has Tried Me, I Shall Come Forth as Gold
Dr. Loyd Clay Harris

As to the background of the book and the text, there was a real place called Uz. There were real people called Uz, in fact, there were several. Since cities and regions were often named for their founders, or progenitors, it stands to reason that there might have been an Uz land or city. Then Jeremiah specifically mentioned Uz as a location during his time in Jeremiah 25:20 (ESV) and Lamentations 4:21 (ESV). There are even map locations for this land. Though we do not know when the story took place, we do know that the message of the story is true. We know it because it is a real truth that we identify with and because it is captured in the divine writings. We know the message is true because it is sprinkled throughout the Scriptures from the suffering of Isaac, who repeatedly had his wells taken away, to the journey of Jacob and his descendants in Egypt who were subjected to slavery but were delivered by God through the hand of Moses. We know it is a true message with the known history of so many righteous men who, despite doing all they could to honor the biblical and medical and social codes of conduct, were stricken without reason (known to man) with sickness, calamity, suffering at the hand of evil men, and hideous death while serving others. The story rings true in our spirits and in the depths of our souls.

The book of Job is written like a real three-act drama in Theodicy pitting Job against Satan and the elements with his friends as antagonists. Job is the protagonist even though he is oblivious of the plot. Without knowing it, he is fulfilling God's goal of the defeat of Satan without props and without knowledge of whether or when help will come. This is faith hidden in the drama, but is not made visible until the epilogue. Job's friends are the antagonists because they fight for the way things have always been perceived and they judge Job on the basis of claiming righteousness while suffering the way no man has been known to suffer.

Throughout the story, Satan does what he always does. He instigates and then lets the drama play out in real time in human experience. We tend to ignore or may even be oblivious to the fact that it all began with an accusation from the devil himself. He started it and men keep it going until there is no one left. But this is who and what he is, as pointed out by scholars. Satan is called "the great dragon . . . that old serpent" (Revelation 12:9 KJV), and his name is *Lucifer*. Many scholars insist that he was the highest angel ever created by God, but he fell because of selfishness and pride. He is *an angel of light* with such deceptive and seductive power that even some ministers follow him, ministers who are "transformed as the *ministers of righteousness*" (2 Corinthians 11:14-15 ESV). Throughout Scripture, Satan is described as "the god of this world" who blinds men's minds (2 Colossians 4:4 KJV). He is "the prince of this world" and:

> "the prince of the power of the air. He is Satan, which means the adversary. He is the devil, which means the slanderer. He is the deceiver of the whole world (2 Colossians 11:3 KJV; Revelation 12:9 KJV). He is the tempter. He is the evil one, the father of lies, the accuser of the brethren, a murderer, Beelzebub, Belial, Abaddon, the angel of the bottomless pit, Apollyon, the enemy, the lying spirit, that old serpent, the prince of devils, the ruler of the darkness of the world, and the wicked one."[10]

Introduction

For years, we have been taught, teaching and believing, that God will hear and grant the requests of His children if they "do those things that are pleasing in his sight"

---

[10] *Job*, The Preacher's Outline & Sermon Bible, vol. 17 (Chattanooga, TN: Leadership Ministries Worldwide, 2010).

(1 John 3:22 KJV). We have also believed that God does all things for good to them that love Him and do His will (Romans 8:28-30 ESV). As far back in my experiences as I can remember, this rule has seemed to manifest itself in a real sense in my life. When my mother died, I felt like it was not only the will of God, but somehow it worked out best for all concerned. I could see how God was working to mother's good to end the suffering and even to my good by freeing me to my life's work. I also knew that death was an appointment of man which all must face and therefore is certainly a just act of God.

Then years into my full-time ministry something happened that I could not explain. A young man named Charles V. Dorsey was in a baseball accident that broke his neck and left him paralyzed from his shoulders down. He and another young man collided in mid-air while running to catch an outfield high-fly ball. It had been a hard game, and this could mean the game. This kind of accident never happens in baseball (football or basketball, yes). His mother was a devout Christian and her children have been instructed in the way of the Lord. Charles, though a Christian, was not as dedicated as his mother. When this accident happened, the church held prayer meetings and went into fasting and prayer for them, asking God to give him back the use of his limbs. We prayed earnestly for weeks and fasted religiously.

The mother was a single mom and was providing for the children alone. She was struggling to support them on a meager salary while having a difficult employer to face at work (we had talked several times about the problems her employer had been giving her). She was doing all she could and had even accepted her difficult times in deep and abiding faith and trust in God. Even if things were bad, she felt good about the God she served. And now she will have to give up her job to stay home with a son who could do nothing.

The son was brilliant, according to reports from his school. He played ball and had won several scholarships. He had a high grade-point average and had just graduated from high school. He was planning to major in engineering in college. When all of this happened, his dreams and hopes became nightmares. He was first frightened, then he wanted to die. He became angry, hostile, and finally indifferent. His mother suffered some of the same emotional changes though she tried to hide them for his sake. She wanted some relief in knowing why or what God expected her to gain by it.

My problem: How do you really explain to this family how to take and understand this? We held up hope to the family as long as we could. If the son was paralyzed for life, the mother may lose everything.

Our question: Why would God not do what His people, the church, were asking, begging and pleading for Him to do? What possible good can come from a young man paralyzed for life and is now only eighteen years old? Are not there enough righteous people in the church for God to hear their cry and grant their petition? Is intercessory prayer of any real value today?

If one believes in God as an all-powerful being whose essence can be described as love, and if this God is both desirous of that which is for the good of man and is committed to grant to man his requests on the condition that man does that which is pleasing in the sight of God, how can one explain the paralysis of a son, coupled with the imprisonment of a mother as his caretaker, as a just and merciful act of a helpful God? This is the theological question. How to answer the question without condemning the suffering family or rejecting the justice, love, and mercy of God? How does the Christian, especially, maintain his integrity in such difficult times?

I became frightened because I wanted to reach out and really help someone and yet I had seen what making allowance to question God can do. I saw what it did to Wiesel who turned from a believer to an atheist. I saw what it did to two other people I knew. One rejected religion and shouted, "Where was God when I needed Him?" The other rejected the church and said, "what has God ever done for me?" So, I enrolled in graduate school and studied Providence and Suffering seeking answers that would help those whom I would serve.

And now here we are wrestling with Job as he cried out of his suffering soul:

> "Today also my complaint is bitter, my hand is heavy on account of my groaning. Oh, that I knew where I might find him, that I might come even to his seat! I would lay my case before him and fill my mouth with arguments.

I would know what he would answer me and understand what he would say to me. Would he contend with me in the greatness of his power? No; he would pay attention to me. There an upright man could argue with him, and I would be acquitted forever by my judge. Behold, I go forward, but he is not there; and backward, but I do not perceive him; on the left hand when he is working, I do not behold him; he turns to the right hand, but I do not see him. But he knows the way that I take; **when he has tried me, I shall come out as gold**" (Job 23:2-10 ESV).

By the time we get to chapter 23, Job is deep in suffering and great anguish because he is struggling more with the reason than the reality of it.

At one point, Job was certain that he would get an answer from God, but was baffled by the fact that he could not have a face-off with God because he did not know where to find him, yet he was certain that God was present and he would vindicate him of the charges his friends made against him. Job believed that an "upright man" could reason with God (v. 7) and that the judgment of God would be different from the judgment of men. So, Job concluded that while he may not know which way He is going at any particular moment, He always knows the way that Job goes (vv. 8-10). Hence, his consoling conclusion when He has tried me (tested me, proved me, cross-examined me) is that he shall come forth (come out) and will be pure as gold (I will emerge as pure gold, I will pass the test, He will find me pure as gold as I go forth).

FOCUS: Does the Suffering of Job Eclipse God?

This message is a discussion of suffering and the servant of God with some emphasis on the principle of suffering and the sovereignty of God and the victory of the believer. Victory is not defined as getting what you want in the outcome of the suffering, but rather of retaining your integrity and receiving vindication from God that your faith and relationship with Him is intact. The power of Job's confidence is seen from our perspective because we have a panoramic view of the movement of the entire episode. We, therefore, can see that while God is not the active cause of all suffering,

He does allow us to suffer and the reasons are not always the same. God's purpose is to help men to be established in faith with hope for the journey. Satan's objective is the fatal fall of man and proof that man is as rotten as Satan himself – he will follow Satan to the depths of depravity. Man's purpose must be as Job's, to retain our integrity even in the most trying times and not sin against God nor charge God foolishly. Job's friends' purpose was to bring Job to their own views of life so that all continued to fit and work as they have always seen it or imagined it to be.

To our consolation, David would later cry, "Fret not thyself because of evildoers, neither be thou envious against the workers of iniquity. For they shall soon be cut down like the grass, and wither as the green herb. Trust in the LORD, and do good; so shalt thou dwell in the land, and verily thou shalt be fed" (Psalm 37:1-3 KJV) (There are similar statements in Proverbs 24:19 KJV and Jeremiah 12:1 KJV.)

It is difficult to carve out a single verse or few verses in this document and seek to interpret it apart from the full corpus of the book. The narrative associated with the text and its application deals with seven images with which Job struggled and in which we also struggle today.

1. *Hope rooted in deep desire and firm faith in God and coupled with a sense of righteousness.* Job shows us that hope is not lost simply because one does not understand what is happening, why it is happening, or how it will end. Hope is rooted in the sovereignty of God and the faith that recognizes that God is not powerless to achieve His purpose and therefore is not limited by either love for man or ability to deliver. His will and purpose determine how He will handle any situation.

2. *The depth of suffering and feeling of aloneness and anguish of the soul because of not being able to comprehend the cause or make sense of the purpose of it.* Job's aloneness was caused by the loss of offspring and possessions, the foolish suggestion of his wife, and the judgmental distance created by friends who condemned him. Their words put them together and placed him all by himself on the other side.

3. *A struggle with the righteousness, sovereignty, and justice of God over against the perfect love and uprightness of God.* For a moment, Job seemed to think that God was unjust but during the debate and

his reasoning he admitted to the justice and righteousness of God and admitted his own shortcoming. Job would finally get it and understand that he did not have the knowledge for the questions he was asking (Job 42:1-6 KJV). We learn that when we do not understand, don't stop believing, don't stop seeking God for help; but know and trust that even if perfect understand does not come, we can come to a place where we are okay with our limited clarity: God is in charge and he and I are alright. That is enough for me.

4. *Is suffering the revelation of divine retribution or a breach of the divine love and omnipotence of God?* Job answered this question by pointing out that both options are at times true for God. Evil men suffer for their evil and at times they seem to be prosperous and contrariwise for the righteous. But God is just in His sovereignty and is fulfilling His purpose.

5. *Is it ever possible to be at peace with suffering without turning cold toward God, being envious of fellowmen who remain whole and even set themselves in judgment over us because of our struggle?* Job works his way to this point with phrases like: The Lord giveth and the Lord taketh away and blessed be the name of the Lord. Or shall we receive good from the Lord and not evil. Or, though he slay me, yet will I trust in him.

6. *The text confirms the openness of friendship and the growth through struggles that do not require a resolution of the case, clarity of the differences, or abandonment of the hope and belief in God and oneself.* Though Job once called them pitiful friends, he did not abandon them, and they did not leave him. By staying together to the end of the debate, God brought clarity for all of them.

7. *The text answers the question raised by atheists, infidels, and agnostics, and even by suffering believers, "If God can heal, or deliver, why does He not do it?"* His answer was, "when he has tried me, I shall come forth as gold" (Job 23:10 NASB1995). He seemed to be saying, "I won't know exactly what I am made of until the test has been performed." A great part of that test comes through suffering.

For us as Christians, we can often see what God was doing with someone in biblical times and we can appreciate it and praise God. But when we are Job and have Eliphaz, Bildad, and Zophar as friends who act as prosecutors against us, and then we have to listen to Elihu who condemns everyone, we often forget the reason for the story and the conclusion of it. We focus on the struggle and the darkness and lack of vision for an acceptable outcome. At this point, we need not forget that Satan is not only the instigator, but he is always fueling the flames of doubt and fear and worry that tend to eclipse God when and while we wrestle with faith and integrity.

Eliphaz's argument against Job was based on experience (4:8-9; 5:17-27; 22:5-13 KJV).

Bildad based his charges on tradition (8:6-8, 20 KJV).

Zophar based his theory on assumption (11:5-6 KJV; 20:4-6 KJV).

Job insisted that he was upright, but he was still suffering (6:27-30 KJV). The friends argued that the wicked always suffer, but Job countered that the righteous suffer also (19:25-26 KJV; 21:7 KJV). Job further argued that the wicked often prosper in this world (24:6 KJV). Job was broken (16:12-14 KJV), melted (23:10 KJV) and softened (19:21 KJV; 23:16 KJV).

Elihu claimed that Job was too arrogant. He tried to convince Job that he must become humble and teachable and more patient. He said Job was sinning because of suffering (33:8-11 KJV; 35:15-16 KJV).

Yet, the real issue for Job, and so often for us, is "where is God in the midst of all this and how do men come up with their diagnosis of the heart of men and the decision of God when looking at the struggles of those around us who suffer more than us, who prosper less than us, who die sooner than us?"

Faith and integrity says, "I do not know what the outcome will be, but I know who will still be there when it is over. So, live or die, stay sick or get well, be liberated or remain in bondage – 'I know that my redeemer lives and that I will see Him for myself. Though he slay me, yet I will trust in him.'"

Despite the early date of the book, it perfectly paints the struggles of men in dealing with most, if not all, issues. We tend to follow Satan's lead and divide over our own convictions and judge everyone who seeks to bring us to a divinely-led conclusion that brings hope to the experiences of life.

Job becomes our teacher in dealing with suffering when we see how he handles his situation. His answer to the charges made by his friends pressed him to a conclusion that becomes the key to the story: HOW WILL THIS

END? Job, though not yet at the end, predicted how it would play out. In his expectation, he was only claiming moral, spiritual, and theological victory. He was not claiming medical, social, economic, or terminal victory over the prospect of extended suffering or even death. He accepted whatever physical outcome there may be, but he did not see it as defining him. He saw the fire of testing and trial and purification and argued that the result would be the shinning brilliance of purified gold. "Behold, I go forward, but he is not there; and backward, but I cannot perceive him: On the left hand, where he doth work, but I cannot behold him: he hideth himself on the right hand, that I cannot see him: But he knoweth the way that I take: **when he hath tried me, I shall come forth as gold**" (Job 23:8-10 KJV).

This is not a claim of purity or perfection. It is not a claim of divine intuition. It is a claim of faith in God due to a knowledge of righteousness and the acceptance of suffering as a refinement to a carefree existence. Job confirmed that his faith in God did not exist because he had never sinned or that he knew how his life will turn out.

Job was weary of debating with men and now wanted to present his case to God Himself. He had concluded what we too often fail to recognize: it is not man we must convince, and it is not man who can vindicate us or even forgive our faults and take away the suffering. We must appeal to God because our case lies with Him. This calls for a level of faith that acknowledges the truth about our lives. We cannot lie to ourselves claiming how faithful we have been when God, and everyone, has seen our rebellion against God without repentance.

To plead a case before God leaves one with nothing hidden, no rock to hide under, no shield to cover us, no secrets to hold back, and no hidden pride paraded as false humility.

Job's desire was to get God's answer, but he wondered if God would be gentle or forceful in His judgment. He convinced himself that God would not be like friends who can only condemn, who can only confirm the status quo, who can only look at things the way he feels, who can only see defeat, who are not willing to admit that they do not know why and they do not know what the outcome will be. All we know is that it is God, but His ways are above finding out; His love is without measure and He is always ready to forgive. When He is ready, He can and will forgive if men will surrender to His truth.

At this point, one of Job's biggest struggles was the fact that no one could know or contain the whereabouts of God. You know He is there and always near, but you have to appeal to Him, pray to Him, wait on Him, and know that He will come to you in His time.

You can see His handy work all around you and try to pinpoint His location, but it does not work. You need to submit to Him, turn to His will, give in to His way, abandon your righteousness, and admit that at your best you are still "you."

Verse 10 becomes one of the pivotal verses that provides an examination of the message of the book because it gives us one of the purposes for suffering and tragedy and disappointment – God's testing, proving us, and interrogating our life, our resolve, our faithfulness, and our proving that Satan is wrong:

1. Not everyone wants to be God as he tried to suggest to Eve in the Garden.
2. Not everyone serves God only because he is never denied a blessing or struggled without knowing why.
3. Not everyone is so influenced by those around them that they abandon faith in the providence of God.
4. Not everyone thinks that nobody is righteous, so it is impossible for me to be righteous.
5. Not everyone cares more about possessions and figures and favor among men than they do for acceptance by God.

Job's reason for believing in how he will fare is based on several facts that he mentioned in his defense:

1. I followed in His tracks and have not turned back or away (v. 11 ESV).
2. I have kept his commands on my lips and treasure his words more than food (vv. 11-12 NKJV). "Man shall not live by bread alone; but man lives by every word that proceeds from the mouth of the Lord" (Deuteronomy 8:3 NKJV; Matthew 4:4 NKJV).
3. God is unchangeable and cannot be defeated because He will carry out His will and He will certainly accomplish what He has directed for me (v. 13 NKJV).

4. This statement is evidence that Job believed that even if it takes death and resurrection, he was in God's plan and the plan would be achieved. He believed that God had a decree over his life, and it would happen (v. 14 NKJV).

5. So, for him, whatever else was happening, he was being tried so the pure gold would emerge. Somewhere down in him, in his heart and soul, in the reigns of his existence, in the relationship he has had with God, there was pure gold and these trials and sufferings would reveal it and it would shine in the presence of God Himself.

Job's position is expressed by B. H. Carroll: "Conscious of my integrity, I expect final vindication, but am puzzled and grieved to be held in the dark at this helpless distance from God (23:3-17). . . . The traditional and prevalent doctrine that all sin is punished in this life and that all suffering is punishment of specific sin, is confuted by Job. . . . The explanation of his calamities he has not found."[11]

This image of God gives me hope amid my personal suffering. I finally get Job's heart. I don't know God as I want to know Him. I know He will do as He pleases. I even fear him – that is, fear the outcome of my circumstances. I don't want to be sick, don't want to die with my condition. I don't want to be in poverty because I lost everything. I don't want to be friendless. I don't want to be abandoned by my wife. I don't want to be broke, sick, dying, and alone. But I will not give God up. I will not deny Him. I will not stop trusting Him and seeking Him. Because I still believe He has something in store for me, whether now or in my new life, and my new body and my new home.

But I am not destroyed by the darkness that covers my face (v. 17). Thus, Job's expectation was fulfilled. **"WHEN HE HAS TRIED ME, I SHALL COME FORTH AS GOLD!!!** (Job 23:10 RSV)

God did three things for Job (Job 42:8-10 RSV):

1. He gave him a transformation – "him will I accept."
2. He vindicated him – called him "my servant Job."
3. He restore him – "the Lord gave Job twice as much.

---

[11] B. H. Carroll, *Job*, An Interpretation of the English Bible, vol. 2, repr. (Grand Rapids: Baker, 1978), 24-25.

I FINALLY HAVE THE ANSWER TO MY QUESTION REGARDING CHARLES DORSEY AND HIS FAMILY, AND THE STRUGGLES WE ENCOUNTERED. I DON'T HAVE TO KNOW WHAT IS GOING TO HAPPEN, I JUST NEED TO KNOW WHO IS GOING TO TAKE CARE OF IT.

Charles did not recover from his paralysis, but he did live a useful life. He still needed a wheelchair the rest of his life. Yet, he started a business and had employees, owned a vehicle and drove himself around. He had children and dreams and a life. God did not remove what we feared, but he did give what was needed. The family's struggle did not end, but their ability to cope grew. I discovered that the believer wants what everyone else wants, but he survives and flourishes by accepting what God gives and using it the best he can and allowing God to bless the effort. If the gold standard for life is being productive, following a course of honor and integrity, and not being despondent and bitter and hating everyone who was overlooked when misfortune and tragedy and suffering were passed out, then Charles could say, **"WHEN HE HAD TRIED ME, I CAME FORTH AS GOLD."**

> Dr. Loyd Clay Harris is minister of McAlmont Church of Christ, North Little Rock, Arkansas. He and his wife Ora are the parents of three children, eight grandchildren, and three great grandchildren.
>
> This sermon is a development and expansion of a study in theodicy at Harding Graduate School in an attempt to help a family and the minister come to grips with God and the Suffering Saint. The original title was: "Why Was an Innocent Boy Paralyzed and a Devout Mother Forced to Suffer?" It was preached in a couple of congregations and used as study material for a course taught at SRS College of Bible and Religion under the heading of Providence and Suffering.

PSALM 27:1-6
The Power of Praise in Stressful Situations
Dr. David L. Lane

Scripture Text:

"The LORD is my light and my salvation; whom shall I fear? the LORD is the strength of my life; of whom shall I be afraid? When the wicked, even mine enemies and my foes, came upon me to eat up my flesh, they stumbled and fell. Though an host should encamp against me, my heart shall not fear: though war should rise against me, in this will I be confident. One thing have I desired of the LORD, that will I seek after; that I may dwell in the house of the LORD all the days of my life, to behold the beauty of the LORD, and to enquire in his temple. For in the time of trouble he shall hide me in his pavilion: in the secret of his tabernacle shall he hide me; he shall set me up upon a rock. And now shall mine head be lifted up above mine enemies round about me: therefore will I offer in his tabernacle sacrifices of joy; I will sing, yea, I will sing praises unto the LORD" (Psalm 27:1-6 KJV).

Introduction

To be sure these are turbulent times, filled with difficult days. Those of us who have walked with the Lord awhile recognize that life can be difficult and demanding, even for the faithful.

- Just because you are *Saved doesn't mean you won't suffer.*
- Just because you are *Sanctified doesn't mean you won't be victimized.*
- Just because you are *Pure* doesn't mean you won't have to deal with pain and problems.
- Just because you are Holy doesn't mean you won't have haters.

This coronavirus really does not care if you are saved, sanctified, and on your way to heaven. This virus does not regard just how long you have been faithful. My brothers and sisters, these are real stressful times. May I suggest to you that it is not an act of faith to disregard and ignore the impact of this virus on our everyday living. **Do not be presumptuous in your decision-making or in tempting God.**

When the devil tempted Jesus to jump from the pinnacle of the temple, he was tempting the Lord to act presumptuously. The devil declared that the angel would hold Jesus up. While it is true that the Father would always come to the rescue of His Son, if He ever needed it, it would be an act of unnecessarily tempting God by acting presumptuously if Jesus would have yielded to the devil's temptation. **Never tempt God's laws of gravity or good health hygiene.**

I suggest to you lovingly, but truthfully, it is presumptuous not to take all necessary precautions during this health crisis. Hear me when I tell you it is not the will of God for His children to ignore evidence and to take unnecessary risk.

1. Wash your hands and sterilize them often.
2. Practice social spacing.
3. Cough into the sleeve of your arm and cover your mouth when you sneeze.

On the other hand, don't lose your faith during this crisis. I declare, if you are not careful the crises and challenges of life will try to rob you of your joy, steal your enthusiasm, AND snatch your song away.

During times of trouble and when experiencing periods of pain and problems, we need encouragement. The mistake so many people make when they experience the dark night of the soul is **they fail to seek the God who is able and ever present, even in the darkest of night.**

Oh, my brothers and sisters, night happens to everyone. You cannot keep the sun from going down. The good news is if you are a child of God you don't have to get down just because the sun goes down.[12]

Only those who have faith in the Lord are able to face the troubles

---

[12] William Jones, sermon on 2 Samuel 22:1-4 titled, "A Timely Song for These Stressful Times."

of life with praise in their hearts. Psalm 27 shows us how to praise God in stressful situations. In every stressful situation, He says, you need to remember to do three things:

1. Understand the Personality of God
2. Seek the Presence of God
3. Rest in the Protection of God

1. Understand the Personality of God

A. In this psalm, David referred to the trouble that he was facing because of his enemies.

David speaks of false witnesses and those who were "violent men." There is no doubt that David was in the midst of an intense attack, but even with trouble all around him, David had great confidence in the Lord. Not only did he have confidence in the Lord, he was able to praise the Lord even in the midst of such difficulty.

In the middle of the psalm, David said something that was the main focus of our message for today: "And now shall mine head be lifted up above mine enemies round about me: therefore will I offer in his tabernacle sacrifices of joy; I will sing, yea, I will sing praises unto the Lord" (Psalm 27:6 KJV).

David was filled with praise, thanksgiving, and adoration for all God had done in his life. He was filled with praise because he had come to know God personally and intimately. The longer you know someone and the more time you spend with them, the more you will learn about their personality.

When you begin to recognize and understand the many attributes of God's personality, you will become more and more confident in His abilities. When you have confidence in the Lord, you will be able to trust Him, even in the tough times of life.

Listen to what David declared about the personality of God in verses 1-3:

> "The Lord is my light and my salvation; whom shall I
> fear? the Lord is the strength of my life; of whom shall I

be afraid? When the wicked, even mine enemies and my foes, came upon me to eat up my flesh, they stumbled and fell. Though an host should encamp against me, my heart shall not fear: though war should rise against me, in this will I be confident" (Psalm 27:1-3 KJV).

B.   David described the Lord as: "my light," "my salvation," and "the strength of my life."

Though trouble surrounded David, he knew that he was not in darkness because the Lord was his light. Though danger was all around him, David knew that the Lord was his "salvation." He trusted that the Lord would deliver him from his enemies. **David's confidence came from the fact that the Lord had delivered him in the past.** He could talk about what the Lord will do based on what the Lord had already done.

Not only is the LORD our light and our salvation, He is "the strength of our life." Think about this for a moment: David was known as being a great warrior. He not only slew that great giant Goliath, but he had many noted victories against the Philistines. Even with his skill and personal abilities, **David looked to the Lord as "the strength of his life."**

I believe that this was the secret to David's success in battle. Though he was skilled and strong, he trusted in the Lord to secure victory. Listen to what David said to Goliath just before he slew him:

> "Then said David to the Philistine, Thou comest to me with a sword, and with a spear, and with a shield: but I come to thee in the name of the LORD of hosts, the God of the armies of Israel, whom thou hast defied. This day will the LORD deliver thee into mine hand; and I will smite thee, and take thine head from thee; and I will give the carcasses of the host of the Philistines this day unto the fowls of the air, and to the wild beasts of the earth; that all the earth may know that there is a God in Israel. And all this assembly shall know that the LORD saveth not with sword and spear: for the battle is the LORD's, and he will give you into our hands" (1 Samuel 17:45-47 KJV).

David's strength was the Lord. In the middle of your mess and your misery, the Lord is the strength for your struggle. When you are Encountering your enemy, Facing your foes, and Dealing with your difficulty, THE LORD WILL . . .

- *aid you when you are in agony*
- *bless you when in burdens*
- *comfort you when in crises*
- *deliver you when in despair*

In every stressful situation, (1) understand the personality of God, then (2) seek the presence of God.

2. Seek the Presence of God

A. David did not just live off of past victories.

David didn't just spend his time reflecting on what God had done for him. He continued to seek the Lord. "One thing have I desired of the LORD, that will I seek after; that I may dwell in the house of the LORD all the days of my life, to behold the beauty of the LORD, and to enquire in his temple" (Psalm 27:4 KJV).

He said that he would seek after the LORD that he may dwell in His house all the days of his life. David knew just how sweet it was to fellowship with the Lord.

1. It is a great thing to know that we can run to the Lord in times of trouble.
2. It is very encouraging to know that we can trust Him to conquer our enemies and secure victory in the battle.
3. It is comforting to know that we can trust Him to protect us in the midst of the storm.
4. There is great assurance in knowing that He will walk with us through the valleys of life.

But we don't have to wait until our world is falling apart to seek the Lord. In fact, we should have the desire to seek Him and to experience His presence all the days of our lives!

B. There is something about the presence of the Lord that reminds me of His power.

If you lean on:

- *Possessions, it will give way on you.*
- *Prestige, it will give way on you.*
- *Popularity, it will give way on you.*
- *People, even they will give way on you.*

Seek the presence of the Lord, with His presence comes His power. In every stressful situation, (1) understand the personality of God, (2) seek the presence of God, and (3) rest in the protection of God.

3. Rest in the Protection of God

A. There is no indication anywhere in the Bible that God's children are to be exempt from trouble in this life.

But when we walk with the Lord, we can trust Him to protect us. "For in the time of trouble he shall hide me in his pavilion: in the secret of his tabernacle shall he hide me; he shall set me up upon a rock. And now shall mine head be lifted up above mine enemies round about me" (Psalm 27:5 KJV).

In the Lord Himself, we find comfort and rest even in the worst of times. He is our refuge in times of trouble. David said that's a truth worth repeating, and he says it over and over; "God He is our refuge in times of trouble."

> "The LORD of hosts is with us; the God of Jacob is our refuge. Selah" (Psalm 46:11 KJV).

"But I will sing of thy power; yea, I will sing aloud of thy mercy in the morning: for thou hast been my defense and refuge in the day of my trouble" (Psalm 59:16 KJV).

"In God is my salvation and my glory: the rock of my strength, and my refuge, is in God" (Psalm 62:7 KJV).

When it is dark... HE IS OUR LIGHT! When we are weak, HE IS OUR STRENGTH! When the fiery darts of the wicked come our way, HE IS OUR SHIELD! When the enemy pursues us, HE IS OUR REFUGE!!

B. Praise is the expression of approval, commendation, or admiration.

To praise is to "glorify, exalt; acclamation, approbation, compliment; laud. In simple English, TO PRAISE SOMEBODY IS TO BRAG ON THEM.

1. We know that praising a child helps a child behave better and to excel because it will build up the child's self-esteem.
2. We know when a wife praises her husband, he will break his neck trying to live up to it, though he knows he doesn't deserve it.
3. When a husband praises his wife, it makes things a little better at home. If you praise your wife, will feel better, she will make the food taste better, the marriage will be sweeter, and the bed will sleep better.
4. If you praise a student, that student will perk up and become more diligent in his studies.
    If you praise a teacher, that teacher will give more.
    If you praise a team, it will win more.
    If you praise a horse, he will run better.
    If you praise a dog, he will behave better.
    If you praise an enemy, he may turn out to be your best friend.

WE OUGHT TO PRAISE GOD; WE OUGHT TO BRAG ON GOD.
After all, God is God, God is Good, God is Great, and God is Gracious.

But why praise the Lord?

1. You praise people in order to win friends and influence people, but why should you praise the Lord? That doesn't make God good because he's already good.
2. It doesn't make God better because he can't get any better. Why praise God? I'll tell you why. You ought to praise God because IT'S GOOD FOR YOU.
3. I need to give thanks more than God needs to receive thanks.
   I need to praise the Lord.
   It will bless me to bless Him.
   It will prosper me to pay Him tribute.
   It benefits me to praise Him.
   It will strengthen me to shout for Him.

> PRAISE WILL... elevate your mind
> PRAISE WILL... clarify your thinking
> PRAISE WILL... strengthen your body
> PRAISE WILL... revolutionize your attitude
> PRAISE WILL... lighten your load
> PRAISE WILL... clear your sky
> PRAISE WILL... fortify your faith
> PRAISE WILL... beautify your life
> PRAISE WILL... satisfy your soul

Praise gives you a transcendence over every problem. It will thrill your spirit to rejoice in God and enjoy Him for Himself.

> Oh, that men would praise the Lord . . .
> It's my highest privilege, just to praise the Lord!
> It's my greatest honor, just to praise the Lord!
> It's my biggest blessing, just to praise the Lord!
> It's my richest joy, just to praise the Lord!
> It's my sweetest pleasure, just to praise the Lord!

OH, THAT MEN WOULD PRAISE THE LORD[13]

Dr. David L. Lane is the CEO of Ja Kem Consorts and Leadership Institute. Because of his artistic and oratorical skills, he is affectionately called "THE GOLDEN VOICE OF THE SOUTHWEST." He is a native of Paris, Texas. Drs. David and Stephanie Lane are the proud parents of three adult children; David Le'Marcus, Stephen Antoine, and Lorna Davette; one grandson, Elijah Jadon, and an adopted grandson, Brendan Jacar Baldwin.

---

[13] David L. Lane, sermon titled "Diamonds from the Mine/Praise."

MAJOR PROPHETS
Jeremiah 38:7-13 – *A Black Man Comes to the Rescue*
Dr. Edward J. Robinson

Jeremiah, whose name meant "The Lord throws" or "The Lord hurls," was called by God to preach to the nation of Judah. The Lord hurled Jeremiah into a hostile world for the "throwing down the nations in divine judgment for their sins." Jeremiah's prophetic ministry began around 626 BC and ended around 586 BC (*NASB Study Notes*, page 1049). The rescue mission of Ebed-Melech is situated during the reign of Zedekiah (597-586 BC).

Even though the United States elected its first African-American president in 2008, there remains many negative views about the black man. Derogatory stereotypes about black people have a long history in this country. In 1905, Thomas Dixon Jr., a white Baptist minister-turned-novelist, wrote a novel titled *The Clansman*, which characterized black men as criminals and rapists. Ten years later, D. W. Griffith developed Dixon's book into a movie, *The Birth of a Nation*, which portrayed black men as immoral and incompetent even as it celebrated white womanhood and glorified the KKK.

Such racist and preconceived notions have lingered long into the twenty-first century. Therefore, President Barack Obama observed that many Americans have "painted a broad brush about black men." American society has been ingrained and indoctrinated to view all black men as: criminals, dope heads, drunkards, foul-mouthed rappers, gang-bangers, rapists, and sexual abusers. Some of the aforementioned stereotypes might be true of some black men, but it is not true of _all_ black men.

In today's text, we see how God used a black man to help rescue His prophet Jeremiah. Yes! A black man who became a hero. Ebed-Melech was a black man who came to the rescue of the prophet Jeremiah.

Somebody might ask: "How do you know Ebed-Melech was a black man?" The Bible refers (in Jeremiah 38:7) to him as "the Ethiopian" (KJV) or "the Cushite" (NIV). In other words, he was from Africa; he was an African. *BLACK FOLK ARE ALL OVER THE BIBLE!*

The black man in our text was Ebed-Melech, whose name in Hebrew meant the "king's servant." I want us to note three things about this man.

I. The Regard of Ebed-Melech

A. According to Jeremiah 38:1-6, Jeremiah was thrown into a dungeon because he told God's people the truth. Hear the Word of the Lord in Jeremiah 38:1-6: "Now Shephatiah the son of Mattan, and Gedaliah the son of Pashhur, and Jucal the son of Shelemiah, and Pashhur the son of Malchijah heard the words that Jeremiah was speaking to all the people, saying, 'Thus says the Lord, "He who stays in this city will die by the sword and by famine and by pestilence, but he who goes out to the Chaldeans will live and have his own life as booty and stay alive." Thus says the Lord, "This city will certainly be given into the hand of the army of the king of Babylon and he will capture it."' Then the officials said to the king, 'Now let this man be put to death, inasmuch as he is discouraging the men of war who are left in this city and all the people, by speaking such words to them; for this man is not seeking the well-being of this people but rather their harm.' So King Zedekiah said, 'Behold, he is in your hands; for the king can do nothing against you.' Then they took Jeremiah and cast him into the cistern of Malchijah the king's son, which was in the court of the guardhouse; and they let Jeremiah down with ropes. Now in the cistern there was no water but only mud, and Jeremiah sank into the mud" (NASB).

Speaking the truth can get you in trouble, as the Apostle Paul put it in Galatians 4:16: "So have I become your enemy by telling you the truth?" (NASB).

1. Jeremiah was there sinking in the mud with no food, no water, no help. He was about to die a miserable death. So, what did he do? Jeremiah cried out to God: "I called on Your name, O Lord, from the lowest pit. . . . You drew near on the day I called on You, and said, 'Do not fear!'" (Lamentations 3:55, 57 NKJV).
2. God heard and answered his cry. How did God rescue Jeremiah?
3. By sending him a black man, Ebed-Melech. *Thank God for a black man!*

B. When Ebed-Melech learned that Jeremiah was in trouble, he showed his regard, his care, and concern for God's prophet. Look at his regard: "Now Ebed-Melech the Ethiopian, one of the eunuchs, who was in the king's house, heard that they had put Jeremiah in the dungeon. When the king was sitting at the Gate of Benjamin; Ebed-Melech went out of the king's house and spoke to the king" (Jeremiah 38:7-8 NKJV). Note what Ebed-Melech did:
1. He "heard" (Jeremiah 38:7 NKJV)
2. He "went" (Jeremiah 38:8 NKJV)
3. He told somebody who could do something about the problem – people in power.

C. The Application: Just like the prophet Jeremiah, many of our people are sinking in the mud of life:
1. People in our community are sinking in the mud of health difficulty because of COVID-19. COVID-19 has sliced through the façade of political and racial pretense and has exposed lingering disparities in economics, education, housing, legal justice, and access to health care.
   a. Men hooking with men . . .
   b. Women marrying women . . .
   c. Parents abandoning their children . . .
2. People in our community are sinking in the mud of racial strife and racial violence. The tragic murders of Ahmaud Arbery, Breonna Taylor, George Floyd, among others have stirred up the ire of people across the country who are striving to get black people out of the mud.

3. People in our congregations are sinking in the mud of despair and despondency. Some preachers have quit the ministry, some elders have abandoned the eldership, and some deacons have walked away from the deaconship because they are sinking in the mud of distress and discouragement.

4. Some of our senior saints are sinking in the mud of financial and monetary hardship. Some of our young people are sinking in the mud of immorality and irresponsibility. Some young men father children and refuse to take care of them. Others walk around with their pants hanging off their waists, sinking in the mud of disrespect. Some young people wallow in the mud of laziness, expecting others to do for them what they must do for themselves.

D. Just like Ebed-Melech, we've got to show enough regard and resolve to get up and do something to get our people out of the mud. We can't depend on the government to do it for us. If we are depending on President Trump and the Republican Party or Vice-President Biden and the Democrat Party to rescue our people, we will be sadly disappointed. Black men have to get up and do something for their own families and own communities.

II. The Rescue of Ebed-Melech

A. Ebed-Melech went to the king and told him about Jeremiah's predicament. The king then told him to get "thirty men" to get Jeremiah out of that pit: "Then the king commanded Ebed-Melech the Ethiopian, saying, 'Take from here thirty men with you, and lift Jeremiah the prophet out of the dungeon before he dies" (Jeremiah 38:10 NKJV).

B. Ebed-Melech could not do it by himself. He needed help. One man can't do all the lifting by himself. Regardless of how educated or eloquent a preacher is, he cannot do the work of God alone. He has to have help.

C. If we could get just thirty good men, we could turn this world upside down and right side up.

1. 30 committed, dedicated, and faithful men can touch 300 lives.

2. 30 committed, dedicated, and faithful men can touch 3,000 lives.

3. 30 committed, dedicated, and faithful men can touch 300,000 lives.

4. 30 committed, dedicated, and faithful men can touch 3,000,000 lives.

D. Notice how they got Jeremiah out of that pit. They used "old rags and worn out clothes." Hear the Word of the Lord in Jeremiah 38:11-13: "So Ebed-Melech took the men with him and went into the house of the king under the treasury, and took from there old clothes and old rags, and let them down by ropes into the dungeon to Jeremiah. Then Ebed-Melech the Ethiopian said to Jeremiah, "Please put these old clothes and rags under your armpits, under the ropes." And Jeremiah did so. So they pulled Jeremiah up with ropes and lifted him out of the dungeon. And Jeremiah remained in the court of the prison" (NKJV).

E. Be careful about tossing out all the "old" stuff. We live in a new era in which people are always clamoring for something "new" – a new beat, a new car, a new dance, a new rhythm, new songs, new technology, and a new wardrobe.

F. But in order to get our folk out of the mud, we need to go back to some of the old stuff. By "old stuff," I mean old school customs of respect for authority. Whatever happened to saying, "Yes ma'am and yes sir"? By "old stuff," I mean the old tradition of fidelity and commitment, when one man stayed with one woman and when we had hard-working men and pretty women. Now, we have hard-working men and hard-working women. By "old stuff," I mean disciplining children with a "rod of correction" (Proverbs 22:15 NKJV).

G. Even in the church, we must not discard all the "old stuff," that is, the old hymns such as "The Old Rugged Cross" and "The Old Ship of Zion." May we never abandoned the "old time Gospel," for Paul said: "For I am not ashamed of the gospel of Christ, for it is the power of God to salvation for everyone who believes, for the

Jew first and also for the Greek" (Romans 1:6 NKJV). If there was ever a time our world needed the "old stuff," that time is now. Our nation is engulfed in three viruses – a medical virus (COVID-19), an economic virus (record unemployment and loss of income), and a racial virus of police brutality. The Gospel of Jesus Christ is the only cure for these moral, social, and spiritual ills.

H. If we returned to some of the "old stuff," we can get our people out of the quicksand of sin and shame. Hear the Word of the Lord in Jeremiah 6:16: "Stand in the ways and see, and ask for the old paths, where the good way is, and walk in it; then you will find rest for your souls. But they said, 'We will not walk in it'" (NKJV).

III. The Reward of Ebed-Melech

A. Ebed-Melech reaped what he had sowed. Hear the Word of the Lord in Jeremiah 39:15-18:

> "Meanwhile the Word of the LORD had come to Jeremiah while he was shut up in the court of the prison, saying, 'Go and speak to Ebed-Melech the Ethiopian, saying, "Thus says the LORD of hosts, the God of Israel: 'Behold, I will bring My words upon this city for adversity and not for good, and they shall be performed in that day before you. But I will deliver you in that day,' says the Lord, 'and you shall not be given into the hand of the men of whom you are afraid. For I will surely deliver you, and you shall not fall by the sword; but your life shall be as a prize to you, because you have put your trust in Me,' says the Lord'"" (NKJV).

B. Ebed-Melech blessed Jeremiah, and the Lord in turn blessed Ebed-Melech. Ebed-Melech helped Jeremiah, and God consequently helped Ebed-Melech. Ebel-Melech rescued Jeremiah, and the Lord subsequently rescued Ebed-Melech.

C. When you help others, you are really helping yourself. When you bless others, you are actually blessing yourself. There is a biblical principle that says: "You always reap what you sow." The wise man Solomon said: "The generous soul will be made rich, and he who waters will also be watered himself" (Proverbs 11:25 NKJV). The Apostle Paul declared: "Do not be deceived, God is not mocked; for whatever a man sows, that he will also reap. For he who sows to his flesh will of the flesh reap corruption, but he who sows to the Spirit will of the Spirit reap everlasting life. And let us not grow weary while doing good, for in due season we shall reap if we do not lose heart. Therefore, as we have opportunity, let us do good to all, especially to those who are of the household of faith" (Galatians 6:7-10 NKJV).

D. When we reach out and labor to get our people out of the mud, we will surely receive blessings from the God of heaven.

Conclusion

*   Ebed-Melech was an African who cared enough about Jeremiah to come to his rescue.
*   God answered Jeremiah's prayer by sending him Ebed-Melech.
*   There are people in our homes, in our communities, and in our congregations who are sinking in mud.
*   Somebody has to get up and do something about the miry situation.
*   Lord, give us more men like Ebed-Melech!
*   His regard, his rescue, and his reward.
*   Homework: Go home and get your family out of the mud.
*   Go home and help your neighbors, relatives, and friends out of the mud.
*   More importantly, what Ebed-Melech did for Jeremiah is exactly what Jesus did for all mankind. Jesus came to rescue sinful humanity from the muck and mire of sin (Matthew 1:21).
*   That is why we sing the song: "Love Lifted Me" – James Rowe, 1912

I was sinking deep in sin, far from the peaceful shore

Very deeply stained within, sinking to rise no more.
But the Master of the sea heard my despairing cry
From the waters lifted me, now safe am I.
Love lifted me!
Love lifted me!
When nothing else could help
Love lifted me!

Dr. Edward J. Robinson, pulpit minister at the North Tenneha Church of Christ in Tyler, Texas, also teaches History and Religion at Texas College in Tyler, Texas. He is married to Toni R. Caruthers and they have three daughters, Clarice, Ashley, and Erika.

MINOR PROPHETS

Jonah 1:1-4, 17 – *A Disobedient Child, with a Compassionate God*

Bryan C. Jones

Jesus Although there have been countless critics and numerous attacks on its content, the book of Jonah is arguably one of the most fascinating books to read, not only in the Old Testament, but throughout the entirety of the biblical canon. Though it is named after the 8th century prophet Jonah, its content is really not about Jonah at all, it's about the God of Jonah. The revelation of the Lord's *communication, commission, and compassion* for Jonah, and the wicked people of Nineveh, gives readers a fascinating glimpse into the mind of God. These poignant pages of inspiration in this historical narrative have become a paramount reflection of the Sovereign God of Israel's awareness, attention, and responsive action toward sin, human frailties, grace, disobedience, destruction, deliverance, and salvation. The book of Jonah can literally be summed up in one word – compassion – which is the Lord's sympathetic pity and concern for one's misfortunes. One of the more interesting occurrences in human history takes place in this Old Testament minor prophet book of Jonah, which has proven to be theologically tenable throughout time.

COMMUNICATION

"The word of the LORD came to Jonah the son of Amittai saying, 'Arise, go to Nineveh the great city and cry against it, for their wickedness has come up before Me'" (Jonah 1:1-2 NASB 1995).

The word of the Lord was communicated to Jonah, the son of Amittai, an eighth century BC prophet (Jonah 1:1 NASB 1995). The transmission of Jonah's mission was unmistakably communicated through God's Word, presumably by inspiration, solidifying God's commission for Jonah to preach to the Ninevites seeking their repentance. As recorded in Jonah 1:2, Nineveh was the "great city," a capital of Assyria, now modern-day Iraq, close in geographic location to Mosul, east of the Tigris river, 550 miles northeast of Samaria. The narrative of Jonah distinguishes the people of Nineveh as wicked and violent persons behaviorally (Jonah 1:2; 3:8 NASB 1995). The Ninevites also worshiped idol gods of love and war, committed violent atrocities against humanity, and harlotry was perpetually rampant among the population of more than 120,000 persons whose hearts were devoid of spiritual acumen, those whose documented actions proved they possessed no moral compass (Jonah 4:11 NASB 1995).

COMMISSION

"The word of the LORD came to Jonah the son of Amittai saying, 'Arise, go to Nineveh the great city and cry against it, for their wickedness has come up before Me'" (Jonah 1:1-2 NASB 1995).

The substance of the text theologically teaches how God commissioned Jonah by calling him to save the lost people of Nineveh (Jonah 1:1-2 NASB 1995). Interestingly, in like manner, God has also commissioned Christian believers to save the lost people even today in modernity. Notice the process of the commission and calling of Jonah in verse 2: God called a **leader** (Jonah), God gave the **leader** a **lesson** (arise, go), God gave the **leader** a **lesson** and a **location** (Nineveh) and God demonstrated His **love** (saving wicked people). It becomes quite clear that God's intended purpose was to use a "called person" to save "lost persons." After reading these four short chapters, if one performs behavioral exegesis on Jonah's rebellion toward his commission, it becomes quite clear that God doesn't call the qualified, He qualifies those whom He calls. For the Christian readers who are digesting the depth of this declaration, let's be clear, SAVING LOST PEOPLE IS WHAT GOD HAS CALLED YOU TO DO! Then the question becomes, HOW SHOULD I RESPOND WHEN GOD CALLS ME TO SAVE THE LOST?

Notice two requirements for those who've received God's commission and desire to adopt His commission as their mission.

God's Commission Requires an Immediate Response

"But Jonah rose up to flee to Tarshish from the presence of the LORD. So he went down to Joppa, found a ship which was going to Tarshish, paid the fare and went down into it to go with them to Tarshish from the presence of the LORD" (Jonah 1:3 NASB 1995).

God's commission required Jonah to "arise and go" because God is indeed a God of not only assignment, but action. We can safely speculate that the majority of persons living in the 21st century are acutely aware of the communication devices through cell phones, calls, emails, instant messages, text messages, and the urgency upon which people expect a timely reply through our acts of communication. God is no different, His calling requires ACTION as an acceptable response, with a sense of urgency as well. Just as people receive favorable communication and respond quickly to *obtain blessings*, we must also respond with rapidity to the Lord's instructions as a requirement upon respectfully receiving communication to *be a blessing* by obeying His commands despite the assignment and who it is the Lord assigns for us to save. Nonetheless, many people have prolonged the inevitable by refusing to move in the direction that the Lord has commanded. Jonah was one of those people. After being commissioned, he rose up, but journeyed in the opposite direction of the Lord's commission (Jonah 1:3 NASB 1995).

God's Commission Requires a Faithful Response

Jonah was specifically commissioned by God to *"arise, go to Nineveh the great city,"* but Jonah's GPS navigation system took him on a detour to Tarshish! It appears Jonah was not pleased with his new job description, so instead of tendering his two weeks' notice, Jonah decided to quit. Jonah's response to God was an unfaithful one as he responded by rising up and heading in the opposite direction of Nineveh as God had requested (Jonah 1:2 NASB 1995). Jonah went to Joppa and found a ship there that was destined to go an estimated 2,500 miles west to Tarshish.

The text teaches us that Jonah was trying to flee from the presence of the Lord (Jonah 1:3 NASB 1995). I'm not sure about you, but the last time I checked, God was omnipotent, omniscient, and omnipresent, which means that the possibility of escaping God's presence is absolutely, unequivocally zero. You can't escape God's presence, but people try it. This is not the first time mankind has tried to flee from the presence of God, as there is a biblical commonality concerning this reality. After Adam and Eve ate off of the forbidden tree of the knowledge of good and evil, they became intellectually aware of their nakedness, felt ashamed, and attempted to hide *"themselves from the presence of the LORD God among the trees of the garden"* (Genesis 3:8 NASB 1995). Another instance occurred after Cain killed Abel: *"Cain went out from the presence of the LORD"* (Genesis 4:16 NASB 1995). Contrastively, King David was a man who was after God's own heart who knew the value of being in the presence of the Lord. The wisdom literature of the psalmist recorded these words from David, *"Do not cast me away from your presence and do not take Your Holy Spirit from me"* (Psalm 51:11 NASB 1995). When mankind attempts to leave the presence of God because of disobedience, one leaves much to be desired. Woven within the tapestry of the presence of the Lord is not only God's PRESENCE, but His PROVISION, POWER, PROTECTION, and PROMISES. A heart of disobedience leaves God's presence, but a heart of obedience remains in God's presence!

As you are reading this, it's possible that your mind is reflective of your own instances where you may have neglected to respond faithfully to God's commissioning in your life. With that reality, one can easily reflect on the cost of those decisions. Notice what refusing to comply with God's instructions to save the people of Nineveh and his attempt to flee from the presence of the Lord cost Jonah.

The Cost of an Unfaithfulness Response

1. Jonah wasted both EMOTIONAL and PHYSICAL ENERGY by deliberately attempting to flee from the presence of the Lord (Jonah 1:3).
2. Jonah wasted TIME by deliberately attempting to flee from the presence of the Lord (Jonah 1:3).

3. Jonah found a SHIP headed in the wrong direction of the Lord's commissioned destination by deliberately attempting to flee from the presence of the Lord (Jonah 1:3).
4. Jonah wasted MONEY by deliberately attempting to flee from the presence of the Lord (Jonah 1:3).
5. Jonah BOARDED onto a ship to assemble with people who were headed in the opposite direction of God's assignment by deliberately attempting to flee from the presence of the Lord (Jonah 1:3).

COMPASSION

"The LORD hurled a great wind on the sea and there was a great storm on the sea so that the ship was about to break up"
(Jonah 1:4 NASB 1995).

Because of his attempt to flee from the presence of the Lord after he boarded the ship headed in the opposite direction of God's instructions, Jonah finds himself in a storm, one of catastrophic proportion. It is here that the Lord reveals to the reader of this historical narrative His nature to demonstrate compassion to those in relationship with Him. The Hebrew word for *compassion* is חוס, which is transliterated as the word *chus*. This verb compassion is mentioned twice in Jonah 4:10-11 and defined as *sympathetic pity and concern for one's misfortunes*. Although the word compassion is only mentioned twice in chapter 4 of the book of Jonah, God demonstrates this compassion through His actions throughout the entirety of the narrative. What becomes fascinating is the method God used to distribute His compassion toward Jonah.

God Demonstrates His Compassion When He Causes a Storm

"The LORD hurled a great wind on the sea and there was a great storm on the sea so that the ship was about to break up"
(Jonah 1:4 NABS 1995).

God demonstrated His compassion to Jonah through a great storm (Jonah 1:4). Interestingly, it is typically antithetical to associate a storm with God's compassion, but the Lord reveals a powerful principle in Jonah 1:4

that is pregnant with relative truth concerning mankind's anthropological history with disobeying His instructions. This narratological discourse informs us that sometimes it's not the devil that is causing the storms, it's the LORD causing a storm to demonstrate His compassion! When a called individual disobeys God, refusing to submit to His calling, one method God uses is to allow storms in that person's life. God never intended for Jonah to be on that ship headed to Tarshish, but what we find woven in this passage is the fact that if God cannot change the heart of that individual, the Lord will CHANGE the atmospheric conditions (great wind/storms) to change the individual's direction. The same God who calmed the sea when He spoke to it is the same God who can weaponize the sea to halt and hinder disobedient movements, enforcing travel restrictions. The LORD demonstrated His ability to change and rearrange situations through a great storm if God isn't successful in His attempts to change your mind. Though the ship hadn't broken up at the point of the tornadic storm, it was well on its way to breaking up. The principle is that there are metaphoric ships in everyone's life that God has the power and prerogative to "break up" if those to whom He has commissioned are rebellious to His intended calling for their lives.

Another glaring principle in the text is that many people won't do what they know they need to do unless they are forced to or have no other options. This mindset is critically dangerous because it suggests that when some people have OPTIONS, they tend to be complacent, prolonging the inevitable, as complacency is the enemy of ACTION, ACTIVITIES, and AGGRESSION. When God wants His people to move, but they are reluctant, God has a historical track record of removing their OPTIONS so that His people have no choice but to comply with God's selected course of action. In the year 2020, the global Coronavirus (COVID-19) pandemic claimed hundreds of thousands of lives. By God allowing the pandemic to occur, it was a clear indication of how God uses such opportunities to get people to DO what they were previously complacent in doing when options were available. Those who deserted God for selfish reasons, money and other priorities, finally came to grips that they had a need for God's presence when their options were stripped, finding themselves quarantined in their homes with nothing to do but pray to God for help as Jonah did (Jonah 2:1). An adequate application appropriate in response to this principal is to simply become obedient, before you have your options taken away due to a lack of spiritual movement. Having options has always been an example of God's grace.

God Demonstrates His Compassion
When He Cares for You during a Storm

"And the LORD appointed a great fish to swallow Jonah, and Jonah
was in the stomach of the fish three days and three nights"
(Jonah 1:17 NASB 1995).

Jonah was confident that God's compassion would result in Him calming the very storm that He caused if Jonah removed himself as a passenger on the ship, thus saving the other passengers from imminent storm-related deaths. Having a dual purpose of an attempted suicide and rescue plan for those accompanying Jonah on the ship, Jonah asked the innocent passengers to throw him overboard (Jonah 1:11-12; 15). However, the Lord, once again, demonstrated His compassion for Jonah by caring for him during his storm. Sometimes the real reason why we go through these storms is not because God is trying to punish us, but because He is trying to PROTECT us to save us from ourselves, keeping us in His presence, provisions, power, promises, and protective custody even during our disobedience! The Lord appointed a great fish, which many scholars believe to be a sperm whale, to swallow, not to eat or chew him, but to save him (Jonah 1:17). It's evident that if God was able to appoint a great fish and the fish had enough sense to obey the Lord, surely every person in the world should!

In Jonah 1:17 we see God's **protection** (swallowed by great fish), God's **patience** (compassion with disobedience), and God's **purpose** (Jonah's repentance/Jonah's proclamation/Nineveh's repentance). Although Jonah was ANOINTED, his behavior was consistently ANNOYING! However, we all can learn how compassionate God is when what we thought was the Lord's punishment was in actuality His PREPARATION. What we think is a PENALTY is really His PROTECTION! When God ultimately has a calling over your life, God still has the ability to demonstrate care for you even when you don't deserve it. Jonah's destiny was connected to God, but he avoided the Holy One who could help him, so God gave him a storm to get him to stop his movement in the opposite direction of his godly destiny. Jonah had to be quarantined, isolated in the stomach of the great fish, a dark place, for three days and nights before he finally realized through contemplation and prayer what a compassionate God he served, and obedience was his best option (Jonah 2:1-10). Sometimes we find ourselves in that nasty, disgusting, uncom-fortable, dark place before we realize obedience to our communication and commission to God is the best response to such a compassionate God's providential care.

Since the fall of mankind in the Garden of Eden with Adam and Eve and through man's anthropological existence, evil has consistently spoken. But evangelism has been silent of recent years among evangelicals in modernity. Just as the gruesome atrocities and crimes against humanity by the Ninevites pained the heart of Jonah, our current cultural climate in America boasts the same atrocities against humanity and pains our hearts as we have witnessed the senseless loss of too many lives in the African-American community. The world we live in today is one big Nineveh. So, today, God needs a Jonah in every country, God needs a Jonah is every city, a Jonah in every community, a Jonah on every corner, and a Jonah in every church! The world won't repent until someone comes preaching the Name of Jesus Christ, our Risen Savior, our Redeeming and Reigning King, the Prince of Peace who has the power to forgive sin and turn hearts of hate to hearts of love. This world is in desperate need for someone who understands that God is not only compassionate with the behavior of those in relationship with Him, but also equally compassionate toward those who are in need of a relationship with God, so that they can save the wicked from God's wrath as the Ninevites who repented were (Jonah 3:1-10). Can God send you? Will you go proclaim the gospel of Jesus Christ to save people whose behavior is abhorrent and despicable? Are you willing to help the lost receive the same level of compassion from God as you received, or will you keep running like Jonah, going through storm after storm because you hate the thought of God's compassion being distributed on the wicked? Jonah's repentance ultimately led to the wicked Ninevites' repentance and eliminated God's wrath toward the Ninevites (Jonah 3:1-10).

APPLICATION: Obey the instructions of our compassionate God of heaven by seeking to save that which is lost. Time is running out; lives are at stake.

> Bryan C. Jones serves as the Senior Minister for the Newburg Church of Christ, a purpose-driven congregation of the Lord's people, in Louisville, Kentucky. Bryan is married to Mrs. Danielle P. Jones.

NEW TESTAMENT SYNOPTICS
Mark 10:46-52
The Compassionate Christ Will Hear You If You Holla
William Jones

Scripture Text:

"And they came to Jericho: and as he went out of Jericho with his disciples and a great number of people, blind Bartimaeus, the son of Timaeus, sat by the highway side begging. And when he heard that it was Jesus of Nazareth, he began to cry out, and say, Jesus, thou Son of David, have mercy on me. And many charged him that he should hold his peace: but he cried the more a great deal, Thou Son of David, have mercy on me. And Jesus stood still, and commanded him to be called. And they call the blind man, saying unto him, Be of good comfort, rise; he calleth thee. And he, casting away his garment, rose, and came to Jesus. And Jesus answered and said unto him, What wilt thou that I should do unto thee? The blind man said unto him, Lord, that I might receive my sight. And Jesus said unto him, Go thy way; thy faith hath made thee whole. And immediately he received his sight, and followed Jesus in the way" (Mark 10:46-52 KJV).

Introduction

The good news about Jesus is, no matter what has you blind, and no matter what has you bound, no matter your condition, and no matter your desperation, Christ can undo all that has you undone. In the book of Mark, we encounter a long procession of hurting people who found their help and hope in Jesus.

Mark's theme is not to show Jesus as the King of the Jews, as in Matthew; nor as the son of man, as in Luke. It is not his purpose to show Jesus as the eternal *Logos* who was manifested in the flesh, as in John.

Mark's gospel, the shortest one and believed to be the first one, has as its purpose to present the Master as the suffering Servant who came into the world to sacrifice Himself for the world. Mark shows us Jesus in action. He emphasizes the Lord's movements and ministry rather than His message.

Two words recur in the King James' translation of Mark, *immediately* and *straightway*. Both words are translations of the Greek word *euthos*, which conveys the idea of action that is swift and decisive.

Mark's story rushes on in a kind of breathless anticipation of the next incident in the life of Christ. He adds statement-to-statement connecting them simply with the word "and." For instance, in Greek in the third chapter there are 34 clauses or sentences, one after the other, introduced by "and" after one principle verb.

In Mark's gospel we see Jesus encountering all kinds of hurting people who needed His help. I think I ought to declare even today there are a whole lot of people who need the Lord's help. I declare this invisible, insidious virus is still causing serious health and financial challenges. We need help.

In the text before, us we meet such a man. His name was Bartimaeus. He was a blind beggar who sat by the roadside looking and hoping for assistance.

Jesus the Lord of life, and the best the world has ever seen, was on His final and fateful journey to the city of the Prophets, Jerusalem, to offer Himself as the sacrifice for the sins of the world. He is passing through the ancient city of Jericho. He encountered blind Bartimaeus. Bartimaeus is one of the few people healed by Jesus who is actually named. Lazarus was another such person, as was Malchus.

It is the desperate cry of Bartimaeus that captures our attention. It reminds us that our Savior is the compassionate Christ. If we call out for help, He will answer. I declare, if we holla, He will hear.

As we unpack the passage to uncover the principles, there are two truths threaded into the tapestry of the text. They form the substance of the sermon and offer the homiletical hinges on which this message swings. Notice, HIS CRY INDICATES A GROWING PERCEPTION, and notice HIS CRY DEMONSTRATES A GENUINE PERSISTANCE.

I. HIS CRY INDICATES A GROWING PERCEPTION

Bartimaeus is sitting there by the roadside, a man in a crisis that is beyond his control or ability to correct OR change. He had little hope of ever having a better life. His main concern from one day to the next was just survival – to survive one more day. He is stuck in his situation, there is nothing that he can do. I wonder if I'm talking to someone who knows a little something about being or feeling stuck. Stuck:

- *With a bad habit you can't seem to break.*
- *With a bad relationship you can't seem to improve.*
- *With an obstacle you can't seem to overcome.*
- *With a crisis you can't seem to conquer.*
- *In some mess that you can't seem to manage.*
- *Inside with your parents' grandkids and you are just about to lose your mind up in here.*

Bartimaeus could not plan his way out of his situation. He could not educate his way out of it. So…he chose to go to a higher source, to a source outside himself.

Something inside of him realized that this Nazarene could do something for him that he had done for other sick people. A hunger and a desire for change was stirring inside of this blind beggar and it drove him to go against conventional wisdom. In his despair, in his hopelessness, he had found hope. He called out to the one who could heal him and make him whole. He made up his mind that he no longer wanted to remain in the condition he was in.

What about you today? Are you just trying to survive one more day? Are life's problems bearing down on you? Do you feel that the world is closing in around you? Do you feel that no one else has ever had your problems? Are you tired of being in the condition you are in day after day? Then you need to do what Bartimaeus did. CRY OUT FOR MERCY!

Some people never get beyond their present condition because they are not desperate enough. They fail to recognize what Bartimaeus recognized. If his blindness was to be alleviated, he needed to cry out to Christ.

A. He Perceived Who He Needed –

Some people never get the help that they need because they fail to realize who they need. They fail to recognize their need for Jesus.

Bartimaeus cries out to Christ, declaring "thou Son of David, have mercy on me." By calling Jesus the son of David, he was acknowledging that Jesus was the Messiah. The designation "Jesus of Nazareth" is used to describe Jesus' humanity. "Jesus Son of David" appeals to Jesus' divinity. Jesus of Nazareth was used by unbelievers, mockers, and detractors like those who arrested Jesus, or like the soldiers who beat Jesus. You see, Nazareth was the hood. Even the girl who confronts Peter in the courtyard during Jesus' interrogation refers to him as Jesus of Nazareth. After Jesus is risen, He is referred to as Jesus Christ of Nazareth, with Christ being the term of Lordship. But, the designation Bartimaeus uses, "Son of David," is a messianic term used to describe the messiah. This is the messianic title that we see expressed in Isaiah 11:1, Jeremiah 23:5f, Ezekiel 34:23f. (KJV).

The title "Son of David" is a very specific Jewish title. And it was reserved for only one person in all the world . . . the Messiah. So when Bartimaeus called Jesus the Son of David, the whole crowd knew what he was saying. Bartimaeus was saying, "I believe this is the one we've all be waiting for, the savior of the world and the deliverer of God's people." Bartimaeus was smart enough to know that no one could give him his sight except God Himself. And so he turned to Jesus and he wasn't disappointed.

I think I ought to tell somebody that it does not matter what you have – if you don't have Jesus, you don't have enough. You may have:

- *Possessions, position, and prestige, but you need Jesus.*
- *Status, station, and standing, but you need Jesus.*
- *Recognition, resources, and renown, but you need Jesus.*

Yes, oh yes, hallelujah yes, you need Jesus! He alone is the 'way' – from...

- darkness unto light
- despair unto delight
- turmoil unto peace
- anxiety unto assurance
- burdens unto blessings
- sorrows unto joy
- emptiness unto fullness
- selfishness unto compassion
- loneliness unto love
- ashes unto beauty
- misery unto glory
- filth unto purity
- fear unto faith
- desperation unto hope
- deceitfulness unto truth
- nothing unto something
- nobody unto somebody
- wickedness unto righteousness
- weakness unto strength
- vice unto virtue
- hunger unto satisfaction
- yearning unto contentment
- failure unto fruitfulness
- bondage unto liberty
- defeat unto victory
- pain into power
- sadness unto gladness
- sin unto salvation
- death unto life
- earth unto heaven!

B. He Perceived What He Needed –

Bartimaeus somehow knew that he couldn't approach the Lord on the basis of what he deserved. So, he cried out instead for mercy. The Greek word is *eleeo*, and means to "have compassion on the undeserving."

I find it striking that although he was blind, he does not ask for sight initially. Although he was a beggar, he does not ask for food. He asks for mercy. That is what he needed most.

I think I ought to tell you that mercy is the only basis by which we can seek help from the Lord. We need mercy because many are:

- *Lost and need to be saved.*
- *Down and need to be lifted.*
- *Imprisoned by their past and need to be set free.*
- *Bound by a stubborn habit and need to be liberated.*
- *Fatally sick with sin and need to be cured.*
- *Completely dominated by the devil and need to be delivered.*

We must cry out to God with the same spirit that publican approached Him when, in the parable of Jesus, he cried "have mercy on me a sinner." Have mercy Lord is the cry we need to make. Have mercy Lord:

- *I deserve so little, but I need so much.*
- *I have so much guilt, but I need your grace.*
- *I know how I have fallen, but I need your forgiveness.*
- *I know I have let you down, but I need you to pick me up.*
- *I know I deserve condemnation, but I need salvation.*

II. HIS CRY DEMONSTRATES A GENUINE PERSISTANCE

This helpless, sightless, hopeless man possesses a persistence born of desperation. He had no concern for whether he was breaking decorum. He gave no thought to whether or not his cry was against custom. He was blind and knew that Jesus could do something about his condition.

A. The Insistent Crowd –

The crowd did not appreciate this unscheduled interruption. They insisted to Bartimaeus that he should be quiet. They told him to hush. The word "charged" is *epitimao*, "to rebuke, censure severely." "Hold his peace" is *siopao*, "to be silent, to hold one's peace." It is ingressive aorist, speaking of entrance into a new condition. Luke says that it was the crowd in front that rebuked the blind man. That was easy for them to do because they had their sight.

I declare there are people who don't want you to cry out to Jesus. They prefer that you stay blind. They are more comfortable if you remain in the condition that you are in. They have no interest in you getting better.

People got in his way, told him to be quiet, and did their best to keep him from Christ. But this sensible man – aware of his need, sure of the saving power of Christ, and conscious that it was now or never for him – refused to be intimidated by the crowd. It was indeed his one and only chance. Jesus was on His way to Calvary. He would not be back that way again. Somehow, Bartimaeus knew that if change was to ever be accomplished in his life, it was now or never.

I think I might ought to mention that there are some people who, when they cry, it is not the cry of desperation, it is the cry for attention. Some folks shout but they are just making some noise. They don't want to be better, they don't really want to change. They are just calling out for attention. They can't stand it when the focus is on someone else. They cry but it is not the cry that leads to positive and productive change.

B. The Persistent Cry –

This blind man could care less about this crowd. He knew they probably wouldn't do anything for him even if they could. The one person who could forever alter his condition was about to pass by. So, in spite of the crowd, he made his cry.

Many among the crowd tried to hush Bartimaeus, but he was desperate and determined and in dead earnest. He would not be discouraged, silenced, or stopped. He repeatedly cried to the top of his lungs: "Thou Son of David, have mercy on me."

The point is that Bartimaeus persevered, he persisted in his cry. He had need, and he would not stop seeking to have his need met. Note the voices raised against him, and they were "many." His faith in Jesus was strong. He believed Jesus could really help him. His faith stood against all the voices of *discouragement* and against the feelings of so many that it was *useless*.

We have voices all around us who try to block our connection with Jesus. They say things like, "You don't take the Bible seriously, do you?" They insinuate that being spiritual has something to do with being organic or being in touch with yourself. They say to us: "This whole faith thing must not be real, God hasn't done what you asked – so you might as well give up." They tell us that taking the spiritual world seriously is foolishness. What they do is, they shout ignorance our way . . . don't buy it. Don't listen to those detractors. The reality is this: Jesus is real, Jesus is powerful, Jesus is ready to act on your behalf and change your world. Voices may try to cut off your path to God, but they can never cut off your heart for God. Bartimaeus seems to instinctively know this and he keeps calling for Jesus. Follow his example.

If you want Jesus to change your life you have to keep looking to Christ and stop listening to the crowd. The crowd can't help you. Often the crowd won't help you. Christ can and will help you if you cry out in desperation. "Father, I stretch my hands to you, no other help I know, if thou withhold thyself from me where can I go?"

There is somebody listening who needs a miracle in their life. You are facing a situation, which is apparently hopeless. You are facing a situation in your marriage and you think there is no help, you are facing a situation on your job, you are facing a situation in your own life and you believe there is no hope. But the reason there is hope is that Jesus is passing by today. I declare, don't let Jesus pass you by. The compassionate Christ will hear you if you holla. The Bible declares:

> "Nevertheless He regarded their affliction, when He heard their cry; and for their sake He remembered His covenant, and relented according to the multitude of His mercies" (Psalm 106:44-45 NKJV).

Today is your day. Jesus is passing by, so if you need a miracle for your mess, if you need a change in your condition, cry out to Christ.

1. Pass me not, O gentle Savior,
   Hear my humble cry;
   While on others Thou art calling,
   Do not pass me by.
   o *Refrain:*
      Savior, Savior,
      Hear my humble cry,
      While on others Thou art calling,
      Do not pass me by.-Fannie Jane Crosby, 1868

I think I ought to tell you that Bartimaeus' persistence paid off. The Bible declares that Jesus stood still and called for the blind man. Jesus heard the man when he hollered and stopped in His tracks to come to the man's rescue. The Bible still says:

"For the eyes of the LORD are on the righteous, and His ears are open to their prayers; but the face of the Lord is against those who do evil" (1 Peter 3:12 NKJV).

Bartimaeus was blind and a beggar, but when he made his cry and answered the Lord's call, he got blessed. Oh, my people, that can happen to you, yes it can.

Conclusion

Yes, Oh Yes, Hallelujah Yes. The Compassionate Christ Will Hear You If You Holla. Go Ahead, Holla At Him, He Will Hear You: He Will Give:

- *The Comfort of His Presence*
- *Sufficiency of His Grace*
- *The Power of His Blood*
- *The Availability of His Spirit*
- *The Certainty of His Word*
- *A Sure Foundation That Never Shakes*

- *A Bright and Morning Star That Never Dims*
- *The Rose of Sharon That Never Fades*
- *Peace for Your Perplexities*
- *Hope for Your Despair*
- *Deliverance for Your Bondage*
- *Glory for Your Gloom*
- *Wisdom for Your Decisions*
- *Guide for Your Journey*
- *Shelter for Your Storm*
- *Blessings for Your Burdens*
- *Help for Your Hurt*
- *Balm for Your Bruises*
- *Strength for Your Weakness*
- *Power for Your Problems*
- *Answers for Your Anxieties*
- *Fullness for Your Emptiness*
- *Joy for Your Sorrow*
- *Love for Your Loneliness*
- *A Resource That Can Never be Depleted*
- *A Well That Will Never Run Dry*
- *A Heart Revived*
- *A Joy Renewed*
- *A Peace Restored*
- *A Soul Redeemed*
- *A Future Secure*

Holla at Him, Holla at Him, The Compassionate Christ Will Hear You If You Holla.

William Jones is a native of Memphis, Tennessee, but spent his formative years in Racine, Wisconsin. He has been married to the former Brenda Briscoe for 35 years. They have three children – Christopher, Christina, and Christian. He has been preaching the gospel of Christ for 42 years. Bro. Jones faithfully served as ministering evangelist to the Reynolds Street Church of Christ in Rochester, New York, for 15 years. He served with distinction at the Boulevard Church of Christ of Memphis, Tennessee, for 22 years. He has returned to Rochester to serve with the North Greece Road Church of Christ (formerly Reynolds Street) as minister for the last 3 years.

LUKE 7:36-50 – SIMON SAYS

Michael L. Dublin Sr.

Scripture Text:

"One of the Pharisees asked Jesus to eat with him, and He went into the Pharisee's house [in the region of Galilee] and reclined at the table. Now there was a woman in the city who was [known as] a sinner; and when she found out that He was reclining at the table in the Pharisee's house, she brought an alabaster vial of perfume; and standing behind Him at His feet, weeping, she began wetting His feet with her tears, and wiped them with the hair of her head, and [respectfully] kissed His feet [as an act signifying both affection and submission] and anointed them with the perfume. Now when [Simon] the Pharisee who had invited Him saw this, he said to himself, "If this Man were a prophet He would know who and what sort of woman this is who is touching Him, that she is a [notorious] sinner [an outcast, devoted to sin]."

"Jesus, answering, said to the Pharisee, "Simon, I have something to say to you." And he replied, "Teacher, say it." "A certain moneylender had two debtors: one owed him five hundred denarii, and the other fifty. When they had no means of repaying [the debts], he freely forgave them both. So which of them will love him more?" Simon answered, "The one, I take it, for whom he forgave more." Jesus said to him, "You have decided correctly." Then turning toward the woman, He said to Simon, "Do you see this woman? I came into your house [but you failed to extend to Me the usual courtesies shown to a guest]; you gave Me no water for My feet, but she has wet My feet with her tears and wiped them with her hair [demonstrating her love]. You gave Me no [welcoming] kiss, but from the moment I came in, she has not ceased to kiss My feet. You did not [even] anoint My head with [ordinary] oil, but she has anointed My feet with [costly and rare] perfume. Therefore I say to you, her sins, which are many, are forgiven, for she loved much; but he who is forgiven little, loves little." Then He said to her, "Your sins are forgiven." Those who were reclining at the table with Him began saying among themselves, "Who is this who even forgives sins?" Jesus said to the woman, "Your faith [in Me] has saved you; go in peace [free from the distress experienced because of sin]" (Luke 7:36-50 AMP).

There are three principle characters and billions of onlookers since the story has been told for 2,000 years. The Lord Jesus is always the central point in any New Testament story. The woman was once a baby and grew into adulthood while Jesus watched her story unfold; therefore, love and forgiveness were already prepared for this moment for her. It was not the self-righteous religious order of the day that attracted Jesus' attention for the right reasons, but those soulfully aware of their need for God.

"The woman no doubt waited near the door for Jesus to arrive. She probably expected that Jesus' feet would have been washed by one of Simon's servants. After His feet were washed, the woman would then likely have planned to anoint His feet with the perfume she had brought. Imagine the look on her face when she realized that Jesus' feet were not going to be washed. She did not let the dirty feet of our Lord keep her from what she had intended to do. She dared not kiss Jesus on the face, as Simon should have done, but she could kiss His feet, His dirty feet. She had come with no basin, no water, and no towel. Nevertheless, as she began to kiss His feet, the tears began to flow, something most unusual for a woman of her profession. As the tears began to flow, the woman must have noted that the little streams of tears carried the dirt of the road as well. She used the water of her tears to wash His feet, something she could hardly have planned in advance. Since there was no towel available to her, she used her hair to dry Jesus' feet. Imagine this, the woman used her hair, the most glorious part of her body (cf. 1 Cor. 11:15), to dry the feet of Jesus, the most ignoble part of one's body! She did not do her duty quickly, so as to quickly finish an unpleasant task. She persisted at kissing the feet of our Lord (cf. v. 45)."[14]

"This woman's worship of Jesus was at a great cost to her. It cost her the expensive vial of perfume, and the humility to kiss, wash, and dry the dirty feet of the Lord Jesus. But there was a higher price than this paid by the woman. Most likely, the greatest price which she paid was facing the scorn and rejection of the self-righteous Pharisees and other dinner guests at that meal. Jesus did not give her a 'dirty look,' but it is inconceivable to think that all of the others did not. Simon's disdain, revealed by his inner thoughts, must also have been evident in his eyes, and so too for the other guests. 'What in the world are **you** doing here?' must have been etched on the faces of the guests. It could hardly be otherwise for a Pharisee, whose holiness was primarily a matter of physical separation from sin and from 'sinners.' The woman's desire to see and to worship Jesus was greater than her fear of these guests. Their scorn was a high price to pay, but to the woman it was worth it."[15]

"Simon's Thoughts and Jesus' Teaching (7:39-43)"

"No doubt a great part of Simon's motivation was to 'check out' Jesus. Was this man really a prophet? Was His message to be believed? And how did His message compare with that of the Pharisees? Was He a threat, or an ally? Just who did Jesus claim to be and what was to be done about Him? Should He be resisted, opposed, put

---

[14] Bob Deffinbaugh, "Wordless Worship of an Unnamed Woman (Luke 7:36-50)," *Bible. org*, https://bible.org/seriespage/23-wordless-worship-unnamed-woman-luke-736-50.
[15] Ibid.

to death, or should be ignored? Could He be recruited to their side? These may have been some of the questions in Simon's mind, suggesting some of his motivation for having Jesus over to dinner."[16]

"Simon's reasoning is most illuminating. It went something like this:

Premises:

- If Jesus were a prophet, he would know people's character
- If Jesus knew this woman was a sinner, He would have nothing to do with her

Conclusions:

- Since Jesus has accepted this woman, He does not know her character
- Since Jesus does not know this woman is a sinner, He cannot be a prophet
- Since Jesus is not a prophet, I/we can reject Him, His message & ministry"[17]

"Simon, like many of us, was being very logical about his thinking and his response to the Lord Jesus. The problem with logic is the same as the problem with computers: your output is only as reliable as your input. To put it differently, there was nothing wrong with Simon's logic, other than the fact that he based his conclusions on a faulty premise. His first premise – If Jesus were a prophet, He would be able to discern the character of those around Him – was correct. Jesus, in fact, went beyond Simon's expectations. Jesus was not only able to detect the woman's character (". . . her sins, which are many," v. 47), He was also able to know the thoughts of

---

[16] Deffinbaugh.

[17] Ibid.

Simon, His host (v. 39). By conveying to Simon that He knew His thoughts, Jesus proved that He was at least a prophet."[18]

"Simon's second premise was entirely wrong, a reflection of his erroneous thinking as a Pharisee. Simon, like his fellow-Pharisees (remember that the word Pharisee means 'separate'), assumed that holiness was primarily a matter of separation. Holiness was achieved by keeping oneself separate from sin and from sinners. According to this view, Jesus would have to shun this sinful woman in order to remain holy. Simon concluded that either (1) Jesus didn't know this woman's character, or (2) that whether or not He knew about her sinfulness, He was physically contaminated by her, and thus could not be holy."[19]

"Our Lord knew exactly what Simon was thinking, as well as why his thinking was wrong, although Simon didn't know those things himself. Jesus' words to Simon in verses 40-47 expose the error of Pharisaical thinking, and explain why the "Holy One of Israel" would draw near to sinners, even to the point of touching them and being touched by them [as the promises of redemption had always been prophesied]."[20]

Simon's religious teaching and foundation would not allow him to conceive of the promised Messiah allowing a woman to touch him, let alone a woman known as "a sinner"! Simon knew who the woman was and that has led some to speculate that she was either a former wife or a disgraced daughter.

Jesus used his masterful teaching skills to show Simon what was going on in that situation and within Simon, where only God can go.

Luke 7:41-42

Simon is asked a question based on the story and answers, "I supposed

---

[18] Ibid.

[19] Ibid.

[20] Deffinbaugh.

the one who had the bigger debt forgiven," and Jesus stated that Simon answered correctly. Jesus then took Simon and his religiosity to task by contrasting how the woman treated Him with the way Simon treated Him as the invited guest in his home.

Jesus turned his back to Simon to face the woman, which seems trivial, but is quite significant. Simon had rejected Jesus, the woman worshipped Jesus!!! Jesus turned to and away, although he loved both.

> "Simon was more interested in passing judgment on God than he was on God's judgment of him. Simon felt that his home would be more righteous by keeping sinners, like this woman, out, than by inviting sinners in. Many churches feel the same way. Simon was inclined to see some sins as greater than others in the eyes of God. Sexual sin was unforgivable, but pride was acceptable."[21]

> "Simon thought of religion as something to be preserved; Jesus thought of true religion in terms of penetration. Simon wanted to keep sinners out, Jesus went out to sinners. Some of Simon's error is the failure to grasp the change from the old covenant to the new. The Old Testament dealt with sin as incurable, and thus the principle defense was simply to avoid contact with sin and sinners. The new covenant came with a solution for sin. The new covenant could change hard hearts to soft ones. Thus, Jesus did not feel compelled to deal with sinners the way the Old Testament taught – seek to destroy or to avoid them."[22]

> "The Pharisee looked at sin something like the way we look at AIDS [or any incurable disease]. It has no cure, and thus the best course of action is to avoid any and all contact. But, you see, the gospel teaches that Jesus is the cure for sin. Thus, Jesus did not need to avoid sinners."[23]

---

[21] Ibid.
[22] Ibid.
[23] Deffinbaugh.

The Pharisee, with a strong belief in keeping the Word of God to the letter, had missed the goal of the Word, which was to point the lost to the coming Messiah. The first and greatest commandment was eventually minimized by the emphasis on outward appearance in religion, rather than the inward, changed heart!!!

The Pharisees did social programs and good work in communities for years, but became distracted by battles with Sadducees and, over a period of time, lost their way in the Scriptures and fell into the ways of divided spirituality, unable to relate to the marginalized such that they couldn't "touch a sinner" even when they knew who they were and their circumstances. Simon lost the drive to love as the Creator had willed for him or may not have had that drive due to the teaching he received as a Pharisee.

Simon says:

- You are unworthy to be saved.
- Your past defines your future.
- Your previous circumstances don't matter.
- Your background does not matter.
- Your repentance isn't real so it does not matter.
- Your contrite heart does not matter unless you prove it to us.
- What's love got to do with this sinner?

"What Did Jesus Reveal to Us about God in This [story within a story]?

- That God wants to reach the moral, upright sinner as well as the flagrantly immoral sinner. He associated with both. He ate with tax collectors and Pharisees.
- That there are no hopeless cases with God. He extends His grace to everyone!
- That God loves and forgives women equally with men.
- There are no second-class members of His family.
- That God knows our hearts and motives even when we do not say anything.
- That God will never stay in the box we put Him in.

- That God hates hypocrisy and self-righteousness.
- That God fully forgives ALL our sins and gives us peace.
- That God accepts us individually
- He accepts our love and worship and the manner in which we express it."[24]

No matter what religious self-righteousness and or strong doctrine says or which version one uses, the message to us from John 6:37 should always be:

New International Bible

"All those the Father gives me will come to me, and whoever comes to me I will never drive away."

New Living Translation

"However, those the Father has given me will come to me, and I will never reject them."

English Standard Version

"All that the Father gives me will come to me, and whoever comes to me I will never cast out."

Berean Study Bible

"Everyone the Father gives Me will come to Me, and the one who comes to Me I will never drive away."

Berean Literal Bible

"All that the Father gives Me will come to Me, and the one coming to Me, I shall not cast out."

New American Standard Bible

"All that the Father gives Me will come to Me, and the one who comes to Me I will certainly not cast out."

---

[24] Vickie Kraft, "Lesson 5: Invitation to Dinner (Luke 7:36-50)," *Bible.org*, https://bible.org/seriespage/lesson-5-invitation-dinner-luke-736-50.

New King James Version

"All that the Father gives Me will come to Me, and the one who comes to Me I will by no means cast out."

King James Bible

"All that the Father giveth me shall come to me; and him that cometh to me I will in no wise cast out."

How can we start the process of developing a caring heart that pushes us to connect with others as a means of moving beyond our religious tendencies that are exclusive rather than inclusive, as Jesus taught and demonstrated?

Each message demands an examination of who we are at this juncture in our walk with God. Set aside time within the next week and answer these questions as best as you can using a true or false measure:

> I do not regard others as inferior to me.
> I value human relationships more than material goods.
> I stick to my core principles.
> I actively take a stand for my moral principles.
> My actions are consistent with my values.

Once you have taken this brief evaluation, pray for God to open you to truth and a willing spirit to sustain you as David asked in Psalm 51:12.

It will be an added strength to take one more self-examination to support and sustain your convictions that you want to connect to others beyond religious trappings. Again, set aside quiet time and answer these questions as honestly as you can:

> I usually have empathy for others.
> I want to help people less fortunate than I am.
> I feel what others are feeling.
> I feel a commitment to caring for others.
> I put myself in other's shoes as I attempt to see their side.
> I work toward peace and elimination of suffering in areas open to me.

I want to work for the good of my community.

I help people regardless of their ethnicity, faith, or politics.

Don't allow excuses like these examples to stop your search for maturation in Christ through service to the people as he did: I can't empathize with that person. I don't have time. I have to deal with my family. People should grow up. What's in this for me?

The Lord Jesus Christ will send the Holy Spirit to lead you to people in need of a compassionate heart, humility, and gratitude. You will begin to experience the love of God through others as you remember, "All those the Father gives me will come to me, and whoever comes to me I will never drive away" (John 6:37 NIV)

References

Deffinbaugh, Bob. "Wordless Worship of an Unnamed Woman (Luke 7:36-50." *Bible.org.* https://bible.org/seriespage/23-wordless-worship-unnamed-woman-luke-736-50.

Kraft, Vickie. "Lesson 5: Invitation to Dinner (Luke 7:36-50)." *Bible.org.* https://bible.org/ seriespage/lesson-5-invitation-dinner-luke-736-50.

"Pharisees." *Wikipedia.* https://en.wikipedia.org/wiki/Pharisees.

Brother Michael L. Dublin Sr. has served in the pastoral role at South Central Church of Christ for the past thirty years. Bro. Dublin was baptized in 1979 and began his service to Christ Jesus in ministry as an Associate Minister at Brooks Avenue Church of Christ in 1985. Brother Dublin has been married to Cecelia (Crim) Dublin for 33 years. They have a lovely blended family of two adult sons, four adult daughters, thirteen grandchildren, and eight great grandchildren.

JOHANNINE LITERATURE
John 8:38-44 – *The Day Jesus Called for a Paternity Test*
Jonathan W. Morrison

This sermon was delivered at the 73rd Annual
Church of Christ National Lectureship in Atlanta, Georgia, in 2017.

Scripture Text:

"I speak that which I have seen with my Father: and ye do
that which ye have seen with your father. They answered
and said unto him, Abraham is our father. Jesus saith unto
them, if ye were Abraham's children, ye would do the works
of Abraham. But now ye seek to kill me, a man that hath
told you the truth, which I have heard of God: this did not
Abraham. Ye do the deeds of your father. Then said they
to him, we be not born of fornication; we have one Father,
even God. Jesus said unto them, If God were your Father,
ye would love me: for I proceeded forth and came from
God; neither came I of myself, but he sent me. Why do ye
not understand my speech? even because ye cannot hear my
word. Ye are of your father the devil, and the lusts of your
father ye will do. He was a murderer from the beginning,
and abode not in the truth, because there is no truth in him.
When he speaketh a lie, he speaketh of his own: for he is a
liar, and the father of it" (John 8:38-44 KJV).

Jesus One of the ugly realities birthed in the moral decline of our
culture is the rise of paternity disputes. And for an increasing number of

parents and children, the question, "Who's the daddy?" is frequently left unanswered. In fact, a recent study estimated that 6.7 million children in the United States alone do not know who their biological father is. People are left wondering who the father is because 31% of the 300,000 paternity tests performed every year come back without a match, leaving over 100,000 children who are tested wondering who their father is!

And while the proliferation of paternity disputes and DNA testing signal a turn for the worse in our moral direction as a society, it has led to the birth of a new industry, and the peculiar popularity of TV personalities like Maury Povich and others who have made a living offering tests to those who have been left wondering who their father is!

But here in this discourse we find that debates and disputes over paternity are not a new thing. In fact, as we pick up the storyline of this passage, Jesus and some unbelieving Jews are debating sonship in God and Abraham. Jesus has created a whirlwind of controversy in the process of declaring that life and freedom was found in Him alone, and that the only way to overcome the power of sin was in the Father through the Son. And it was those conditions of true sonship that challenged the Jews' own religious pride and ecclesiastical elitism. Their resulting disdain and distaste for these conditions of sonship exposed the spiritual corruption of those who would rather die in their sin than live in the Son.

And it is for that reason that Jesus begins this discourse with a startling contrast between his paternity and the paternity of the Jews who rejected Him. Jesus says, **"I speak that which I have seen with my Father** [or while at the side of my Father]**: and ye do that which ye have seen with your father"** (v. 38 KJV). Now, what cannot be ignored is the irony of that statement, seeing that both Jesus and these disputing Jews were both seeds of Abraham according to the flesh. If they performed a search on Ancestry.com, they'd find common ancestry because they shared the same bloodline of their father in the faith, Abraham. Yet, in a strange twist, Jesus says your father and my father are not one in the same. Now, if you're like me, you have to wonder how both Jesus and these Jews could be of the seed of Abraham, and at the same time be the sons of two different ancestral fathers.

Jesus suggests that, while the difference is subtle, the fact that they have different fathers is the result of one being a son . . . and the other being a seed. Jesus suggests that the reason their fathers were not one in the same is because He was a son, but these Jews are simply seeds. Jesus, speaking of himself, says it this way, **"If the Son therefore shall make you free, ye shall be free indeed"** (v. 36 KJV). But describing the Jews in the very next verse, He says, **"I know that ye are Abraham's seed"** (v. 37 KJV). And the idea here is that being a seed simply implies insemination; but being a son implies influence. In the truest sense, seed alone doesn't make one a father or son. Fatherhood and sonship in the truest sense requires influence. While these Jews (including Jesus) were all the seed of Abraham, because of opposing influences, they were not all sons of God.

Put another way, Jesus suggests that a person's true father can be determined by who is influencing their thinking and behavior. To that point, the Jews doubled down on their heritage as the legitimate descendants of Abraham, "[the Jews] **answered and said unto him, Abraham is our father"** (v. 39 KJV). That was to say that, unlike those they considered to be in the bastard line of Ishmael or a tainted bloodline of the Samaritans, they were of the pure bloodline of Abraham. But Jesus pushed back, and asserted, **"if ye were Abraham's children, ye would do the works of Abraham"** (v. 39 KJV) (which included loving, worship, and embracing Jesus). **But now ye seek to kill me, a man that hath told you the truth, which I have heard of God: this did not Abraham. Ye do the deeds of your father"** (vv. 40-41 KJV).

In other words, while these Jews were Abraham's descendants, they lacked Abraham's disposition. Their origin could be traced to the house of Abraham, but they were spiritual runaways from the house of God. Pausing parenthetically, the greater tragedy was not that they were spiritual runaways. Truth is, at some point, we've all lost our way or been on the run from God. The greater tragedy was that they were runaways and didn't know it. The parenthetical lesson here is that trouble becomes tragedy when your heart becomes so hard, and your eyes become so blind, that you believe you're in the house of God when, in reality, you're in bed with the devil. Trouble becomes tragedy when your conscience becomes so numb, and your mind becomes so wicked, that you assume you're doing the Lord's work, but you're actually doing the devil's business.

Jesus keeps talking, and he asks a good question, **"Why do ye not understand my speech?"** (v. 43 KJV). Another translation puts it this way, "Why do you not understand My language, the language of the father you claim." And the idea here is that in the same way that a natural son understands the language of his natural father, a supernatural son understands the language of his supernatural father.

It is both unusual and uncommon for there to be a language barrier between a father and his offspring because a child ordinarily and instinctively adopts the language of its family of origin. Jesus seems to be suggesting here that another means of concluding that God was not the father of these Jews was their inability to recognize, receive, or reciprocate the language that Jesus spoke on behalf of God the Father. And the implication for us today is that a true child of God speaks and understands the language and message of God. One of the best ways to distinguish a child of God from an imposter is the ability to both recognize the truth and speak God's language.

Describing those who had become calloused in their thinking, Jesus says, **"Why do ye not understand my speech? even because ye cannot hear my word"** (v. 43 KJV). Taken in context, the phrase "cannot hear" carries the idea of being unable to tolerate the truth in Christ's teaching because it is too offensive. In other words, these Jews' problem was not a lack of intellectual capacity to understand the truth, the problem was their lack of spiritual integrity to embrace the truth. It was not that they could not hear what Jesus was saying, they didn't want to hear what Jesus was saying! And their paternity was being called into question as a result of their rejection of the gospel.

It can be safely said that, at this point, Jesus has successfully delegitimized and debunked these arrogant Jews' claim as true children of God. In my imagination, Jesus' patience is exhausted, and his patience has run out. The theological banter, spiritual sparring, and religious retorts have gone on long enough. Now, it is time to cut the corner, say what needs to be said, and drop the mic. Without biting his tongue, Jesus says, **"Ye are of *your* father the devil, and the lusts of your father ye will do"** (v. 44 KJV).

It's worth mentioning that Jesus chose His words very carefully. Notice that Jesus says "he *lusts* of your father" or "the evil *desires* of your father you will pursue." Notice that Jesus does not accuse them of being the devil's children because they had a casual *lapse* with the devil, he accused them of being the devil's children because they were consumed by the *lusts* of the devil. Jesus was describing the wickedness they were seeking after, not a sin they stumbled into. Let me pause again parenthetically and humbly say that there is a clear and distinguishable difference between having an appetite and having an accident, having a desire and taking a detour, being careless and having a craving, and having a lust versus having a lapse. Spiritual paternity is not necessarily compromised by lapses in our focus, but it is always compromised in our lusts through our flesh.

Finally, speaking of the common nature they share with their father, the devil, Jesus mentions two tell-tell signs of Satan's spawn. First, Jesus says they are just like their father who **"was a murderer from the beginning"** (v. 44 KJV). While Jesus did not bother to pinpoint the time or define what he calls "the beginning," we can be sure that from the very moment God created man in his image, the devil deployed a plan to destroy that image. Beyond that, Jesus suggests that where God's truth abides, the devil's lies are added. Speaking of the devil, Jesus says, "[he] **abode not in the truth** [or has no footing in the truth]**, because there is no truth in him. When he speaketh a lie, he speaketh of his own: for he is a liar, and the father of it"** (v. 44 KJV). Taken together, Jesus says the language Satan speaks is nothing more than the language of his essence and engineering . . . lies.

As I close, I told you a few moments ago that Maury Povich made a career by revealing paternity test results during his program. Two or three times during every episode, the show's producers hand Maury an envelope as the words "The test results are in!" flash across the screen. But what I didn't tell you is that the high demand for paternity testing is the result of a recent spike in what is called paternity fraud. In many recent cases, the father and child are knowingly lied to, and told they are "father and child" when they're not.

In the same way, the devil, the father of lies, is guilty of paternity fraud. And one of the biggest lies the devil ever told us was that he is our father. He whispers lies like, "God could never love you that much. He is too Divine, and you are too depraved! God is not your father. I am your father."

But tell the devil that the test results are in! They've run his DNA against our DNA, and the test results are in! Tell the devil that in the case of every child who's been washed in the blood and sealed by the Spirit . . .

who's walked by faith and not by sight . . . and who's been saved by grace through faith!

In the case of every child who's more than a conqueror through Christ who loves them . . . who put their trust in the Lord and leaned not to their own understanding . . . who loves the Lord and is called according to His purpose!

In the case of every child who's been given a spirit power, love, and a sound mind, who loves the Lord with all their heart, soul, and strength . . . and walks in the light as He is in the light!

In the case of every child who can do all things through Christ who strengthens them . . . who has not been conformed to this world but transformed by the renewing of their mind . . . who's joyful in hope, patient in affliction, faithful in prayer . . . and who runs their race to the end! Devil . . . you are not the father!

You told us God's grace was insufficient, but the
lie detector determined that was a lie!
You told us He'd leave us and forsake us, but the
lie detector determined that was a lie!
You told us He'd leave us comfortless, but the
lie detector determined that was a lie!
You told us spiritual blessings in heavenly places are in
you, but the lie detector determined that was a lie!
You told us in the end you win, but the lie
detector determined that was a lie!
Devil, you are not the father!

Minister Morrison is happily married to the former Lataria Andrews of Dallas. They have four children: Jostyn, Jensyn, Juliyn, and Jiliyn. Prior to working with the Cedar Crest congregation, he was privileged to serve the Marsalis Avenue Church of Christ (Dallas, Texas) as Associate Minister and the West End Church of Christ (Terrell, Texas) as Senior Minister.

JOHN 10:7, 11 – I AM, THE GOOD SHEPHERD
Dr. Robert Davis

There is a bit of a discrepancy in our text this morning. In verse 7, Jesus declares his third I AM statement – "I am the door of the sheep" – and then just four verses later he declares his fourth I AM statement – "I am the good shepherd." Beloved, what may seem like conflicting and incongruent statements to us, would not have been negated by the first century audience. For us, out of all of the I AM statements, I would be willing to argue that these two I AM statements are the most underappreciated and overlooked of the seven I AMs. People get excited when you start to talk about "I am the light of the world." People quote right alongside you when you start with "I am the way, the truth, and the life." You would be hard pressed to make it through a funeral without hearing, "I am the resurrection and the life." But rarely do folk get riled up when you remind them that Jesus is the good shepherd. And let me tell you why – because you don't live in an agrarian society and you don't understand sheep farming.

Come here. You will never understand the title of the good shepherd unless you understand the nature of sheep. The number one fact that you need to know about sheep is that, out of all the animals that God created, sheep are arguably the dumbest animals on the planet. When you think sheep, you should immediately think dimwitted – feebleminded – thickheaded – idiotic. Before you get upset, let me explain. Sheep are so dumb that when they graze, they won't even lift up their eyes while they are walking and will walk directly off a cliff into a ravine. Sheep are so thickheaded that if they see something they want, they will forsake the flock and will wander off by themselves. Sheep are so dimwitted that even if they are dehydrated, they will not drink water from a stream unless it is static. Sheep will stick their heads in insect nests. Sheep will stick their head in a snake burrow. Sheep when frightened will forsake safety in numbers. Sheep will not defend themselves when being attacked. Sheep can stress out so much over a predator that they die from panic.

Sheep are one of the only animal species who could not and would not survive without a shepherd intervening. The shepherd feeds them. The shepherd has to guide them to new pastures to eat. The shepherd has to pull them out of the ravine. The shepherd has to run after wandering sheep. The shepherd has to treat parasitic infections. The shepherd has to relieve their constipation. The shepherd has to find them still water. The shepherd has to protect them from danger because sheep are defenseless, dependent, and endangered – if there is no shepherd. Beloved, if you're like me and amazed by how dumb sheep are, you will be even more amazed that when Jesus is talking about sheep, he is NOT talking about the animals – he is talking about us – because a sheep is God's perfect symbol for everyone in this room.

I'm not calling you dumb, but I am saying that we can be so fixated on something that we can't even see the cliff up head. I'm not calling you dumb, but I am saying that all of us at some point and time are prone to wonder. I'm not saying you're dimwitted, but I am saying that we all put our nose where we have no business putting it. I'm not calling you thickheaded, but some of still don't understand that when trouble comes, and problems arise, we should pull together instead of tearing apart. The *reason* why God calls us sheep is because he knows that we cannot make it on our own. We don't know which way to go on our own. We don't know what is good for us. We don't know what is safe for us. We don't even know what we don't know. But I thank God we have a Good Shepherd who does not give up on us when we wander – will come get us out the depth by which we have fallen – that protects me from me. Thank God Jesus is the Good Shepherd because we owe everything to Him.

Transition: When we last left Jesus, he was in chapter 8 at the feast of tabernacles. It was the illumination of the temple ceremony, and Jesus makes the declaration, "I am the Light of the World." If you were here last week you know this set people off, particularly the Pharisees and scribes. They begin to question Jesus about who He is. He tells them I come from the Father. They begin asking him about his father, and things get contentious. Here is how the conversation goes in the Robert Davis translation: Jesus essentially says even if I told you, you wouldn't even know Him. They shoot back, well "we were not born out of sexual immorality" and "we know our father, his name is Abraham." Jesus says, "no, your father is the devil because I know Abraham and he was glad when we met." They say, "this dude is crazy because how are you going to meet Abraham and you're not 50." Jesus says, "Truly, Truly," I say to you, before Abraham, I AM." In other words, Jesus is making it plain in

Jerusalem that "I am the great I am." And they knew that is what Jesus was saying because the Bible says they pick up stones to throw at Him. That is how chapter 8 ends.

Chapter 9 opens up with the Jesus encountering a blind man and healing the blind man. But he does it on the Sabbath. And, for the next 41 verses of chapter 9, there is controversy surrounding the miracle because Jesus is the crazy young rabbi leading people astray and wanted by the Sanhedrin Council. Yet, they can't reconcile it with the fact that this man who has been a blind beggar for years is now able to see. Beloved, what makes this miracle so special is that the blind man testifies that "since the beginning of the world nobody has been able to bring back sight to a person born blind." Now you would think that people would rejoice. You would think that people would take a closer look at Jesus. You would think that they would simply investigate this young man. Investigate where he is from, and the claims he is making. Instead, people kept Jesus at a distance because the religious elite had let it be made known that if you confess Jesus to be Christ, you will be put out of the synagogue. Listen, for a Jew to be put out of the synagogue means that you lost your Jewishness. You lost communion with God. You lost access to God. You were not able to participate in the temple worship. But I thank God for the blind man, because when he is asked to testify who Jesus is, he says, "I don't know who he is, all I know is that he comes from God." And the Bible says that they kicked him out of the synagogue. Here it is, he has lost his identity, he is labeled a blasphemer, he has just lost everything all **because of Jesus**. At that moment, Jesus shows up and reveals himself. Now the man has a choice to make – reject him – or receive him – and the Bible says the man begins to worship him!

And what I find interesting about that is if you have been *blind* your whole life, how do you know what worship looks like? Well. let me help you – worship isn't supposed to look like anything. Worship is what happens when you think about everything that you have been through – and when you think about where you have come from – and when you think about all the things you are blessed with and don't deserve – and your spirit can't help but to – wave a hand – fall to your knees – shed a few tears – holler thank you Jesus. Beloved, whether you shout or cry – clap or rock side to side – tap your foot or shake your head – worship is between you and the God that has touched your life.

Note Jesus does not stop him, but there are some Pharisees that see and decide to challenge Jesus again and the chapter closes with Jesus making the case that they think they see, but are blind. He proves it in chapter 10. It is the same day, the same event, the same crowd as chapter 9. And so, in the first 6 verses, John says Jesus uses a *figure of speech* – in Greek – *paroinia*, which is literally a *word picture* for them. He describes a common scene that would have been in virtually every village. **He gives 4 characters: Sheep in a sheepfold or pin – a gatekeeper who opens the door – a shepherd who cares for the sheep – and thieves who seek to do harm to the sheep.** Everyone who is listening to Jesus would have understood the imagery, would have understood its religious undertones. The Hebrew Bible is filled with sheep/shepherd imagery. Here is the way the Pharisees would have seen the world picture: the flock are the people – Moses or Messiah are the shepherds who will come for the flock – and they serve as gatekeepers protecting the flock until the shepherd shows up. As gatekeepers they are in charge of the access between the shepherd and flock.

But they are missing the point that Jesus is trying to get them to see. Jesus is making the point that you are so blind that you think you're the gatekeepers, when really you are the thieves and robbers. You have done damage to the people. You have caused fear among the people. You have run people out the synagogue. You have destroyed people's identity. You have killed people's faith. You have put heavy burdens on people who don't belong to you. You have made them feel less than worthless – rejected – and you think you are gatekeepers, but you are thieves and robbers.

Beloved, this is how I know Jesus is making the point because verse 6 says they don't understand, so in verse 7 He clarifies with *another word picture*. Instead of four characters, he only gives three: there are sheep, which are the people – there is the shepherd – and there are thieves. To make his point clear, He gets rid of the gatekeeper all together as if to say, "you don't control the door to the sheep because *I am the door of the sheep* – and before you get crazy – I *am the shepherd too* – which means that you are thieves that come to steal, kill, and destroy!" But here is Jesus' point to them – for those that walk around with the pharisaical mindset – for those that think they can determine the relationship one has with God – for those that believe they can determine righteous and unrighteous – for those that believe they can make the decision of who is in and out. Hear me, you are not the door! You don't make decisions for God. You can't see what God sees. You don't know what God knows. You don't love like God loves, and before you keep running folk off –pushing folk out the door, killing folk spirit, bestowing who is a child of God and who is not – please understand God does not need your help putting people in hell – God does not need your help reading the hearts of men – God does not need your help being God because, truth be told, there is not a day that goes by where *you yourself are not struggling* with your mouth – temper – lust – desires – envy – sin. *If* you make it, it will be because *Jesus opened the door for you*. Preach the Gospel and let God be God.

Jesus' "I am the door" statement is more than an indictment against the pharisaical spirit, but it denotes that Jesus is responsible for giving access to eternal life. If you come by *me*, you will be saved and will go in and out and find pasture. Then Jesus transitions and says, "I am the Good Shepherd." If we can harken back to the introduction, this begs the question *how* can you be the door *and* the shepherd? Those seem like incongruous statements. But if you notice the Pharisees and scribes don't challenge Jesus like usual, because they understood something that we do not. What you have to realize is that after the harvest, the pasture is bare because of the heat. The shepherd would have to lead the sheep along the western side of the Jordan River Valley into the wilderness of Judea to find pasture in the midst of the wilderness. Life is rough in the wilderness, but the shepherd's job is to sustain life. Whatever happens to the sheep, the shepherd will take care of it. If the sheep is sick, he will nurse it. If the sheep is injured, he will mend its injuries. Before the sun goes down, he will take rocks and thorns, and build a small sheepfold around the sheep. In this makeshift sheepfold, there would be an opening in which he would prop himself up, thus becoming the door to the sheep while simultaneously being the shepherd. It is in this capacity that he puts his life on the line against the wolf – lion – coyote – bear – robbers – thieves – bandits – etc. The shepherd does all of this so that the sheep can live!

So, when Jesus says I come so that you can have life and have it more abundantly, 'abundant' in Greek means "to go immeasurably beyond." He is saying that when you are my sheep, it doesn't matter where you are – I'll come get you. When you belong to me, it doesn't matter how far gone you are – I'll come get you. If you're wounded – I'll come heal you. If you're scared – I'll comfort you. If you're angry – I'll calm you. If you're stuck – I'll free you. If you're under attack – I'll shield you. Beloved, the abundant life has nothing to do with stuff. There are a bunch of people with stuff and they still kill themselves. It's not about power or position. Some of the most important folk still kill themselves. Only God can make life beautiful. Only God can put the right people in your life. Only God can give you satisfaction. Only God can give your life weight. The abundant life is not about stuff, but about have a life WORTH LIVING. Beloved, you know you are living when you don't know how you are going to pay your bills, but still lay down and sleep like a baby. You know you are really living when you don't own a house or a car, but you know you already got more than you need. You know you are living when someone walks away, and your life don't skip a beat because you know if God wanted them in your life they would be there. You know you are living when you wear a smile that is not determined by how you look – what you got on – or your bank account – or your accomplishments – but your joy is simply in knowing that Jesus is the life. He gets sweeter and sweeter as the days go by!

The Jews understood the shepherd imagery. They understood that Abraham was a shepherd. They understood that Isaac was a shepherd. They understood that Moses was a shepherd. They understood that David was a shepherd. They also knew Ezekiel 34. It's in that text that God makes it clear that He is the shepherd of His people. So, when Jesus identifies himself as the shepherd, He says, "I am the Good Shepherd." Not *a* good shepherd but *the* good shepherd. If you are a Bible reader, you know previously that He said nobody is good except God, *alone!* Jesus is suggesting that He is not a shepherd like Abraham, Isaac, Jacob, Moses, David. They could lead the sheep, and guide the sheep, and warn the sheep. However, a shepherd isn't a *good* shepherd unless he can protect the sheep from death. Come here, Church, a shepherd cannot protect the sheep from death if the shepherd dies. And if the shepherd dies, the sheep die. So, if you want to know what Jesus really means when he says I am the Good Shepherd, keep reading when he says, "I have the power to lay down my life and take it back up again." Listen up, sheep, when you are walking through the valley of the shadow of death, nobody can walk with you but the good shepherd. When you need someone to prepare a table in the presence of enemies, nobody can do it but the good shepherd. When you need someone to anoint your head with oil, nobody can do it but the good shepherd. When you need goodness and mercy all the days of your life, nobody can do it but the good shepherd. Goodbye, Church, may God bless you and keep you.

Dr. Robert Davis is a native of Gilbert, South Carolina, and the fourth child of Milton and Lorraine Davis. In July 2016, Robert joined the ministerial staff at Sigsbee Church of Christ in Spartanburg, South Carolina. Robert is a member of Kappa Alpha Psi Fraternity Incorporated. In 2020, Dr. Davis led Sigsbee Church of Christ in the purchase of a worship facility in downtown Spartanburg where they now assume the name Drayton Mills Church of Christ. Robert is currently married to his college sweetheart, Dr. Courtney Davis of Lexington, South Carolina. They have three beautiful children – Wright, Carter, and Carson.

JOHN 11:35-37 – CROCODILE TEARS

Dr. Lovell C. Hayes

"Jesus wept." To me that is one of the most powerful, profound, and propelling statements of the Bible. Jesus!! wept!! Not some frail ordinary man – Jesus wept! Not some scrawny, fearful, cowardly character – Jesus wept! Not some nerdy nobody – Jesus wept! What a profound revelation. For I have heard somebody say that "men are not supposed to cry." They are supposed to be strong, virile, heroic. They are supposed to laugh in the face of danger and rise to the top in the face of calamity, but they are not supposed to cry. Just imagine your greatest hero or some person you admire greatly, breaking down and crying like a baby. You don't imagine the Black Panther crying. You don't imagine Duane "the Rock" Johnson crying. You don't imagine Shaquille O'Neal or Anthony Barr, the rough and tumble linebacker of the Minnesota Vikings, or Russell Westbrook, the hard-driving guard on the Houston Rockets team: you don't readily visualize them crying even under a difficult circumstance, for men are supposed to be tough, to be able to take it, to stand up under pressure.

But now we are not talking about Shaq or the Rock. This is Jesus Christ, the Son of the Living God. The text says that Jesus wept. This is Jesus: the one who came into the temple in John 2 overturning the moneychangers' tables and driving them out with a whip. This is Jesus who in John 4 boldly proclaimed Himself equal with God, even though He knew that they would try to kill Him. On one occasion even, they took up stones and came toward Him and He didn't even run. This is Jesus who in John 6 walked on the sea in the midst of a raging storm and took control of the wind causing it to cease its troubling ways. This is Jesus, who in John 7 withstood the Pharisees and chief priests, the sharpest thinking minds of His day, and outsmarted them all. THIS Jesus wept. This is Jesus: who is God. Who, according to John 1, in the beginning was with God the Father and was God. Jesus is God, a member of the Godhead made up of Father, the Word, and the Holy Spirit. Since Jesus is God, when John reports that "Jesus wept," John is also saying that God cried! What a profound revelation! What a revealing insight into the character of God, the Son!

Now the occasion of this text involves the death of a man named Lazarus.

1. He and his sisters had a very close relation with Jesus. This is evidenced by verse 3. When Lazarus was ill, Mary and Martha sent word to Jesus saying, "Lord, he whom you love is sick."
2. But Jesus did not come immediately. Then later the word came that Lazarus had died. He came to Bethany and each sister greeted Him by saying, "Lord, if you had been here, my brother would not have died" (John 11:21 and 32 NKJV).

   Have you ever had times when you felt that the Lord was far away from you? Have you ever felt that the reason a certain thing happened in your life was because the Lord was not there? Have you ever been so troubled that you said, "Lord, if you had been here, this would not have troubled me?" Have you ever said, "Lord, if you had been here, I would not be depressed?" Have you ever said, "Lord, if you had been here, I would not have faced this sorrow?"
3. Jesus told them to take Him to where Lazarus was buried and when they arrived at the tomb, Jesus wept.

I. THE ACCUSATION OF JESUS' SINCERITY

But some accused Jesus of crying crocodile tears.

1. "Crocodile tears" are defined as insincere tears or a hypocritical show of grief.
2. As Jesus wept, "some of them said, 'Could not this Man, who opened the eyes of the blind, also have kept this man from dying?'" (v. 37). In other words, if you had really cared, you would have come when Lazarus was sick and healed him, thusly preventing his death. They are parroting the words of Mary and Martha who had earlier said to Jesus, "if you had been here, my brother would not have died."

   But these people are essentially saying: Jesus, you could have prevented this death. Jesus, you could have saved Lazarus from suffering. Jesus, you could have saved this family from all this grief and trouble and heartache and pain. You are crying now, you display this emotion and shed these tears, but do you really care?

3. After all, Lazarus was your good friend. Lazarus was "he whom You love." Just a few days ago, you met a blind man you did not even know and healed him that day, but when you got word that Lazarus, whom you love, was sick, you did not come. A few days ago, you defended a woman who was an adulteress, rescuing her from the crowd who had taken up rocks to stone her. You helped that adulteress woman, but when Lazarus, whom you loved, was sick, you did not come. Just a while ago you fed a crowd of over 5,000 knowing that they were fair-weather friends and would desert you the next day. You fed those fair-weather friends, but when Lazarus, one whom you loved, was sick, you did not respond. You are crying, yes, but they must be crocodile tears.

There are probably times in our lives when we doubt the care of God. We are like the writer of the 73rd Psalm (NKJV).

1. In verse 1, he acknowledges God as a God who is good. And, like him, on a general and superficial level, we believe that God is there and that He exists and that He is a caring God. But like the writer expresses in verse 2, we face things that lead us to wonder on a heartfelt, personal level if God really is aware of our problems. He says in verse 1 that God is good, but in spite of that knowledge he is on the verge of stumbling and slipping.

2. Just like in the gospel of John, Jesus was sensitive to the hunger of that multitude even though they were fair-weather friends. He was protective of that woman who was an adulteress, but seemed not to be sensitive to Mary and Martha's message that Lazarus was sick and they needed Him.

3. In verses 3-5, the psalm writer seems to think that the wicked are more fortunate than he is. Others seem to be well off, but what about his problems? What about his troubles and sickness and heartaches? Then in verse 11, he seems to be questioning the care of God. He is asking, doesn't God know? Isn't He aware that I am hurting inside? My spouse and I are having problems: doesn't

God know? I get discouraged and sometimes feel like giving up: doesn't God know?

4. But in verses 23-28, he is able to focus again on the fact that God is good and that God does care.

II. THE ACTUALITY OF JESUS' SYMPATHY

But how can God understand my troubles?

1. How can He know what it is like:
   - to have to live with sickness and have days when you can hardly get up out of bed;
   - to live with a husband or wife who doesn't treat you with any respect;
   - to have parents who don't understand and don't express love toward you that you need;
   - depressed and troubled on every side, both day and night;
   - to be low in spirit and low in faith and feel hopeless and full of despair?

2. The answer comes from Hebrews 4:13-16 (NKJV). Christ "was in all points tempted as we are." He can be touched with the feeling of our infirmities.

   Since God does care, since God does understand, our response should be to keep on working, to stay on the battlefield, to keep laboring in the vineyard. Let God worry about your problems. You concentrate on doing His will, on being faithful, on obeying His commands, on doing what is needed to build up the church and spread His gospel throughout the world.

Going back to John 11, we see that Jesus cares. Remember that the Hebrew writer said that God sees all and that He is touched with the feeling of our infirmities.

This is clearly evident in John 11:33-44 (NKJV). Jesus saw their weeping, and "he groaned in the spirit and was troubled." He was "touched with the feeling of" their infirmities (Hebrews 4:15 KJV). The people were crying tears or "weeping" in verse 33. The word there is *klaio*, which is a loud expression of grief, wailing, bitter crying. "Jesus wept," says verse 35. The word there is *dakruo*, which is to shed tears in silence.

The weeping of Jesus was not "crocodile tears." Jesus saw their trouble, for verse 33 says that Jesus saw the weeping of Mary and the Jews who came with her. But Jesus not only saw their trouble, He was touched by their trouble, for verse 33 and 35 say that Jesus "groaned in the spirit and was troubled" and that "Jesus wept." But not only did Jesus see their trouble and was touched by their trouble, He knew what to do about their trouble, for in verse 34 He said, "where have you laid him" (NKJV).

That's what you need to do with your problems in life: show it to Jesus. First Peter 5:7 (NKJV) says, "casting all your care upon Him, for He cares for you." Is your body in pain? Show it to Jesus! Is your heart troubled within you? Show it to Jesus! Is your spouse making you miserable? Show it to Jesus! Are you lacking in faith? Show it to Jesus! Have you allowed life to get you down? Show it to Jesus! Is despair and depression wrecking your soul? Show it to Jesus!

Then Jesus told them to "Take away the stone." Jesus could have commanded the stone to move, but He did not. There was a part that they had to play in the process. Too many times we do not see God's care and we assume that God does not care. We assume that the Lord is crying "crocodile tears." But the problem is not with God, but with the fact that there is some kind of stone blocking our blessing. And the Lord is waiting for us to show our faith and confidence in Him by moving the stone out of the way so that He can call forth the blessing that is buried in the tomb of lack of faith and absence of trust.

It is after the stone was moved that Jesus said, "Lazarus come forth." Jesus did not call Lazarus until the stone had been removed. We allow the stones of life to block our progress toward our goals. Stones such as: "I give up" or "I'm afraid" or "Nobody cares" and such are what keep us from moving forward to the glory ahead and receiving the blessing that the Lord will call forth. We must "take away the stone!"

If we take away **the stone of**:

- "I give up," then from the grave discouragement, fortitude will come forth;

- "I doubt it," then from the grave of despair, faith will come forth;
- "I can't afford it," then from the grave of insufficiency, blessings will come forth;
- "I'm afraid," then from the grave of fear, courage will come forth;
- "It's too hard," then from the grave of weakness, strength will come forth;
- "I can't make it," then from the grave of death, a reason to live will come forth;
- "I can't go on living," then from the grave of despair, faith will come forth;
- "Nobody cares," then from the grave of loneliness, the Comforter will come forth.

This victory is ours because Jesus cares. No matter the trouble, Jesus cares! No matter the pain, Jesus cares! No matter the heartache, Jesus cares! No matter the problem, Jesus cares! No matter how dark the night, Jesus cares!

The words of the songwriter ring true!

> Does Jesus care when my heart is pained Too deeply for mirth or song?
> As the burdens press, And the cares distress,
> And the way grows weary and long? Does He care enough to be near?
>
> O YES, HE CARES, I KNOW HE CARES,
> HIS HEART IS TOUCHED WITH MY GRIEF;
> WHEN THE DAYS ARE WEARY,
> THE LONG NIGHT DREARY,
> I KNOW MY SAVIOR CARES!-Frank E. Graeff and Joseph Lincoln Hall

Dr. Lovell C. Hayes is the pulpit evangelist for the East Jackson Church of Christ in Jackson, Tennessee, where he has served since 1994. Under his ministry, the church has shown a steady increase in ministry development, contributions, and attendance. He and his wife, Patricia, have been married for 49 years. They have two children and two grandchildren.

BOOK OF ACTS

Acts 8:26-40 – *The Conversion of a Black Man*

Dr. Cleavon P. Matthews Sr.

INTRODUCTION

In observance of African-American history month, we will be preaching texts with characters of color. It is a grave oversight and misunderstanding to assume all of the people of Scripture reflect and only represent Europeans.

I want people of color to understand we are not second-class citizens. Although we have experienced great injustices, slavery, segregation, lynchings, bombings, afflictions, and continue to be mistreated with all manner of evil, God loves you and you are not inferior to any people. Blackness is not a curse. Blackness is not a crime. Blackness doesn't mean you finish last.

Many of our boomer and builder generations lived in homes with pictures of important figures such as MLK and JKF. But then they would also have another picture of the wall depicting Jesus. One of my favorite television sitcoms as a child was called *Good Times*. There is a memorable episode in which JJ painted a picture that his little brother Michael insisted looked more like the real Jesus. Their mother demanded that the picture of Jesus on their wall with long blonde hair and blue eyes was the correct image.

God is neither black nor white, nor Asian, nor Latina, nor Irish, nor Scottish, nor African. The Bible is not a white man's book and Christianity is not a white man's religion. The gospel is for all nations. The Bible is a multicultural book. God is the Creator of all nations, therefore it only makes sense for there to be some people of color in the biblical story. God didn't create everyone European. Our God is a master creator. He's an artist. He's the Creator of Van Gogh. Just like you can't tell the true story of American history without Native and African-Americans, neither can you tell the true story of redemption without people of color.

I. THE PURSUIT OF THE EVANGELIST

> "Now an angel of the Lord spoke to Philip, saying, "Arise and go toward the south along the road which goes down from Jerusalem to Gaza." This is desert. So he arose and went. And behold, a man of Ethiopia, a eunuch of great authority under Candace the queen of the Ethiopians, who had charge of all her treasury, and had come to Jerusalem to worship, was returning. And sitting in his chariot, he was reading Isaiah the prophet. Then the Spirit said to Philip, "Go near and overtake this chariot." So Philip ran to him, and heard him reading the prophet Isaiah, and said, "Do you understand what you are reading?" (Acts 8:26-30 NKJV).

It was a time of persecution against the church at Jerusalem. Stephen was stoned. The saints were scattered abroad. Saul was making havoc of the church. Those who were scattered went everywhere preaching the Word. Philip, a man of honest report, full of the Holy Spirit and wisdom, went down to Samaria and preached Christ.

There was great joy in Samaria because the people gave heed to the Word and they heard and saw the miracles done by Philip. Philip had a great ministry in Samaria. Numerous men and women were baptized when they believed Philip preaching those precious things concerning the kingdom of God and the name of Jesus Christ.

Leaving fruitful ministry to go to a desert is foolish from man's perspective, but wise if directed by God! He had a big church in a thriving city and God told him to quit and take a small church with five sisters and one brother in the rural country. But instead of wrestling with God, Philip showed humility and followed the plans of God.

The focus shifts from the metropolitan of the masses to the significance of the singular. During the time when the angel of the Lord spoke directly to men, He said to Philip **"Arise and go toward the south unto the way that goeth down from Jerusalem unto Gaza, which is desert. And he arose and went"** (Acts 8:26-27 KJV).

Philip was an awesome man of God. We first met him in Acts 6. He is a man of good reputation, full of the Holy Spirit and wisdom. He was chosen by the people. The apostles laid hands on him and prayed. He was a prototype deacon, but went on to do the work of an evangelist. Philip was also a #GIRLDAD. "On the next day we who were Paul's companions departed and came to Caesarea, and entered the house of Philip the evangelist, who was one of the seven, and stayed with him. Now this man had four virgin daughters who prophesied" (Acts 21:8-9 NKJV).

The Lord arranged a meeting between Philip and a man of Ethiopia. We can't keep waiting on people to find us. We must go to them. This is not present-day Ethiopia. This is the ancient area of Nubia. Ethiopia literally means 'burnt faces.' This region represented to both the Greeks and Romans 'the uttermost parts of the earth.' **The Ethiopian was undoubtedly a black man from the continent of Africa.**

> This Black man is somebody.
> This Black man is intelligent.
> This Black man is a god-fearer.
> This Black man is a worshipper.
> This Black man is being chauffeured.
> This Black man is a man of faith.
> This Black man reads the Scripture.

He was a eunuch of great authority under Candace, queen of the Ethiopians, who had the charge of all her treasure. Candace was not her name. Candace was her title. Just as Pharaoh was not his name, but his title. There were many Pharaohs and Candace's. Furthermore, Herod was not a name, but a title. Caesar was not a name, it was a title. Mr. President is not his name, it's his title. Some of you know what I'm talking about! The hood gives you a nickname like 'little pistol shooter' – it's not your name, it's a title. His name isn't 50, it's Curtis. His name isn't Jay-Z, it's Shawn.

Candace was the title for the Queen mother who governed their nation. Her son was considered the royal son and he was worshipped by the people because they believed he was the offspring of the Sun. Therefore, his time must not be wasted with such trivial things as governing a nation.

This eunuch was a man with great authority. This Black man was the minister of finance. He had great authority over all her treasure. He was somebody in Ethiopia. This Black man had power, respect, prestige, and influence. He must have been thoroughly equipped, intellectually astute, morally accountable, and trustworthy.

When Philip meets him, he is riding in his chariot on his way back home. He has been to Jerusalem to worship. He has traveled a great distance to worship the Lord. He respects the Lord. He values the Word of the Lord. He is likely what they called at this time a 'god-fearer.' **But he had two problems: he was cut off and confused!**

He could not become a full Jewish proselyte because he had a problem. He is a eunuch. The Old Testament Law prevented him from gaining access to the Lord. He could worship, but he could not come near. He could pray from afar. He could give his money, but he must by all means remain on the outside. Deuteronomy 23:1 says, **"He that is wounded in the stones, or hath his privy member cut off, shall not enter into the congregation of the LORD"** (KJV). His physical condition prevented him from entering the congregation of the Lord. The eunuch had been to church, but he was still cut off. He had a problem that he could not overcome. There was nothing he could do to change his condition! There are three categories of eunuchs. **"For there are some eunuchs, which were so born from their mother's womb: and there are some eunuchs, which were made eunuchs of men: and there be eunuchs, which have made themselves eunuchs for the kingdom of heaven's sake. He that is able to receive it, let him receive it"** (Matthew 19:12 KJV). The eunuch was cut off! His dinner plate was broken! His key no longer worked to the house! He was no longer invited to dinners! Paul said it this way, **"That at that time ye were without Christ, being aliens from the commonwealth of Israel, and strangers from the covenants of promise, having no hope, and without God in the world"** (Ephesians 2:12 KJV).

The eunuch was also confused. He was reading aloud from the prophesy of Isaiah which was customary at this time. When Philip obeyed the spirit and joined himself to the chariot, he asked the eunuch, "do you understand what you are reading?" (v. 30 NKJV). The eunuch said, "how can I, except some man should guide me?" (v. 31 AKJV). This man had been to worship at the capital of spiritual knowledge. This man had been to worship where the doctors of the law reside. **He had been to church, but he left church confused!** He left church cut off and confused!

> He left church without feeling grace.
> He left church without feeling wanted.
> He left church without being filled.
> He left church without his faith being revived.
> He left church with the same problems he came with.
> He left church with people who played church.

He left cut off and confused because when he went to Jerusalem to worship, he worshipped with the wrong people! He obviously worshipped with those who were hanging on to the Law of Moses! There are some people in this church hanging on to old traditions. No Bible for your belief system whatsoever! How are you supposed to draw all men to Jesus if you shun, condemn, and call every method used to draw men sinful! You won't invite your friends to church because you don't want them at church! Some of you have the audacity to say I don't care.

The truth is right now, bold believers, we are the wrong people to be worshipping with! He was worshipping with the people who had rejected the only hope of salvation. He didn't know any better. He was sincere. He was genuine. But he was still cut off and confused!

II. THE PONDERING OF THE EUNUCH

> "And he said, "How can I, unless someone guides me?" And he asked Philip to come up and sit with him. The place in the Scripture which he read was this: "He was led as a sheep to the slaughter; And as a lamb before its shearer is silent, So He opened not His mouth. In His humiliation His justice was taken away, And who will declare His generation? For His life is taken from the earth." So the

eunuch answered Philip and said, "I ask you, of whom does the prophet say this, of himself or of some other man?" (Acts 8:31-34 NKJV).

This text lets me know that God is better than good. God will come to where I am. Church is not the only place God can meet you. God will come to you in the crack house. He will come to you in the trap house. He will come when the needle is still in your arm.

The eunuch was reading the prophesy of Isaiah 53. He was confused. He didn't know if Isaiah was talking about himself or some other man. The eunuch identified with the man. He was interested in the man because he could relate to him. This man was rejected just like the eunuch. He was cut off just like the eunuch. He was despised just like the eunuch. Listen to the prophecy:

> "He is despised and rejected of men; a man of sorrows, and acquainted with grief: and we hid as it were our faces from him; he was despised and we esteemed him not. Surely he hath borne our grief, and carried our sorrows: yet we did esteem him stricken, smitten of God, and afflicted. But he was wounded for our transgressions, he was bruised for our iniquities: the chastisement of our peace was upon him; and with his stripes we are healed. All we like sheep have gone astray; we have turned everyone to his own way; and the LORD hath laid on him the iniquity of us all. He was oppressed, and he was afflicted, yet he opened not his mouth: he is brought as a lamb to the slaughter, and as a sheep before her shearers is dumb, so he opened not his mouth. He was taken from judgment: and who shall declare his generation? For he was cut off of the land of the living: for the transgression of my people was he stricken" (Isaiah 53:3-8 AKJV).

Philip wanted the eunuch to understand what Jesus did for him! You need to understand what Jesus did for you. Jesus was...

Bruised for your benefit
Rejected for your reconciliation
Despised for your deliverance
Shamed for your salvation
Hurt for your healing
Penalized for your pardon
Humiliated for your honor
Grieved for your grace
Tortured for your transformation
Struck for your safety
Pierced for your preservation
Wounded for your welfare
Crucified for your cleansing
Afflicted for your acquittal
Flogged for your forgiveness

Philip preached Jesus because . . .

Salvation is in no other name
Jesus destroyed the works of the Devil
Jesus broke down the middle wall of separation
Jesus took the handwriting of ordinances away
Jesus spoiled principalities and powers
Jesus is the Head of the body, the Church
Jesus is the Savior of the body
Jesus is the faithful witness
Jesus is the first begotten of dead
Jesus is the prince of the kings of the earth
Jesus loved us
Jesus washed us in His own blood
Jesus put all things under Him
Jesus snatched the sting out of death
Jesus took the victory from the grave
Jesus brought grace and truth
Jesus stilled the storms of life
Jesus gave water when the wine ran out

Jesus gave sight to the blind

Jesus evicted demons from the possessed

Jesus fed the famished

III. THE PERSUADING OF THE EUNUCH

"Then Philip opened his mouth, and beginning at this Scripture, preached Jesus to him. Now as they went down the road, they came to some water. And the eunuch said, "See, here is water. What hinders me from being baptized?" Then Philip said, "If you believe with all your heart, you may." And he answered and said, "I believe that Jesus Christ is the Son of God." So he commanded the chariot to stand still. And both Philip and the eunuch went down into the water, and he baptized him. Now when they came up out of the water, the Spirit of the Lord caught Philip away, so that the eunuch saw him no more; and he went on his way rejoicing. But Philip was found at Azotus. And passing through, he preached in all the cities till he came to Caesarea" (Acts 8:35-40 NKJV).

The eunuch had an urgency! He didn't delay. The eunuch had an understanding now! He made no excuses. In fact, he made the observation, see here is water! When you have an urgency for Christ, you will look for the opportunity to obey Him! When the eunuch heard the Gospel of Jesus Christ, he understood there was no longer a barrier cutting him off from the Lord. Jesus made it possible for Him to be accepted by the Lord and receive full access.

The eunuch didn't allow anything further to 'hinder him from obeying the Lord.' He didn't allow anyone or anything to hinder him. He didn't allow the queen of Ethiopia to hinder him. He didn't allow his prestige, power, or wealth to hinder him. He didn't allow his physical condition to hinder him. He didn't allow his ethnicity to hinder him. Don't allow anything or anyone to hinder you from obeying the Word of the Lord.

Notice the condition and the confession! Philip said "if thou believest with all thine heart, thou mayest." The condition for baptism was 'believing with all thine heart.' Believing was essential, but it was not the stopping point! If anyone is going to be saved, they must believe with all their heart!

Then the cleansing! After the eunuch confessed his belief in Jesus Christ, the text says, "he commanded the chariot to stand still." He didn't wait until he talked to his family and friends. He didn't need to talk to the doctors of the law in Jerusalem. He wasn't ashamed of getting into the water. He was not too high to come down from the chariot! He wasn't worried about clothing. Somebody today needs to understand the urgency of doing God's will and you need to stop your chariot! Stop your chariot of excuses. Stop your chariot of procrastination. Stop your chariot of rebellion. Stop your chariot of stubbornness. Stop your chariot of indifference. Stop your chariot and submit yourself to the Lord. Stop your chariot and surrender to the Almighty! Stop your chariot and humble yourself in the sight of God!

The text says both Philip and the eunuch went down into the water. Philip didn't pour water on him. He didn't sprinkle him. They went down into the water and Philip buried the eunuch in the water. He dipped him. He covered him. He submerged him. In the water the eunuch's sins were washed away. In the water, the eunuch died, buried, and rose again a new creature in Christ!

CLOSING

It's something about being new in Jesus. Whenever a person meets Jesus, they are never the same again! Can I call the roll this morning?

> Saul met Jesus, and he was never the same again.
> Cornelius met Jesus, and he was never the same again.
> Before the Cross, Nicodemus met Jesus and was never the same again.
> Zaccheus met Jesus and was never the same again.
> Lepers met Jesus and were never the same again.

The poor in spirit...the brokenhearted...those who were blind...those held captive, all met Jesus and were never the same again.

Jesus specializes in taking our old, beat-up personality and making us new.

Dr. Cleavon P. Matthews Sr. is a prolific orator, communicator, and author. He is highly sought after and accomplished as a person of influence. He and his family currently reside in Dayton, Ohio. He ministers to the Bold Believers Church of Christ in Dayton, Ohio, where he has served for the last sixteen years.

PAULINE EPISTLES
Welcome to Ephesians
Dr. Luis R. Lugo Sr.
Taken from the book, *Help from Heaven: Expositions of Ephesians*

We are introduced to the city of Ephesus in the book of Acts (18:19), Paul's second missionary journey. Paul was on his way back from Athens after tarrying for a while (v. 18). He set sail for Syria. Accompanying him to Cenchera was Priscilla and Aquila. While there, Paul took the vow of the Nazarite. This vow was undertaken when a Jew wished to thank God for some blessing. This vow, if it was carried out in full, meant that for thirty days the person would not eat meat or drink wine, allowing his hair to grow. At the end of that time, they would make certain offerings at the temple, the head would be shaven, and the hair burned on the altar as an offering to God. As to what it was that led to this vow, we are not certain.

From Cenchera, Paul then comes to the city of Ephesus. Ephesus was a celebrated city in Ionia in Asia Minor about forty miles south of Smyrna. He leaves his traveling companions there and enters into the synagogue "to reason with the Jews" (v. 19 KJV). As he reasons with the Jews, they desired that he would tarry with them a little longer. More than likely they wanted to continue the discussion that Paul had introduced to them. But he "consented not" and "bade them farewell" (vv. 20-21), although he promised that after he kept the feats that was coming up in Jerusalem he would return if God permitted. He thus set sail from Ephesus, arriving at Caesarea; he goes in and salutes the church. From there he goes to Antioch. After spending time there, he departs and goes all over the region of Galatia and Phrygia for the purpose of strengthening the brethren.

In the meanwhile, an Alexandrian Jew by the name of Apollos, one who Luke says was "eloquent," "mighty in the scriptures," "fervent in the spirit," who "taught diligently the things of the Lord," but he only knew "the baptism of John" (vv. 24-25). As he began to speak boldly in the synagogue through the providence of God, Aquila and Priscilla heard him. As they heard him speak, they took him aside and taught him the way of God more perfectly. As he desired to pass into Achaia, the brethren there at Ephesus wrote letters exhorting the disciples to receive him. Upon his arrival and acceptance of the letter, he "helped them much which had believed" (v. 27).

The might of Apollos in the Scriptures was seen in his ability to convince the Jews, and this he did by showing that Jesus was the anointed Messiah. In Acts 19, we have the beginning of Paul's longest stay and development of the great congregation at Ephesus. This congregation would have some of the more renowned preachers of the New Testament. When Paul first came to Ephesus, he discovered some disciples there to whom he asked if they had "received the Holy Spirit?" (v. 2). Their response was "we have not so much as heard whether there be any Holy Ghost." Paul is stunned at their response and wanted to know "unto what then were ye baptized?" They answered "unto John's baptism" (v. 3). His baptism was one unto "repentance," preparing them for the coming of Jesus Christ. From the text, we see that the reason they had not received the Holy Spirit was due to the fact that their baptism was not for the purpose of putting them into Christ by washing their sins away. Thus, upon hearing this they were baptized for the right reason, in the right manner, and received the expected promised Holy Spirit!

For the second time after Pentecost there is a manifestation of the gift of tongues, as well as prophecy. Here, Paul lays his hands upon them and the results of the tongue-speaking and prophecy are manifested. The church at Ephesus had its difficulties. It began seemingly with twelve men, but Paul went into the synagogue continuously and spoke boldly, seeking to persuade the synagogue of the Kingdom of God. This he did "for the space of three months" (v. 8). Soon there was a hardening of some who did not believe and began to speak "evil of that way before the multitudes" (v. 9). So, the apostle Paul "departed" from them and separated the disciples, "disputing daily in the school of Tyranus" (v. 9). He continued there for "the space of two years," and Luke records that those who "dwelt in Asia heard the word of the Lord Jesus; both Jews and Greeks" (v. 10). There would be two incidents at Ephesus that would cement the church and the preaching of the gospel.

The first was the Sons of Sceva. God, according to the Scriptures, wrought special miracles by the hands of Paul" (v. 11), so much so that he did not have to touch an individual for healing to take place. They could have "handkerchiefs or aprons" brought to them and upon being touched they would be healed (v. 12). There were those who were called "vagabond Jews" who practiced exorcism, and they believed that they could exorcise the power of Paul. These vagabond Jews were known as strolling Jews or wondering Jews; they had no fixed place. They took it upon themselves because they were the offspring of one named Sceva who was "chief of the priests" and adjured a man possessed with an evil spirit to come out. They adjured the spirits by the name of Jesus whom Paul preached (vv. 13-14).

Much to their surprise, the evil spirit responded and said, "Jesus I know, and Paul I know; but who are ye?" (v. 15). Upon him saying these words, the evil spirit "leaped on them, and overcame them, and prevailed against them." The result was that they fled the house "naked and wounded" (v. 16).

The result of this incident was on both the Jews and Greeks for "fear fell on them all, and the name of the Lord Jesus was magnified. And many that believed came, and confessed, and showed their deeds" (vv. 17-18). Also, many of those who had practiced magic "brought their books together, and burned them" in the sight of all. They counted up the value of them and it totaled "fifty thousand pieces of silver" (v. 19), depending on Jewish currency, $35,000, or Greek $9,300. So, the result was that the Word of the Lord grew and multiplied and prevailed (v. 20).

The second event that earmarked the church and Paul's ministry was a riot. According to the historian, Luke records for us Paul's desire to visit Rome. According to Luke, Paul had finished preaching in the parts that led to Rome. If we study Paul's missionary journey, we discover his great plan for world evangelism. He had launched his mission to the great cities of South Galatia (Acts 13:1–14:28). After this, he wanted to reach Ephesus quickly, which was the link between the east and the west, but God had a future generation in mind and led Paul to Europe (Acts 15:36–18:22).

After Europe, Paul left immediately for Ephesus, the vanity fair of

Asia. With the evangelism of Ephesus, he said that he would go to Rome by way of Spain (Romans 15:28). Before he left for Spain, he had to go to Jerusalem that he might minister to the Saints. The purpose of traveling to Jerusalem had to do with the collection for the poor saints in Jerusalem given by the Macedonian and Achaia congregations. Paul explained that the Gentiles felt a debt to the mother church in Jerusalem. He dispatched Timothy and Erastus into Macedonia, but he stayed in Asia.

About this time there arose a great commotion (Acts 19:23). The name of this man was Demetrius, who was a silversmith who made shrines of Diana, which brought great wealth to the craftsman. Demetrius called all those of the same craft and explained to them that they made their living by the manufacturing of those shrines. Charges were brought against Paul and the believers, not only at Ephesus, but also in the surrounding area. Paul had persuaded and turned many people away from the goddess by preaching that there are no gods made with hands. So, he charged that if something was not done, their "trade" was in danger of falling into disrepute and "that the temple of the great goddess Diana should be despised, and her magnificence should be destroyed, whom all Asia and the world worshippeth" (v. 27).

When they heard this, "they were full of wrath, and cried out, saying Great is Diana of the Ephesians. And the whole city was filled with confusion" and rushed "into the theater" and seized the traveling companions of Paul (vv. 28-29). Paul, having the desire to go out and confront the people, was hindered by the disciples. The officials of Asia who were friends of Paul, sent to him pleading with him not to go into the theater because the assembly (*ekkleseia*) was in a state of confusion and the majority of the people did not know why they were there (vv. 30-32). The Jews "drew Alexander out of the multitude" (v. 33). He wanted to make his defense to the people, but when they discovered that he was a Jew, "all with one voice about the space of two hours cried out, Great is Diana of the Ephesians" (v. 34). The city clerk seemed to be the only one with some sense, and quieted the crowd and sought to bring some calm to the situation. He began to inform the crowd who did not know that the city of Ephesus was the temple guardians of the great Goddess Diana and of the image that fell down from Zeus. He assured them that these things could not be denied and because they could not be denied, they needed to be quiet and not act in a rash manner. He further exonerates the believers as being neither "robbers of the temple, not blasphemers of their goddess. He lets them see that if they had a legitimate problem when the courts opened they needed to take it to the courts. He accuses them of being an unlawful assembly and they were on the brink of bringing the law down on themselves for the disorderly manner of the assembly (vv. 35-41). Thus, we see the power of the Word of God that seeks to show the evil from the truth. Christianity is vindicated in this culture at this time.

The third event that transpired with this church and Paul is recorded for us in Acts 20:17-38. After the uproar had ceased, Paul took leave of the disciples and set out to Macedonia. He came to Greece and stayed there three months. Later, there was a plot to take his life and he left for Syria, but decided to return by way of Macedonia. There, he was accompanied by men like "Sopater of Berea; and of the Thessalonians, Aristarchus and Secundus; and Gaius of Derbe, and Timotheus; and of Asia, Tychicus and Trophimus" who went with him to Asia (v. 4). These men went ahead at Troas and waited for Paul. It is here that Paul spoke to the disciples until midnight and the young man fell out of the window and died, but Paul restored his life (vv. 7-10). From there, they went to Assos, then to Mitylene. They arrived at Miletus after staying at Chiss, Samos, and Trogyllium.

After arriving at Miletus, Paul wanted if possible to be at the feast of Pentecost in Jerusalem. It was from Miletus that Paul would demonstrate to the universal church the primary function of the eldership as a unit in instructing the church so that Satan could be defeated as he sought to take the church down! Here, Paul lets the elders know of his past (20:18-35). He reminded them of his "lifestyle" and how "he served God with all humility." He reminded them of his tears and how the Jews plotted against him, but he was faithful in his teaching, preaching, and how he did it both publically and from house to house. Then he presented the present to them. In the present, he was going to Jerusalem. He would go there not knowing what to expect other than the Holy Spirit had revealed that chains and tribulation awaited him. He let the elders know that he was not concerned about what would happen to him because his concern was to "finish my course with joy" and to fulfill the ministry given to him by Jesus Christ (v. 24). He pronounces that this departure would be one that they would see his face no more, but that he could depart with a clean conscience for he had taught them "all the counsel of God" (vv. 25-27).

Beginning with verse 28, Paul gives a sober admonition and warning that would plague the Christians' faith down through the corridors of historical times. Paul lets them see that the church is a blood-bought institution, purchased by the sacrificial life of Christ. Thus, they as overseers, bishops, pastors, shepherds, elders, and presbyters must take the oversight of the church for the double reason that:

1. Savage wolves were to enter the flock (a graphic picture of lambs that are waiting for the slaughter from the outside).
2. From within the church there would be those who seek to divide the church with false teaching. Paul then gives the following charge to the eldership:

   a. Be Vigilant – Acts 20:31
   b. Be Studious – Acts 20:32
   c. Be Content – Acts 20:33
   d. Be Industrious – Acts 20:34
   e. Be Generous – Acts 20:3

So, here the elders of the church receive a solemn charge and as we follow the impact of the church in the first century, we will see that Paul's words became all too true. There are five other books and one chapter that address the church and we see a gradual descent from each book. The books that contain the history of the Ephesians church are the pastoral epistles of 1 and 2 Timothy; 1, 2, 3 John; and Revelation 2:1-7. In the first five, we see a plethora of issues, but somehow the church is still holding on to her candlestick. In 1 Timothy, Paul gives a solemn warning to Timothy, his son in the gospel, about a great apostasy that will corrupt the church. First Timothy 4:1-3 says,

> *"Now the Spirit expressly says that in latter times some will depart from the faith, giving heed to deceiving spirits and doctrines of demons, speaking lies in hypocrisy, having their own conscience seared with a hot iron, forbidding to marry,*

and commanding to abstain from foods which God created to
be received with thanksgiving by those who believe and know
the truth" (NKJV).

This philosophy is seemingly a mixture of mysticism and Judaism, which would evolve into what would become Gnostic philosophy that would seek to destroy the church. In 2 Timothy, Paul writes a better encouragement to Timothy about issues that would threaten the peace of the church, thus he should not be ashamed of the Gospel (1:8-12), should be faithful (1:13-18), and should be strong in the grace and salvation that is in Christ (2:1-10). He reminds them of workers who are approved and disapproved (2:14-26). In the third chapter, he warns him about the perilous times that the church would face. Perilous means "grievous." These times would be based upon the fact that men would become:

1. Lovers of themselves
2. Lovers of money
3. Boasters
4. Proud
5. Blasphemers
6. Disobedient to parents
7. Unthankful
8. Unholy
9. Unloving
10. Unforgiving
11. Slanderous
12. Without self-control
13. Brutal
14. Despisers of good
15. Traitors
16. Headstrong
17. Haughty
18. Lovers of pleasure rather than lovers of God
19. Having a form of godliness but denying its power (vv. 1-5 NKJV)

Paul's admonishment for the young preacher is to turn away! He then instructs him about his relationship as the man of God to the Word (3:10-17). He is to preach the Word without fear (4:1-5). He finishes the book with sundry admonishments and farewells.

His own victory, 4:6-8
His loneliness, 4:9-12
Come see me, 4:13
Restitution from God, 4:14-16
The faithfulness of Jesus, 4:17-18
Come before winter, 4:19-21
Farewell, 4:22

Thus, we see that the Ephesians church has come under the assault for which Paul has warned the elders. His encouragement to Timothy is to see if he and his efforts may stem the tide! The church at Ephesus has now been through some historical issues and towards the latter end of the first century the church has seen her best days. John, in the book of Revelation, will seek to admonish the church. In Revelation 2:1-7, Jesus is the one who reveals to John the true condition of the church in Ephesus. They once were a working congregation, a laborious congregation, especially in the realm of doctrine, who stood for good and withstood evil. They were not afraid to put truth to the test, or to investigate those who claimed authenticity of apostleship and found them to be liars. Jesus further commends them for their perseverance, patience, and the fact that they have labored in his name and had not become weary. Jesus commends them on their stand on false doctrine being perpetrated in the church by the Nicolaitans. The problem with Ephesus at this time was that they were theologically straight as a gun barrel and just as empty. They had become all form and no substance; all doctrine, but no love, compassion or kindness. Their actions were not because they loved the Lord, but pharisaical in their walk as Christians. As a church, they had lost the main ingredient for existing, ministering, and evangelizing the lost. Thus, they are commanded to repent and do the first work or the candlestick will be removed. In verse 7, Jesus gives the church the opportunity to revive itself.

As we look at the three epistles of John, we see that the Lord's warning is not heeded and John now validates that the demise of the church as the internal soul of the church (which is love) is now corrupted. John seeks to remind the Ephesian church that God is light. If we recall, in Ephesians 5:8 Paul tells the church that they are to walk in the light. Here, John tells them the same (1 John 1:5-10). God is not only light, but he is love (3:1-3), and through love one is identified as God's child (2:10-11; 3:16-17; 4:7-11; 4:17-21). The lack of love makes one a deceiver. God is also life (1:1). John lets us see that fellowship with God is only possible when we comprehend God's light, love, and life. If we are to enjoy our walk in fellowship with God, we must walk in the light and not darkness. One of the things about walking in the light is that one will recognize his inability to do all things correctly and when he sees his sins because of the light, he will repent and confess. This will allow us to be cleansed by the blood of Jesus (1:7). The one thing that the church in Ephesus lost sight of is the fact that there are two barriers that can hinder one's walk; that is, falling in love with the world and falling for the misguided lies of false teachers.

So, when John writes the first epistle, he is seeking to get the believers to restore their first love. Without this love, you do not know God. This love is not mere words, but it is life in action, it is giving and not getting. It is unconditional and when the believer possesses this type of love, he will discover freedom, righteousness, joy, and peace. Thus, in 1 John, John indicates that they were in the process of losing their eternal life. Why? Because they had lost their spiritual essence!

In John's second epistle to the church at Ephesus, not everyone had fallen down. The recipients of this admonition, along with her children, were still standing, and they were still walking in the truth of the commandments of the father (2 John 4); and to this lady John continues the plea of love. John recognizes that if they are to maintain, they must remember that from the beginning, it was Jesus who imposes that we love one another (v. 5). To John, love is equated with the believer's walk (v. 6). John will deliver to this lady the reason the church is in a stay of apostasy, she has failed to be discerning. He showcases how deceivers "have gone out into the world who does not confess Jesus Christ" (v. 7). To John, the inability to confess Christ is both a sign of deception and the anti-Christ Thus, John seeks to inform this faithful lady, as well as the body, that if someone does not believe the incarnate Christ to be God in the flesh, then they should not accept them nor give an audience to them. If they did, to John this makes them guilty of misdeeds.

In the third epistle of John, we find the church has allowed one individual to have such preeminence to the degree that he is no longer living by love but by selfish arrogance. Pride has become his ruling stick and he has rejected John's beloved Gaius who, in spite of the fallacy at the church, is still walking in love, light, and life (3 John 1-4). He wants them to continue to entertain and fellowship with those who have been missionaries for the cause of Christ at their own expense. There is a fellow there who will go against gains and anyone who would receive these missionaries. Thus, we see why John writes that they as a congregation had lost their first love. Now we seek why the book of Ephesians is such a magnificent book for the church and why the church needs to familiarize itself with it, read it, study it, and seek to implement its teachings to keep the life of the Lord in the body alive!

Dr. Luis R. Lugo Sr. has been married to Andrea C. Geace for 53 years. They are the parents of 5 children – 4 boys and 1 girl. His ministry includes missionary work in the Caribbean, Puerto Rico, Trinidad, Jamaica, and St. Croix US Virgin Islands. Local work includes: Chattanooga, TN; Valdosta, GA; Tampa, FL; Kansas City, KS; Chicago, IL; Jacksonville, FL; and Tampa, FL (Northside Church of Christ). His hobbies include writing, fishing, swimming, and reading.

EPHESIANS 6:10-11 – BE STRONG IN THE LORD

Dr. Nicholas A. Glenn

"Finally, my brethren, be strong in the Lord, and in the power of his might. Put on the whole armour of God, that ye may be able to stand against the wiles of the devil" (Ephesians 6:10-11 KJV).

Introduction: Prior to Ephesians 6:10, Paul has been discussing the believer's walk in the Lord (Eph. 4:1-6:9). Beginning with Ephesians 6:10, he shifts his attention from the believer's walk to spiritual warfare. Paul makes it clear that the believer's walk is a life lived on the battlefield engaged in opposition with the enemy. This series of sermons is designed to equip believers in being victorious in spiritual warfare.

I. The soldier's charge in spiritual warfare (Ephesians 6:10)

   A. Three components of the soldier's charge:
   1. Be strong in the Lord.
      a. The believer's success in spiritual warfare is contingent upon being strong in the Lord.
      b. The imperative "be strong" is in the passive, which means to be made strong or strengthened, which is consistent with the language Paul used in his prayer in Ephesians 3:16.[25]
      c. The actual word "strong" in this verse means "to empower,"[26] to increase in strength "to render strong."[27]
      d. The Christians soldier's strength in spiritual warfare does not come from his own merit, but comes supernaturally from the Lord (Eph. 6:10).
         ➤ The Christian soldier must be strong in the sovereign and unlimited power of God (Ephesians 1:19-23).

---

[25] Peter T. O'Brien, *The Letter to the Ephesians* (Grand Rapids: Eerdmans, 1999), 460-61.

[26] James Strong, *A Concise Dictionary of the Words in the Greek Testament and the Hebrew Bible* (Bellingham, WA: Logos Bible Software, 2009), 28.

[27] W. E. Vine, Merrill F. Unger, and William White Jr., *Vine's Complete Expository Dictionary of Old and New Testament Words*, vol. 2 (Nashville: Thomas Nelson, 1996), 198.

e. In order for the Christian soldier to receive this supernatural strength, a kinship "in the Lord" is necessary.

f. This type of strength exhibited by God is also used in 1 Timothy 6:16 in reference to God's everlasting power.

➢ God's power is so great that He is immortal.

➢ His power in immortality does not imply so "much persistence of life after death, as freedom from death."[28]

2. Be strong in the Lord's power.

a. "Power" in this verse is descriptive of great and "manifested power."[29]

b. The Lord's power is "a power that is demonstrative, eruptive, and tangible."[30]

c. In the arsenal of weaponry for the Christian soldier is God's unlimited power and complete dominion.

d. God's power is designed so that it be demonstrated and expressed outwardly to assist the Christian soldier in combat. The idea is, "in the active efficacy of the might that is inherent in Him."[31]

3. Be strong in the Lord's might.

a. The Lord's "might" refers to His ability and force.

b. This type of power is descriptive of "an extremely strong man, such as a bodybuilder; a man who is able; a man who is mighty; or a man with great muscular capabilities."[32]

c. Paul is inferring that God is more capable, powerful, and able than any human.

d. God's power is essential for success (Zechariah 4:6).

e. In 2 Thessalonians 1:9, this type of strength is described in reference to "the glory of His might," which "signifies

[28] I. Howard Marshall and Philip H. Towner, *A Critical and Exegetical Commentary on the Pastoral Epistles* (New York: T&T Clark, 2004), 667.

[29] Vine, Unger, and White, *Vine's Complete Expository Dictionary*, 180.

[30] Rick Renner, *Dressed to Kill: A Biblical Approach to Spiritual Warfare and Armor* (Tulsa: Teach All Nations, 2007), 172.

[31] Kenneth S. Wuest, *Wuest's Word Studies from the Greek New Testament: For the English Reader* (Grand Rapids: Eerdmans, 1997), s.v. "Eph. 6:12."

[32] Renner, *Dressed to Kill*, 176.

the visible expression of the inherent personal power of the Lord Jesus."[33]

    f.   In spiritual warfare, God will permit the Christian soldier to have access to his mighty strength and might to fight against the enemy.

II. The soldier's responsibility in spiritual warfare (Ephesians 6:11)

A. To follow God's provision.
   1. God has provided protection for the Christian soldier in preparation for battle.
   2. The Christian soldier must be protected prior to entering combat with the enemy and be prepared for the enemy's devices (2 Corinthians 2:11).
   3. The Christian soldier must not walk according to the course of this world but be prepared to follow godly instructions (Ephesians 2:2-3).
B. To put on the whole armor of God.
   1. In response to the God's strength, power, and might, the soldier's responsibility in preparing for war is to put on the whole armor of God.
   2. The Apostle Paul made it clear that proper preparation requires every piece of armor as he indicated by putting on "the whole armor of God."
   3. Without every piece of armor, the soldier is exposed and open prey for the attacks of the enemy.

III. The purpose of the soldier's armor (Ephesians 6:11)

A. The armor is necessary to the soldier for the following reasons:
   1. So the believer may be able:
      a. "Able" is a verb that means 'to be able to do something' and it carries the idea that something is capable and has the ability to be done.

---

[33] Vine, Unger, and White, *Vine's Complete Expository Dictionary*, 2.

b. Paul informs the Christian soldier that in preparing for spiritual warfare, when the complete armor of God is put on, there is nothing that cannot be executed.

2. So the believer may be able to stand:
   a. "Stand" means to stand in place and be set.
   b. Paul is giving attention to the posture of the soldier in warfare, which must be up right, in place, and prepared to hold his ground for the pending battle.

3. So the believer may be able to stand against the wiles of the devil:
   a. "Wiles" is the noun *methodeía*, which means to work by a method.
   b. *Methodeía* is where the English word 'method' comes from and it suggests "craft and deceit."[34]
      ➤ This word in the New Testament is associated with the following:
        (a) Deceit
        (b) Trickery
        (c) Cunning arts
        (d) Method
   c. By Paul using the word "wiles," he is informing the believer to be prepared to the method and technique the enemy will use to attack.
   d. "The plural marks both the multiplicity of the concrete cases, and the obstinacy of the repeated attack."[35]
   e. In order for the Christian soldier to be prepared for battle, the soldier must not be ignorant of Satan's devices (2 Corinthians 2:11).

---

[34] Vine, Unger, and White, *Vine's Complete Expository Dictionary*, 676.

[35] John Peter Lange, Philip Schaff, and J. J. van Oosterzee, *A Commentary on the Holy Scriptures: 1 & 2 Timothy*, trans. E. A. Washburn and E. Harwood (Bellingham: Logos Bible Software, 2008), 221.

Summary:

Paul's command to be strong in the Lord stresses the emphasis on the need for dependence upon God in spiritual warfare. "To be strong means in the Lord to maintain an ongoing awareness that the Lord Jesus has superabundant stores of strength that the Christian soldier has access to draw from continuously."[36] God has provided everything needed to withstand and successfully defeat the enemy. How does the Christian soldier stand and resist the enemy? Victory against the enemy is predicated on being clothed with the entire armor of God. The choice is up to the Christian soldier as to whether or not to take heed to the instructions given and "put on the whole armor of God."

Bibliography

Borgman, Brian, and Ventura, Rob. *Spiritual Warfare: A Biblical and Balanced Perspective.* Grand Rapids: Reformation Heritage Books, 2014.

Lange, John Peter, Philip Schaff, and J. J. van Oosterzee. *A Commentary on the Holy Scriptures: 1 & 2 Timothy.* Translated by E. A. Washburn and E. Harwood. Bellingham, WA: Logos Bible Software, 2008.

Marshall, I. Howard, and Phillip H. Towner. *A Critical and Exegetical Commentary on the Pastoral Epistles.* New York: T&T Clark 2004.

O'Brien, Peter T. *The Letter to the Ephesians.* Grand Rapids: Eerdmans, 1998.

Renner, Rick. *Dressed to Kill: A Biblical Approach to Spiritual Warfare and Armor.* Tulsa: Teach All Nations, 2007.

Strong, James. *A Concise Dictionary of the Words in the Greek Testament and The Hebrew Bible.* Bellingham, WA: Logos Bible Software, 2009.

---

[36] Brian S. Borgman and Rob Ventura, *Spiritual Warfare: A Biblical and Balanced Perspective* (Grand Rapids: Reformation Heritage Books, 2014), 11.

Vine, W. E., Merrill F. Unger, and William White Jr. *Vine's Complete Expository Dictionary of Old and New Testament Words*. Nashville: Thomas Nelson, 1996.

Wuest, Kenneth S. "Ephesians 6:12." In *Wuest's Word Studies from the Greek New Testament: For the English Reader*. Grand Rapids: Eerdmans, 1997.

Dr. Nicholas A. Glenn is a native of Winston-Salem, North Carolina. He was baptized into Christ in January 1987 at the age of 8 at the Redland Church of Christ in Advance, North Carolina. He later began preaching the gospel at age 14.

In November of 2002, he became the Associate Minister at the South English Street (Now Sharpe Road) Church of Christ in Greensboro, North Carolina, and served in that capacity for over 14 years. On January 15, 2017, he was installed as the ministering Evangelist at Sharpe Road. He has been married to the former Nikki Greene of Winston-Salem, North Carolina, since July of 2003. They have one daughter, Nia Symone Glenn.

EPHESUS – FIRST LOVE FORSAKEN – REVELATION 2:1-7

Jeffrey J. Walker

"The Revelation of Jesus Christ" is not a revelation of the person of Jesus but a revelation from Jesus, which the Father gave to Him. It was Jesus' obligation then to show it unto His people. This was accomplished by getting it into the mind of the exiled apostle John. John was to give testimony to the Word of God, recording what he saw and heard. John was then instructed to deliver these inspired writings concerning things which must shortly come to pass to the seven Churches of Asia.

What makes the book of Revelation significant is that those that read and hear the prophecy of it and keep what is written will be blessed! Jesus reconfirms this blessing in chapter 22, verse 7, as one of the seven "beatitudes" found in this last book of the New Testament. Careful observation should lead one to understand that the prophecy of this book is not just about future events. This book, just like the gospels and epistles, is meant to make a change in us now! So, let us see how the letters to the churches of Asia relate to and shape our Christian conduct today.

Characteristics of the Seven Churches

Before actually beginning the exposition of the message to the Ephesian church, it would be beneficial to consider a few of the distinctive and common characteristics that can be observed in each of the "performance reviews" of the seven churches of Asia Minor recorded in Revelation, chapters 2 and 3.

The Selection

First, we need to know that John did not have a choice in which congregations he would address. Christ, the head of the church, specified in Revelation 1:11 that John should write what he sees and hears in a book and send it to the seven churches of Asia, to Ephesus and to Smyrna and to Pergamum and to Thyatira and to Sardis and to Philadelphia and to Laodicea. These were letters to seven historical churches at the time of John's writing. The letters each dealt with actual conditions of church life in John's day. But as God's Word is written to the whole body of Christ for all time, they are also representative of all churches, both in John's day and at any time since then. Just as the letter to the Galatians does not only apply to the church at Galatia, but all churches past, present, and future, so do these letters.[37] Rationale:

1. Though many other churches existed and may have been larger and better known, only these seven were selected. Seven is the number of completion and it may be suggested that these seven perfectly represent conditions that would be characteristic of various congregations of the churches of Christ throughout history. Remember the words of Solomon as he said, "What has been is what will be, and what has been done is what will be done, and there is nothing new under the sun" (Ecclesiastes 1:9 ESV).

2. Though each letter is written to a specific congregation, all the letters close with the words "let him hear what the Spirit says to the churches" (plural). Each message is pertinent to all the churches, not only of John's day, but of ours as well.

3. Because the composition of church membership and leadership are ever changing (members die, move, "place membership," demographics, etc.) and because of the influence of the environment (church culture and traditions), a single congregation throughout its existence may experience one or more of the challenges of the seven churches that Christ addressed through John's writings.

The Sufficiency of Christ

Christ will always be related to the needs, problems, and conditions within the local church. It cannot be stressed enough how Jesus Christ perfectly meets our needs, and is the source of our strength. All the problems and needs of the church are met in Jesus Christ. He alone is the answer to our needs and the solution to our problems. This is why God has Him seated at His right hand and given Him supreme authority over the church (Ephesians 1:20-23 ESV). Please note:

---

[37] J. Hampton Keathley III, *J. Hampton Keathley's Commentary on Revelation.*

- Christ is the Author of each message: it is a special word from Him.
- Christ is the Answer for our every problem: He is our need and solution.
- Christ is the Authority for our lives: we are all answerable to Him.

The Omniscience of Christ

Each letter begins with a statement of the Lord's omniscience – "I know your works" (cf. 2:2, 9, 13, 19; 3:1, 8, and 15). This should cause Christians to be vigilant and walk circumspectly because Christ sees and knows all. As the song says, "There's an all-seeing eye watching you." This should also bring us comfort in knowing that there is no problem or condition that we face that He does not know or care about. We should be eternally grateful to have a Holy Savior that sympathizes with mortal man (Hebrews 4:15).

Chapters 2 and 3 contain seven messages that are extremely practical for us today, both on a personal and a congregational level. For the most part, each letter contains five divisions:

1. The Place of the people.
2. The Lord's Presence among the people.
3. The Lord's Perception about the people.
4. The Lord's Prescription for the people.
5. The Lord's Promise to the people.

Now let's look at the church at Ephesus and the issue of First Love Forsaken in Revelation 2:1-7.

1. The Place of the People

Ephesus was an ancient Greek city located near the Cayster River. It became the capital of Asia Minor (modern Turkey). Ephesus was connected by highways with the interior of Asia and all her chief cities, and became a great commercial center. At the heart of the city's life and economy was the worship of Artemis (also known as Diana), the ancient fertility goddess. The great temple dedicated to Artemis was 450 feet long, 220 feet wide, had more than 120 columns sixty feet high, and was known as one of the seven wonders of the entire world. Ephesus was also known for idolatrous worship. Silversmiths made money selling silver shrines of Diana. Paul threatened their livelihood because he taught that gods made with hands are not gods at all (Acts 19:23-27).

The inception of this congregation at Ephesus occurred on Paul's second missionary journey (Acts 18:18-21). On Paul's third missionary he spent 2-3 years nurturing the church by refuting false doctrine and pagan practices (Acts 19:8-10). Converts to Christianity stopped practicing magic and burned their books of sorcery publicly as a sign of true repentance and word of God grew mightily (Acts 19:18-20). According to Acts 20:17 the congregation had elders and Paul left the young evangelist Timothy there to teach the word of truth (1 Timothy 1:1-4).)

2. The Lord's Presence among the People (verse 1)

It is He who holds the stars (angels/messengers) in His right hand and walks among the candlesticks (churches). The life or death of the churches resides within Jesus. Jesus Christ is the abiding presence in the churches, directing their work, walking and dwelling in their midst, as the central spiritual force in each congregation. He is the guiding presence, the moving energy, the inspiring influence, the infinite indweller in every faithful church, then and in the church today.[38]

3. The Lord's Perception about the People (verses 2-4, 6)

This second epistle to the Ephesians is different from the first. The first was the observations of a servant of Christ, the apostle Paul, the second was the observations of the head of the church, Jesus Christ. The Lord's understanding about the conduct of the Ephesian church came from firsthand knowledge as He stated in verse 2, "I know your works." What Jesus noticed about the work of the Ephesians was both positive and negative.

A. **The Lord's Commendation (verses 2, 3, 6)** – They could not tolerate evil and immoral people and would not listen to false

---

[38] E. M. Zerr, *Zerr's Combined Bible Commentary on Revelation.*

teachers. This aligns with Paul's instructions to Timothy that while he was in Ephesus he should "charge certain persons not to teach any different doctrine" (1 Timothy 1:3 ESV). The work had been difficult, but they had not fainted. In every way, it was a successful church from the human point of view. Being able to forbear or endure in times of difficulty is a characteristic that all churches should possess.[39] Jesus made it clear that all who endure until the end would be saved (Matthew 24:13), and James says that the tying or testing of our faith produces steadfastness (James 1:3).

B. **The Lord's Criticism (verse 4)** – In the KJV, the first word in verse 4 is "nevertheless." This single word conveys a very important truth; namely, while the Lord does not fail to see all the good a disciple (or in this case, a congregation) does, that will not cause Him to accept the service unless it is pleasing in its totality (see James 2:10). The church at Ephesus had works, labor, and patience – but no love for Christ. In contrast, the Thessalonians were commended for their "work of faith, labor of love, and patience of hope" (1 Thessalonians 1:3). It is not "what" we do for Christ, but it is the motive behind what we do that is of the utmost importance. Ephesus had been a busy church with high spiritual standards.

The Ephesians had abandoned their first love. This phrase may be illustrated by the warmth of feeling that exists in the first part of the relation of husband and wife. The word love is from *AGAPE* and its chief meaning is to have that regard for another that will cause one to be interested in his welfare and happiness. Such a love will prompt one even to "go out of his way" to do things to please the other. Likewise, a Christian should have such a feeling for his brother or sister and for Christ who is the bridegroom of the church. There are countless instances where a Christian can make a special effort to show his love for the Lord. The church at Ephesus had fallen into the frame of mind where it performed its services from the legal standpoint only, and it had ceased to be a "labor of love." Christ does not want His church

---

[39] Warren W. Wiersbe, "Revelation 2," in *Wiersbe's Expository Outlines on the New Testament*.

to be robotic, going through the motions without fervent love for Him and humanity! We have to be careful not to become like Martha, so busy "working" for Christ that we don't have time to love Him! (Luke 10:38-42).

4. The Lord's Prescription for the People (verse 5a)

Jesus' spiritual prescription for the Ephesians has three parts: **Remember** from where you have fallen, **Repent** and **Repeat** your first works. Scriptures tell us to remember Lot's wife" (Luke 17:32 KJV) and "Remember now thy Creator in the days of thy youth." (Ecclesiastes 12:1 KJV). There are many things that we should be able to recall into our present state of awareness. People we know, places we've been, birthdays, and anniversaries are just a few. Jesus is reminding the Ephesians that there was a lofty spiritual place they once occupied. Christ's desire was that they recognize how far they had fallen and make the necessary corrections to ascend back to where they had fallen from. This clearly demonstrates that Christians can be condemned either for not doing what is required or for what they are doing if how they are doing it is not pleasing to Christ. We are commanded to give, but the attitude we have when giving is what makes the difference. Paul says that cheerful giving is acceptable, while unwilling, unenthusiastic, and involuntary giving is not (2 Corinthians 9:7). The Hebrew writer asks an important question, "How will we escape if we neglect so great a salvation?" (Hebrews 2:3 NASB). We must be mindful that just as faith without works is dead, works without love are dead also!

How could they reverse this downward spiral? The answer is clear – repent! They had to have a sincere change of heart that would lead to a significant change in conduct. Once the burden of sin was lifted they could get back to doing the Lord's work, the way they did it from the start. They could return to their first works, not the quantity but the quality! Works with the original enthusiasm. The same work they had been doing but with a different motivation. Works motivated by love for Christ and His church! The same is true today, if we regain our first love, we too can repeat our first works!

5. The Lord's Promise to the People (verses 5b, 7)

Jesus now confronts the Ephesians with what would happen if they became noncompliant in following His prescription. Jesus said in the latter part of verse 5, "If not, I will come to you and remove your lampstand from its place, unless you repent" (ESV). Jesus makes it plain that the Ephesians either repent or be removed. This idea is similar to what Jesus told the Jews in Luke 13:3 (NKJV) – "unless you repent, you will all likewise perish." What a terrible thought to be rejected by Christ, losing our redeemed status along with the blessings that come with it! As Moses did with Israel, Christ did with the church at Ephesus, as well as with the church today. He set before them life and death, blessing and cursing! (Deuteronomy 30:19 KJV) and Peter declared He (Christ) is not willing that any should perish but all should come to repentance (2 Peter 3:9 KJV). If the Ephesians make the right choice, they have everything to gain; if not, they lose everything.

The second promise is to those that would pay attention to what the Spirit is saying to the churches, not only those in Asia but to churches throughout all ages. Jesus promises that the overcomers, the conquers, will be granted the privilege of eating from the tree of life, which is in the paradise of God. John describes this tree as having twelve kinds of fruit that yields its fruit every month and the leaves are for the healing of the nations (Revelation 22:2 KJV). This should give every believer the incentive to live a faithful life until death and even in the face of death (Revelation 2:10 KJV) so that we can enjoy the "food" of the faithful in paradise where we will be with Christ and our fellow conquerors for ever more! Until then, I encourage you to remain faithful with the words of our brother Paul, "Therefore, my beloved brothers, be steadfast, immovable, always abounding in the work of the Lord, knowing that in the Lord your labor is not in vain (1 Corinthians 15:58 ESV). Amen, So Let It Be!

Brother Walker currently serves as the minister of the Tonto Street Church of Christ in Phoenix, Arizona. Prior to relocating to Phoenix, in February of 2018, Brother Walker served as the pulpit evangelist of the Northside Church of Christ in Rochester, New York, for 14 years. Brother Walker has been married for 33 years to his lovely wife Laurie. They have three children and five grandchildren.

GENERAL EPISTLES

Hebrews 11:32-40 – *What More Shall I Say? Faith Is the Key*

George Micheal Williams

Jesus The book of Hebrews was written to a group of Jewish Christians who had become so discouraged and disheartened that they were ready to give up on Christianity and walk away from Jesus.

Like most new converts, they started out full of zeal and full of excitement for the Lord, but not long after their conversion to Christ, Satan unleashed a vicious attack against them from all sides.

- The Jewish religious establishment hated Christians and they attacked them.
- The Roman government looked upon Christians with suspicion, and saw them as a threat to the Roman Empire, and they attacked them.

Consequently, because of constant persecution from all directions, these saints had become so discouraged that they were on the verge of leaving Christ and Christianity and going back to the safety of Judaism.

As an aside, let me issue fair warning to every new convert in the Lord – when you become a Christian, you need to expect the devil to attack you. You need to understand that Satan will *never* let anyone leave his kingdom without a fight. And one of the devil's favorite weapons to use against Christians (*both new converts and mature converts*) is discouragement. And sometimes discouragement will come at unlikely times from unlikely sources.

- Sometimes discouragement comes from your own brothers and sisters in Christ.
- Sometimes discouragement comes from your own family who will attack your faith and demean your decision to follow Christ.
- Sometimes discouragement comes from your co-workers who turn on you simply because you became a Christian.

That's exactly why Jesus said if you are going to be My disciple you need to be prepared to **suffer**, to **sacrifice**, and to be **scorned** for His name. Jesus said in Luke 9:23, "If anyone desires to come after Me, let him deny himself, and take up his cross daily, and follow Me" (NKJV). Intrinsic in the concept of taking up a **cross** is the idea of **suffering, sacrifice, scorn**, and even **humiliation**. Jesus said if you are going to follow ME, you need to be ready to endure everything that is implied in the image of bearing a cross.

Why? Because the devil is coming after you with both barrels blasting trying to **weaken** your resolve, trying to **dismantle** your faith, and trying to **destroy** your relationship with Christ. Jesus could speak about this from the vantage point of personal experience because after Jesus' baptism (*which was the beginning of His public ministry, Matthew 3*), Jesus was immediately driven into the wilderness by the Holy Spirit where He was confronted by the devil, who unleashed his barrage of temptations against HIM. The devil attacked Jesus from every angle. He attacked Him by trying to appeal to the lust of the flesh, the lust of the eyes, and the pride of life (cf. Matthew 4:1-11 KJV). But Jesus withstood His spiritual assault by appealing to the written Word of God. Because the Word of God is "the sword of the Spirit" (Ephesians 6:17 KJV), and it is our offensive weapon to go on attack against the devil – because Satan is no match for the Word of God. When God speaks, the devil must acquiesce, whether he wants to or not.

The point is, when we become Christians, we can expect the devil to launch his arsenal of **demonic, deceptive, destructive tricks** and **tactics** upon us.

- Suddenly, old friends that you have not seen or heard from in years (*that you used to hang with and get into mischief with*) will pop up in your life.
- Suddenly, an old girlfriend or boyfriend will show up on your Facebook page, or call you, or text you, or email you.
- Suddenly, everything in your life starts going south:

  o You lose your job
  o You lose your transportation
  o Your spouse starts mistreating you and behaving strange toward you
  o Your family and so-called friends disassociate from you

And that's when the devil moves in for the kill. He first seeks to weaken you, and then he seeks to destroy you! He attacks your faith by pointing out everything that's wrong in your life. He points out everything that's wrong with the church. He points out every hypocrite in the church. And just for good measure, he makes sure that he sends the wrong member in your direction who will inevitably say the wrong thing, in the wrong way, at the wrong time. That's the devil's M.O. (*modus operandi*). Consequently, if you are not careful, the devil will be whispering or shouting in your ear:

- You need to leave the church.
- You were doing better before you became a Christian.
- In fact, look around you – those who are **not** serving the Lord are faring better than you are.

And before you realize what's happening to you, you find yourself ready to walk away from the Lord and disassociate with the church. But the lie that the devil tells you is that you're not leaving the Lord, you're only leaving the church and going back to your old beliefs and lifestyle – where you didn't have all these problems.

That was the lie that these Hebrew Christians were buying into. They were ready to leave Christianity and go back to Judaism where they could practice their religion without fear of molestation, because Judaism was a state-sanctioned religion – but Christianity was not.

However, the author of the book of Hebrews said, if you leave Christ you will be leaving the best thing that ever happened to you. *If you go back to Moses:*

- you will be leaving the **SUPERIOR** for the **INFERIOR**.
- you will be leaving the **BEST** for the **GOOD**.
- you will be leaving a walk for **FAITH** to bear the unbearable burden of the **LAW**.

The Hebrews' author said that everything about Christ and Christianity is superior to Moses and the Judaic system of law. He said Jesus is superior in every way.

- He is superior to the **angels** – because angels bow down and worship Him (Hebrews 1:4-6).
- He is superior to **Moses** – because Moses was a servant in God's house, but Jesus is a Son over His own house (Hebrews 3:6).

In fact, any way you look at Jesus, Jesus is better than everything offered in Judaism – under that old covenant.

- His **name** is better than angels – because He is the Son of God, and angels worship Him (Hebrews 1:4-6).
- His **image** is better – because He is the express image of God (Hebrews 1:3).
- His **Word** is better – because His Word holds everything together (Hebrews 1:3).
- His **position** is better – because He is enthroned in heaven at the right hand of the Father (Hebrews 1:3).
- His **priesthood** is better – because His priesthood is eternal, sinless, and blameless (Hebrews 7:26-27).
- His **covenant** is better – because it is everlasting (Hebrews 8:6).
- His **sacrifice** is better – because it is permanent and all encompassing (Hebrews 9:23-27).
- His **blood** is better – because it is uncontaminated by sin, and it takes away the sins of the sinner once and for all (Hebrews 9:12-14).

- His **promises** are better – because they are everlasting (Hebrews 8:6).
- His **hope** is better – because it is the hope of eternity with God (Hebrews 11:16).
- His **resurrection** is better – because it is the resurrection to eternal life with God forevermore (Hebrews 11:35).

You get the point – I don't care how you look at it, cut it, slice it, or turn it – **JESUS IS BETTER, BETTER, BETTER, BETTER!** In fact, not only is He **BETTER** – HE IS THE **BEST**! Therefore, the author's question to them is, "Why in the world would you leave the **best** for something less than the **best**?" "Why would you leave the **superior** for the **inferior**?"

Brothers and sisters, that's where I stand! I don't care what life brings my direction, or how ill-treated I am (*in the church or out of the church*), I'm sticking with Jesus till the end! David said in Psalm 34:8, "Oh, taste and see that the LORD is good." (KJV) I have tasted of the goodness of the Lord, and there is nothing in the world that tastes better than the goodness of the Lord. Besides that, the stuff that the world offers is like cotton candy – it's sweet to the taste but it quickly dissolves because it has no substance to it. The world offers us **fleeting pleasures, momentary happiness**, and **temporary excitement**. But Christ offers us **eternal joy, infinite happiness**, and **everlasting delight**.

These Hebrew saints were on the verge of leaving Jesus and going back to Judaism, and the writer of the book of Hebrews told them that what they needed was the same thing that has sustained *every* **saint** in *every* **generation** – through *every* **trial**, *every* **tragedy**, *every* **heartache**, *every* **disappointment**, *every* **failure**, *every* **frustration**, *every* **challenge**, *every* **difficult time**, and *every* **disaster** – and that is **FAITH**!

The Hebrews' author took his readers through age after age of men and women who made it through the **most challenging times**, endured the most **difficult of circumstances**, **overcame** the most **intimidating odds**, and **accomplished** some of the **most amazing feats** through **FAITH** (cf. Hebrews 11:4-40).

- **Hebrews 11:4-7** – deals with great examples of faith before the flood.
- **Hebrews 11:8-22** – deals with great examples of faith after the flood all the way to Joseph's death in Egypt.

- **Hebrews 11:23-31** – deals with great examples of faith during the period of the Exodus and up through the period of the conquest of the Promised Land.
- **Hebrews 11:32-40** – deals with great heroes and heroines of faith from the period of the judges, the kings, the prophets, and on to the end of O.T. canon (Malachi).

And the message is that, in generation after generation, the common thread that tied them together, and the common **ingredient** that got them through **every trial** and every **challenge** – was their FAITH!

And the same is true for us today! If we are going to make it through these difficult and unprecedented times – **FAITH** is the key! We need **FAITH** to deal with all the fall-out of this COVID-19 pandemic:

- **Unemployment** is at record highs – jobless claims are at **33 million** as of **July 9, 2020** – according to a source called "Market Watch."
- **Businesses** are closing their doors **permanently** because they cannot survive the revenue loss that they have incurred during this pandemic shutdown.
- There will be **bankruptcies, foreclosures, repossessions**, loss of **pensions, retirement savings depleted**, and massive loss of **medical insurance.**
- One source projected upwards of a **120,000,000 Americans** will be without **health insurance** due to the **job losses** precipitated by this **current pandemic**, coupled with the number of Americans already uninsured.
- On top of that, there's fear of contracting the virus. According to the CDC, in the USA we are now at over **4 million cases**, and over **143,000** dead, and every day that number is climbing.
- Then there's **political** and **social strife, unrest**, and **upheaval**.
- We have government **paramilitary police** engaging in violent attacks on nonviolent protestors.
- We have **violent protestors** and **rioters** who have taken over sections of major cities.

- We have **racial tension** that only seems to be **exacerbated** by the political rhetoric coming out of Washington, State houses, and local governments.
- We have **gun violence** in our communities, neighborhoods, and schools.
- And the list goes on . . .

What we need more than ever to see us through these difficult times – is FAITH!

- Faith gives us endurance
- Faith gives us hope
- Faith enables us to hang tough when it's tough to hang
- Faith enables us to look beyond a bad of today and see a better of tomorrow

FAITH IS THE KEY TO IT ALL

- Faith has always been the key
- Faith will always be the key
- Faith was the key yesterday
- Faith is the key today
- And faith will be the key tomorrow – because **"the just shall live by faith"**

That was and is the message of the writer of the book of Hebrews. And that is the same message that we need right now in 21st century America! And to show them that faith is the key – that faith is the panacea – he takes them on a journey through the museum of faith, and he stops at the "**Hall of Fame of faith heroes**" in Hebrews chapter 11. And his main thrust is that we may not know what the future holds, but by faith we know Who holds the future in His hands – and that is God! God will see to it that in the end (*no matter what happens in between*) His people will triumph and receive all the promises that He has made to His children.

Therefore, the author begins to point out one by one the power of faith in the lives of God's people from of old. He said:

- By faith, the **elders** obtained a good testimony.
- By faith, **Abel** offered to God a more excellent sacrifice than Cain.
- By faith, **Enoch** was taken away so that he did not see death.
- By faith, **Noah**, being divinely warned of things not yet seen and moved with godly fear, prepared an ark for the saving of his household.
- By faith, **Abraham** obeyed when he was called to go out to the place that he would receive as an inheritance. He went out not knowing where he was going.
- By faith, **Abraham, Isaac,** and **Jacob** dwelled in the land of promise as in a foreign country.
- By faith, **Sarah** received strength to conceive seed and she bore a child when she was past the age of childbearing because she judged Him faithful who had promised.
- By faith, **Abraham**, when tested, offered up **Isaac.**
- By faith, **Isaac** blessed **Jacob** and **Esau** concerning things to come.
- By faith, **Jacob**, while on his deathbed, blessed each of **Joseph's** sons.
- By faith, **Joseph**, when he was dying, made mention of the departure of the children of Israel and gave instructions concerning his bones.
- By faith, **Moses**, when he was born, was hidden three months by his parents because they saw he was a beautiful child, and they were not afraid of the king's command.
- By faith, **Moses**, when he became of age, refused to be called the son of Pharaoh's daughter, choosing rather to suffer affliction with the people of God than to enjoy the passing pleasures of sin for a season.
- By faith, **Moses** forsook Egypt not fearing the wrath of the king, for he endured as seeing Him who is invisible.
- By faith, **Moses** kept the Passover.
- By faith, **Israel** passed through the Red Sea on dry land.
- By faith, **Jericho's walls** came tumbling down after they were encircled for seven days.
- By faith, **Rahab** the harlot did not perish with those who did not believe.

And then the author of Hebrews said in Hebrews 11:32 – **"And what more shall I say? For the time would fail me to tell of Gideon and Barak and Samson and Jephthah, also of David and Samuel and the prophets"** (NKJV). In other words, my sermon would be too long if I included everyone that I wanted to include in my sermon on the power of faith in the life of a child of God. There's still: **Gideon, Barak, Samson, Jephthah, David, Samuel, Elijah, Elisha, Daniel, Shadrach, Meshach, and Abednego** – and a host of others, who by faith accomplished great things and overcame staggering odds! The message is loud and clear, faith is the key! Faith is the victory that overcomes the world!

Listen to the rest of my sermon text as I leave you with three salient points to ponder:

> "Women received their dead raised to life again. Others were tortured, not accepting deliverance, that they might obtain a better resurrection. Still others had trial of mockings and scourgings, yes, and of chains and imprisonment. They were stoned, they were sawn in two, were tempted, were slain with the sword. They wandered about in sheepskins and goatskins, being destitute, afflicted, tormented – of whom the world was not worthy. They wandered in deserts and mountains, in dens and caves of the earth. And all these, having obtained a good testimony through faith, did not receive the promise, God having provided something better for us, that they should not be made perfect apart from us" (Hebrews 11:35-40 NKJV).

I.   First, faith is what makes our hope real (cf. Hebrews 11:1-3)

The author tells us in Hebrews 11:1 that faith is the **"substance of things hoped for, the evidence of things not seen."** The noun **"substance"** is from a compound word. **"Sub"** is from the Greek word *hupo* – which literally means "under or beneath." In other words, it is something that serves as a **solid foundation** that runs beneath you and acts as a support.

The second part of this compound word is **"stance"** which comes from the Greek word *histemi* – which literally means "**to stand**." When you put them together it gives us a **DESCRIPTION** of faith, not a **DEFINITION** of faith. Together, the word means that faith is something intangible in us that runs beneath us and acts as a supporting foundation upon which we are able to stand firmly in the toughest of times, and know that the foundation is strong enough to support the weight of our **trials, concerns, burdens, questions, doubts,** and **fears.**

The author goes on to say that it "**is the evidence of things not seen.**" In other words, faith is what puts the meat on the bones of hope! Faith gives solid meaning to what we are hoping for, anticipating, and expecting. Faith is taking God at His word and bringing God's future promises into our present reality.

We don't see what God promised with our natural eyes; nevertheless, we trust His Word to be true because we have all the evidence in the world to believe that His Word can be trusted. All we have to do is look at the physical world (Hebrews 11:3) that was spoken into existence by God's Word from stuff that couldn't be seen, and therein lies our proof.

The very world in which we live is proof that God's Word can be trusted to produce what He has promised out of what cannot be seen.

- Even though I cannot see with my natural eyes – the Lord Jesus coming on the clouds of glory one day in the future.
- Even though I cannot see with my natural eyes – the resurrection of the dead in Christ.
- Even though I cannot see with my natural eyes – that celestial city called heaven, wherein dwells righteousness, where there will be no more **suffering, pain, sorrow, sickness,** or **death.**
- Even though I cannot see with my natural eyes – the streets of **gold**, the gates of **pearl**, the walls of **jasper**, the foundation of **precious stones.**

I can see all them through the eyes of faith – by the Word of God! I know it is all there because God said so, and since I am living **in, around,** and **on** the world that He created by His word, I know I can trust His Word to be real. Therefore, my faith is what holds me up when it's hard to stand up. My faith is what supports me and keeps me from giving up or giving out.

- When loved ones are **sick** – faith holds us up.
- When loved ones **die** – faith holds us up.
- When the money is **low** and the bills are **high** – faith holds us up.
- When the **job** is no more and the **prospects** are few – faith holds us up.
- When **trouble** visits my home – faith holds me up.
- When our current **predicament** with this **pandemic** seems to be getting worse by the day – faith holds me up.

Church, faith is our investment and God's Word is the assurance that what we have invested in is undergirded and underwritten by God Himself. And there is no better guarantee in the world than God!

II. Second, lack of deliverance does not mean lack of faith (cf. Hebrews 11:35-38)

Notice that everyone who had faith was not miraculously delivered. It is important that we know that a lack of deliverance does not mean that you have a lack of faith.

These individuals had just as much faith as the others who stopped the mouths of **LIONS**, quenched **FIRE**, killed **GIANTS**, received their **DEAD** back to life, but God did not deliver them in a miraculous fashion. That is important – because when God chooses not to deliver us from our circumstances, it is easy for us to conclude that:

- Our faith must be weak.
- And the devil gets busy with his attacks on our faith by telling us that God does not love us as much as those that He delivered.
- The devil tells us that maybe God is not real.
- The devil tells us that all this praying and trusting stuff is just a joke, it really does not work.

Look at you:

- You had faith – yet you still lost your health,
- You had faith – yet you still lost your job,
- You had faith – yet you still lost your house,
- You had faith – yet you still lost your loved one,
- You had faith – yet COVID-19 still took your mother, father, sister, brother, spouse, or friend.

Brothers and sisters, faith is no guarantee against trouble of the worst kind coming into our lives. Faith is no guarantee that the worst of things will not happen to us in this present world. However, faith is the guarantee that after the suffering comes the glory (cf. Hebrews 12:2-3).

Brothers and sisters, God can be glorified either by delivering us from a trial, or by sustaining us in a trial. Sometimes, it takes more faith to endure a trial than it does to escape a trial. And we must never forget that our faith is not proven by miraculous deliverance, but by faithful endurance in the time of trial.

- When we have faith (*even doing the most difficult times*) we remain steadfast.
- When we have faith, we keep on keeping on even when we feel like giving up.
- When we have faith, we keep on **PRAYING, STUDYING, WORSHIPING**, and **TRUSTING** in the Lord – even when we do not see the visible results immediately.

III. Finally, we need to understand that faith is not near-sighted it's far-sighted (cf. Hebrews 11:39-40)

When we truly possess faith, we understand that the best is yet to come. The author proves his point by indicating that all the **heroes** and **heroines** of faith spoken of in **Hebrews 11** never received what we have received in Christ.

All they had were **promises**, but we got the **substance**! Nevertheless, we thank God that there is still something else to come beyond this world.

We have the blessed hope of heaven, and one of these days the saints from every generation will go marching in together.

- We will walk in together with the likes of Abraham, Isaac, Jacob, Moses, Elijah, Daniel, Shadrach, Meshach, and Abednego.
- We will walk in with the likes of Peter, Paul, Timothy, Titus, Sarah, Rebekah, Ruth, Naomi, Mary, Martha, Elizabeth, Lazarus, David, Daniel, and all of the others who have gone before us.

The point is, that if we keep on walking in faith, one day we, together with the Patriarchs of old and all the faithful saints of old, will be together in that glorious city with God.

You can obey Christ and begin your journey of faith by putting your faith in the crucified, buried, and resurrected Christ (1 Corinthians 15:1-4 KJV; Hebrews 11:6 KJV); by repenting of your sins (Acts 17:30, 31 KJV); by confessing the name of Christ (Romans 10:9,10 KJV), and by being baptized into Christ (Acts 2:38 KJV); after which He will save you by His grace and add to His body – the Church (Acts 2:47 KJV).

> George Micheal Williams, a committed and devoted servant of God, serves currently and for the past 37 years as ministering evangelist to the Church of Christ at East Side in Austin, Texas. Brother Williams was previously married for 25 before the Lord called his spouse home. He is currently very happily married to his incredibly special gift from God, the love of his life, the beautiful (outwardly and inwardly) Gail March-Williams. Together they share four wonderful grown children and three grandchildren, one adorable granddaughter, Amayah Nicole, and two handsome grandsons, George Micheal III and Harrison Emanuel.

1 PETER 2:11-17 – THIS IS HOW WE DO IT
Dr. Kelvin Teamer

1. The Pursuit of Holiness

This sermon was birthed from a series that I conducted with the Church of Christ at Bouldercrest in Atlanta, Georgia, titled, "Standing on Holy Ground." The aim of the series was to help the body of believers see that the Lord has called His people to aim for holiness in their conduct. With the series, various texts were examined to explore the holy mindset and lifestyle urged by the biblical writers to the people of God, as depicted through ancient Israel, as well as with the church. With this specific sermon, however, I approached the congregation with a charge and an explanation of how to carry it out. The exhortation was to pursue holiness. In order to be successful with such a task, I felt it necessary to understand how to do it. This opinioned truth invited the title of the sermon, "This Is How We Do It."

To the first century church, the holy apostle Peter wrote a series of letters of instruction and exhortation. In the first of these recorded letters, Peter taught the scattered Christians and persecuted Christ-followers about the importance of the lifestyle of holiness. He set the thematic tone early on in his epistle when he instructed them not to be conformed to the passions of their former ignorance, but *"as He who called you is holy, you also be holy in all your conduct, since it is written, 'You shall be holy, for I am holy'"* (1 Peter 1:14-16 ESV).

Pithy, yet inspired statements such as, *"You shall be holy, for I am holy,"* are oft quoted within the realm of the church, but they sometimes seem to lack the real power of expectation, which is truly placed upon the hearers of such words. When Peter wrote his statement, he seemed to write it with the expectation that the church would not only quote it, but that they would also live it.

Living out holiness is the grand challenge of the church. It was so important to the early church that we see the human authors of the great works of the New Testament go through much detail in order to give the believers a sense of what it would take to live out their holiness in the society in which they were living. They seemed to be tapping into a phenomenon of human existence in which humans didn't just want to know *what* to do, they wanted to know *how* to do it.

A little while ago, I had a problem with the freezer section of my refrigerator. For some unknown reason, the freezer stopped . . . well . . . freezing! Long frozen food began thawing out. Water started leaking. The worst thing of all, the ice cream started to melt! As a result, I went to the Internet and started asking the DIY "experts" what the problem could be. Quickly, I ascertained that what was going on was a motor issue. Almost as soon as I discovered it, I was faced with another problem – I didn't know *how* to fix it. Just knowing *what* the issue was proved to no longer be beneficial. I needed to know *how* to deal with the issue.

Holiness, for the church, is a lot like that. We know *what* the issue is or rather what we have been called to do – to be holy; we just don't know *how* to live out holiness in our lives. Since Peter was the one who revealed the issue, we lean on him to show us what to do about it. Before we listen to Peter explain *how*, let's hear him explain, *why* we should be holy.

The pursuit of holiness is the quest of us seeking to be like God. It isn't us seeking to be God, rather it is us seeking to be . . . like God, in a sense. The word 'holy' is the Greek word *hagios*, which expresses the meaning of being separate. There was no God like Jehovah, and there were to be no people like the church. As God is separate, so were His people to be. Their separateness was to be seen in their conduct, in the same way that God's separateness was seen by His actions.

Life can be challenging. It often throws us all a variety of circumstances and situations that will invite us to be anything but holy. Thus, Peter counteracted his invitation with an urging of his own that he shared in the inspired text. Peter intimated that there is a constant struggle to pull believers off of their holy positioning. Since that is the case, the Christ-follower must put some distance between themselves and the lives that they used to live (pre-surrender to Jesus). They must put distance between the holy life and that old life.

2. At War with the Old Life

1 Peter 2:11 (ESV)

"Beloved, I urge you as sojourners and exiles to abstain from the passions of the flesh, which wage war against your soul."

Within this powerful urging, Peter was calling the Christian to distance himself from the passions, lusts, longed for desires, and cravings of the flesh. When one reads a list such as this, it is easy to place them solely in the realm of the sexual appetites of the human existence. However, Peter was referring to any fleshly and worldly behavior. So, his urging was against any hedonistic, self-seeking tendency that characterized the pre-Christian lifestyle.

As he mentioned in 1 Peter 4:2, the Christian should not "live for the rest of the time in the flesh" for human passions, but he should live "for the will of God." In other words, Peter was explaining that once one surrenders to Christ, he or she must live, not for their own will, but for the will of God. To do that, he must put distance between himself and the acts of that old life.

The thing I most like about the Bible is its amazing Holy Spirit-led uniformity. Many of the same themes are reinforced in different books, by different authors. Paul, the apostle, spoke in a similar vein in Galatians 5. There, he encouraged the church to walk by the Spirit and then they wouldn't gratify the desires of the flesh. Paul also gave the ancient Galatians a listing of things that fell into the category of "fleshly desires."

Galatians 5:19-21 (ESV)

"Now the works of the flesh are evident: sexual immorality, impurity, sensuality, idolatry, sorcery, enmity, strife, jealousy, fits of anger, rivalries, dissensions, divisions, envy, drunkenness, orgies, and things like these. I warn you, as I warned you before, that those who do such things will not inherit the kingdom of God."

This listing from Paul tells us something about the works of the flesh and about the attitude required to separate ourselves from it. These works affect the believer from the inside out. They take effect inside our bodies, then they manifest themselves in outward action. Our separation must be as comprehensive as the desire and the act. To walk in holiness, we have to learn to emphatically draw the line!

How do you draw the line, however? How does one make his separation comprehensive and emphatic? Well, it begins when we distance ourselves from any situation where indulgence is probable. For instance, in order to distance self from sexual immorality, one must distance himself from situations where sexual immorality and lust of the flesh are possible.

Such a radical approach is necessary because the Christian is at war. Notice how Peter qualified his audience in verse 11. He said that they were sojourners and exiles. In other words, Christians really aren't from around these parts. We are citizens of heaven (Philippians 3:20). We are foreigners on enemy soil, and we stand in opposition to the culture of the land. As a result, our former conduct has declared war on our soul. No longer can we casually indulge our lusts. Now, that indulgence attacks us like a spiritual cancer. It eats away at our soul. Like a nation at war with another, its aim is our domination and surrender.

War is constant, active, engaged conflict. Temptation, lust, and eventual sin aren't drills for us; they are actual hand-to-hand combat. We are in a constant fight for our lives; thus, we must be vigilant against these ills. Fleshly gratification has set its sights on anyone who desires to live a holy life.

3. Honorable Conduct and Works

1 Peter 2:12 (ESV)

> *"Keep your conduct among the Gentiles honorable, so that when they speak against you as evildoers, they may see your good deeds and glorify God on the day of visitation."*

After telling the Christ-followers about the importance of the separation from their old lives, Peter then spoke to them about the seriousness of living out their holiness in front of those who were still stuck in the existence from which they were delivered. Their holy conduct was supposed to be seen as honorable among the *heathens* of the day. When the heathens spoke evil against them (notice he said, *"When"* and not *"If"*), their conduct – the conduct of the Christ-follower – was to be such that they [the heathen] might see their good deeds and then in turn glorify God.

During the time period that Peter wrote his epistles, it was common for Christians to be "bad mouthed" by the Gentiles. The church was accused of acting against the decrees of the Roman Caesar. Other charges included peddling superstitions, cannibalism, incest, turning slaves against their masters, and having an overall hatred of mankind.

Peter believed that the holy lifestyle characterized by good works would counteract the slanderous words of the ancient society. The good that the church would do would invite others to see God. The same principle applies to the church and the world today. Keep doing good and invite others to see God. After all, the church was created for good works. Paul expressed a similar thought to those in this ancient society.

Ephesians 2:10 (ESV)

> *"For we are his workmanship, created in Christ Jesus for good works, which God prepared beforehand, that we should walk in them."*

Titus 2:14 (ESV)

> *". . . who gave himself for us to redeem us from all lawlessness and to purify for himself a people for his own possession who are zealous for good works."*

Peter gave another qualifying statement relating to the Gentiles' eventual glorification of God because of the good works. He said that it would take place on the "day of visitation." What is meant by this phrase is thought to be either the day Jesus returns or the day that His salvation visits them. I am one to believe the latter, for we work the works of a holy priesthood, so that people might know Jesus before He returns.

4. The Good Life

1 Peter 2:13-17 (ESV)

> *"Be subject for the Lord's sake to every human institution, whether it be to the emperor as supreme, or to governors as sent by him to punish those who do evil and to praise those who do good. For this is the will of God, that by doing good you should put to silence the ignorance of foolish people. Live as people who are free, not using your freedom as a cover-up for evil, but living as servants of God. Honor everyone. Love the brotherhood. Fear God. Honor the emperor."*

Peter continued with his illumination of how to live this holy life. Christians were to be subject to every human institution, whether Caesar or governors. This was a major command by the apostle. The church was being persecuted, in large part, by the very government he told them to subject themselves to.

It is important to note that the church wasn't a collection of anarchists; they were citizens of a different kingdom. They weren't seeking to overthrow the current kingdom. They were seeking to win them over to a better one. They wouldn't do that by rabble-rousing, but they would do it by serving. They would do it, not by resisting the emperor, but by persistently serving King Jesus.

The will of God was that they would continue to do good, and in so doing they would put to silence the aforementioned slander. They were free in Jesus, thus they weren't to answer evil with evil. When you've been set free, there is nothing that anyone can really do to you. When that is the case, you can simply focus on being obedient to the will of God. In this situation, it called them – for the Lord's sake – to be subject to those who worked, whether they knew it or not, on God's behalf to keep order in society. Paul wrote to the Roman church:

Romans 13:1-7 (ESV)

"Let every person be subject to the governing authorities. For there is no authority except from God, and those that exist have been instituted by God. Therefore whoever resists the authorities resists what God has appointed, and those who resist will incur judgment. For rulers are not a terror to good conduct, but to bad. Would you have no fear of the one who is in authority? Then do what is good, and you will receive his approval, for he is God's servant for your good. But if you do wrong, be afraid, for he does not bear the sword in vain. For he is the servant of God, an avenger who carries out God's wrath on the wrongdoer. Therefore one must be in subjection, not only to avoid God's wrath but also for the sake of conscience. For because of this you also pay taxes, for the authorities are ministers of God, attending to this very thing. Pay to all what is owed to them: taxes to whom taxes are owed, revenue to whom revenue is owed, respect to whom respect is owed, honor to whom honor is owed."

The early church would have likely found it too difficult to heed these words, even though they came with apostolic authority. To honor an emperor as vile as Nero would have almost been unthinkable, but Christians often must do the unthinkable. Why? They do so because they fear God. Additionally, according to Ecclesiastes 12:13, this reverence for God – along with keeping His commandments – these things remind us of the whole duty of man. Living in holiness is one of those commandments. It is our duty and we've now been told how to carry out these orders.

5. The Better Life

Ironically, seeking to live this type of life, a life of holiness, will produce failure, disappointment, and discouragement. It isn't actually possible to live a holy existence unless one leans on Jesus. As a matter of fact, allow me to say it more emphatically: a life of this magnitude and nature <u>cannot</u> be lived out without Jesus. He is our model of how to do it, and He is our advocate whenever we don't. Such is the reason that He came and died. He came to show us how to succeed, and He died because we will fail. We will fail without Him.

Because of Jesus, we have a chance. Because of Jesus, we can have a better life, a more abundant life (John 10:10). All of mankind can have that, if they are willing to go from where they are right now to where God wants them to be. Those things that are difficult become easier; that which seems impossible becomes possible – when we follow the pattern already set by Jesus.

Remember that freezer that stopped working? After I discovered what the issue was, I researched how to fix it. I found a wonderful YouTube video that took me step-by-step through the process of fixing it. I learned what part to buy, where to buy it, how to unhook the defective part, and how to install the new one. Once I purchased the needed part, I went to work, but never too far away from the video. I would watch, then I would work. Watch and work. Watch and work. Finally, after about thirty minutes, I could hear the motor starting to run, and I felt cold air blowing out. I figured out how to do it by watching an expert.

Jesus is our expert on how to be holy. He shows us how to do it. Now, it is time to allow His instruction to change our lives.

> Dr. Kelvin Teamer is the Evangelist of the Church of Christ at Bouldercrest. He has served in this position since May of 2015. Prior to serving in this capacity, he served as Youth Minister, as well as the Minister of Spiritual Development for Bouldercrest. Kelvin has been married to Kim for the past 22 years and they have two children, Joshua and Jordan.